Writing the Radio War

Edinburgh Critical Studies in War and Culture

Published titles

Our Nazis: Representations of Fascism in Contemporary Literature and Film
by Petra Rau

Writing the Radio War: Literature, Politics and the BBC, 1939–1945
by Ian Whittington

www.edinburghuniversitypress.com/series/ecswc

Writing the Radio War

Literature, Politics and the BBC, 1939–1945

Ian Whittington

EDINBURGH
University Press

Edinburgh University Press is one of the leading university presses in the UK. We publish academic books and journals in our selected subject areas across the humanities and social sciences, combining cutting-edge scholarship with high editorial and production values to produce academic works of lasting importance. For more information visit our website: edinburghuniversitypress.com

© Ian Whittington, 2018

Edinburgh University Press Ltd
The Tun – Holyrood Road
12(2f) Jackson's Entry
Edinburgh EH8 8PJ

Typeset in 10.5/13 pt Sabon by
Servis Filmsetting Ltd, Stockport, Cheshire

A CIP record for this book is available from the British Library

ISBN 978 1 4744 1359 6 (hardback)
ISBN 978 1 4744 1360 2 (webready PDF)
ISBN 978 1 4744 1361 9 (epub)

The right of Ian Whittington to be identified as the author of this work has been asserted in accordance with the Copyright, Designs and Patents Act 1988, and the Copyright and Related Rights Regulations 2003 (SI No. 2498).

Published with the support of the University of Edinburgh Scholarly Publishing Initiatives Fund.

Contents

Acknowledgements	vi
Series Editors' Preface	viii
Introduction: Projecting Britain	1
1 *Out of the People*: J. B. Priestley's Broadbrow Radicalism	30
2 James Hanley and the Shape of the Wartime Features Department	65
3 To Build the Falling Castle: Louis MacNeice and the Drama of Form	83
4 Versions of Neutrality: Denis Johnston's War Reports	117
5 *Calling the West Indies*: Una Marson's Wireless Black Atlantic	153
Coda: Coronation	185
Bibliography	192
Index	211

Acknowledgements

It is a privilege, after many years, to thank publicly a few of the many people who have helped this book to come into being. This would be a much-diminished volume without the wisdom and verve of Allan Hepburn, who has been the most steadfast of supporters since the earliest days of this project. Debra Rae Cohen, Ned Schantz and Jonathan Sterne have provided astute feedback and professional support over the years, and in doing so have been models of good academic citizenship as well as scholarly practice. Miranda Hickman, Peter Kalliney and Eli MacLaren read an early version of this project with great care and critical attention, and helped me to see the possibilities therein. Similarly, Kate McLoughlin, Gill Plain and the external reviewers for Edinburgh University Press have made this a far better work than it would have been without their keen insights and editorial acumen. At McGill University and the University of Mississippi, I have been lucky to work with generous teachers, colleagues and friends, many of whom critiqued chapter drafts, attended talks, or simply thought to ask the questions I had not: Ben Barootes, Lindy Brady, Ariel Buckley, Paula Derdiger, Erin Drew, Cristie Ellis, Robin Feenstra, Sue Grayzel, Ivo Kamps, Casey McCormick, Sunita Nigam, Dan Novak, Justin Pfefferle, Monica Popescu, Dan Stout, Jay Watson and Caroline Wigginton have all helped, in ways tangible and intangible, to shape this project for the better.

Early archival research for this book was made possible thanks to the generous support of the Social Sciences and Humanities Research Council of Canada. The University of Mississippi contributed significantly to the evolution and completion of this project through Summer Research Grants from the College of Liberal Arts (in coordination with the Department of English) and travel grants from the Office of Research and Sponsored Programs and the Department of English. Research assistants Shertok Lama, Katie Albers and Scott Obernesser helped speed this book along. My thanks to all of these people and organisations, without whose support the archival research at the core of this volume would not have been possible.

Speaking of archives: Louise North, Jacquie Kavanagh and the entire staff of the BBC Written Archives Centre in Caversham provided invaluable assistance in navigating the compendious records of the Corporation. This book would not exist without their gifts of expertise, dedication and time. Acknowledgement is also due to Alison Cullingford and the Special Collections staff at the University of Bradford; Aisling Lockhart and other archivists at the Manuscripts and Archives Reading Library at Trinity College Dublin; and archivists at the National Sound Archive at the British Library, the Harry Ransom Humanities Research Center at the University of Texas at Austin and the Bodleian Library Special Collections at the University of Oxford, all of whom were manifestly professional, courteous and knowledgeable in their dealings with me.

Much of the primary material reproduced in this volume appears courtesy of its copyright holders. The BBC Written Archives Centre has been exceedingly helpful in granting permission to use materials under BBC copyright. My thanks to Rory and Micheal Johnston for our conversations about their father Denis's life and work, and for permission to quote from his unpublished writings; to United Agents, for permission to quote from the correspondence of J. B. Priestley; to David Higham and Associates, for permission to quote from the letters of Louis MacNeice; to Lady Susan Briggs, for permission to quote from an interview featuring Lord Asa Briggs; and to Hilary Sherlock, for permission to quote from Sir Philip Sherlock's poem 'Dinner Party 1940'. Parts of Chapter 3 first appeared in the article 'Archaeologies of Sound: Reconstructing Louis MacNeice's Wartime Radio Publics', in *Modernist Cultures* 10.1 (2015); my thanks to Edinburgh University Press and *Modernist Cultures* for permission to reproduce portions of that essay.

Finally, the book you are holding reflects the unwavering love and support of those I hold closest. Claire Byrne has sustained me through the last two years with her confidence, her deep humour and her deeper kindness, even when those formidable powers had to bridge a distance usually reserved for shortwave. My family, who have been the centre of my emotional and intellectual life since before I can remember, have my gratitude for squeezing more than a lifetime's worth of conversations, laughter and pleasant silences into the days we have shared so far. In addition to being the best of siblings and friends, my brothers Luke and Jesse are a constant source of inspiration and encouragement. This book is dedicated to my parents, Barb and Bruce, who taught me to read and to listen. With love.

Series Editors' Preface

This series of monographs is designed to showcase innovative new scholarship in the literary and filmic representation of war. The series embraces Anglophone literature and film of all genres, with studies adopting a range of critical approaches including transhistorical and intercultural analysis. 'War' in this context is understood to mean armed conflict of the industrialised age (that is, from the late eighteenth century onwards), including not only conventional war between sovereign states but also revolution, insurrection, civil war, guerrilla warfare, cold war and genocide (including the Holocaust). The series is concerned with the multiple, often conflicting, significations that surround the act and event of armed combat, and volumes will also consider the causes, consequences and aftermath of wars; pro- and anti-war literature and film; memorialisation, trauma and testimony. The premise of the series is that new critical perspectives need to be developed in order to understand war representation better. Rather than simply analysing war texts, or even situating those texts in their contemporary cultural contexts, Edinburgh Critical Studies in War and Culture will identify the conceptual categories and forms by which war has been mediated in literature and film, and illuminate the cultural influences that produce them. Wars shape bodies, minds and literary forms; they mediate the possibilities of expression and create discourses of repression; they construct ambivalent subjectivities such as the enemy and the veteran; they invade and distort popular genres from crime fiction to fantasy; they leave tangible scars on the landscape and generate the production of memorials both concrete and imagined. This series explores the role of literature and film in mediating such events, and in articulating the contradictions of 'war' and 'culture'.

Kate McLoughlin and Gill Plain

To my parents

Introduction: Projecting Britain

For this is total war; and total war is war right inside the home itself, emptying the clothes cupboards and the larder, screaming its threats through the radio at the hearth, burning and bombing its way from roof to cellar. (J. B. Priestley, 'Postscript', 22 September 1940 [Priestley 1940c: 78])

J. B. Priestley was not listening when Neville Chamberlain declared war against Germany over the wireless on the morning of 3 September 1939. Driving into London from the Isle of Wight to broadcast the first instalment of his new 'novel for radio', *Let the People Sing*, Priestley could not tune in to hear the Prime Minister announce the arrival of war in a voice tinged with personal disappointment: 'You can imagine what a bitter blow it is to me that all my long struggle to win peace has failed,' Chamberlain intoned. 'Yet I cannot believe that there is anything more or anything different I could have done and that would have been more successful' (Chamberlain 1939). If Chamberlain's transmission marked the exhaustion of appeasement as a viable strategy for the British government, Priestley's broadcast later that day signalled a symbolic transfer of power enacted over the air. The first commission of its kind by the British Broadcasting Corporation (BBC), *Let the People Sing* is a light-hearted comedy centred on a small English town; its simultaneous print and radio publication would, it was hoped, offer listeners and readers a multimedia form of respite from the growing tensions in Europe. For all its levity, however, the plot of the novel bears a message, common to much of Priestley's previous work but newly resonant, about the rights of citizens to take control of their political and cultural lives: the residents of the Midlands town of Dunbury struggle to keep their market hall, bequeathed to the town by a local aristocrat, out of the competing clutches of that aristocrat's jealous descendants and the town's American-owned plastics factory. The residents want nothing more, or less, than to use the hall for their town band.

The producers' decision to allow *Let the People Sing* to go ahead, despite widespread disruptions to broadcasting that day, was intended as a gesture that the conflict would not induce a total upheaval of cultural programming (Nicholas 1996: 26). The gesture is all the more fitting given the novel's crystallisation of many of the themes of what would come to be known, by winter 1940–1, as the 'People's War'. In this account of the war, a myth almost as vociferously debunked as it has been affirmed, a plucky island nation put aside differences of class and politics and rallied together to defeat the Nazis, establishing in the process a new and more equitable social and economic order at home.[1] Priestley's fictional Dunbury, which John Baxendale characterises as 'torn between decadent traditionalism and rapacious Americanisation, and to be rescued only by a national-popular reawakening' (2007: 140), stands in neatly for the nation that would emerge from the war: if the people are to sing, they must reclaim the spaces of their singing. This 'novel for radio' is therefore remarkable today less for its form – essentially a conventional novel read over the air – than for its apposite framing of wartime debates over politics, culture and national identity. Priestley, along with dozens of other writers at the BBC, would play a key role in wartime negotiations over who 'the people' were, and how the BBC might mediate the range of their present experiences and their possible futures.

Though not a new role, it was one amplified by its historical moment. The Second World War was the first 'radio war' in the sense that, for the first time, belligerent nations mobilised wireless broadcasting on a global scale for both domestic and international persuasion and information.[2] And yet for all the globe-spanning, invasive potential of radio, listeners experienced it less as an agent of unwanted aggression than as a lopsided interlocutor: a vital source of entertainment and information implicated in complex networks of transmission, reception and feedback. Reflecting on the war some twenty-five years after its conclusion, novelist and broadcaster Elizabeth Bowen remarked that, during the conflict, radio created, as much as it reflected, its public:

> In the main, the voice proved mightier than the pen. Sound made for community of sensation, was emotive (which was required) . . . The desideratum was not to *address* the masses but speak as one of them. Press and radio combined in keeping the people's collective image constantly in front of the people's eyes, and did well in doing so. It was inspirational; one beheld oneself as one had it in one to be. ([1969] 1986: 184)

Bowen's account of the constitutive relationship between radio and its public captures how the BBC guided listeners' acoustic involvement in the nation at a time of crisis. Geared towards national mobilisation and increasingly responsive to its listeners, the BBC afforded media producers and consumers alike an unprecedented auditory space in which to think through the problem of collective participation in the war effort and the possible configurations of a postwar Britain, with or without its Empire. Considerable constraints of censorship and propaganda meant that, throughout the upheavals of the war, the BBC played a double role: it both channelled official policies and information, and reflected the concerns and aspirations of a broad swath of the British public. If the BBC was to serve the interests of its listening public, it had to tread a line between encouraging officially sanctioned views on the events of the war and addressing the frustrations, confusion and dangers experienced by average Britons. What 'one had it in one to be' was an expression of possibility that shifted along axes of the descriptive and the prescriptive, the individual and the collective, and the present and the future.

The task of projecting Britain over the air and into an imagined future was made newly urgent by the tectonic shifts war brought to almost every facet of British cultural and political life: civilians became combatants as aerial bombardment literalised the 'home front'; the social and financial turmoil of the 1930s yielded to the planned economies of total war and, later, the welfare state; stark divisions of left and right found themselves replaced, however tenuously, by wartime coalitions and the postwar consensus; and the British Empire held together for the duration of the war, only to break apart in its aftermath.[3] If the People's War myth and its instrumentalisation remain subjects of considerable debate almost eight decades after the outbreak of hostilities, it is nonetheless true that Britain left the war a substantially transformed nation. Moreover, as Marina MacKay has pointed out, the social and political changes ushered in by the war and the postwar Labour government were experienced and discussed in revolutionary terms, regardless of whether they actually constituted a revolution in the larger historical sense (2007: 4). Priestley gave voice to this revolutionary sentiment in the preface to his *Postscripts*, published in the bleak months of late 1940: 'Either we are fighting to bring a better world into existence, or we are merely assisting at the destruction of such civilisation as we possess' (1940c: vii). Caught between catastrophe and the possibility of a national rebirth, writers took to the BBC as a pre-eminent site for the public discussion of British cultural and political identity. Questions resounded about what ideologies might fit the normative mould of British political life, how to address the injustices facing Britain's imperial subjects, and most of all, how best to steer the nation through the current crisis and into a more equitable social order than that left in the wake of the First World War.

Central to the task of projecting Britain to itself and to the world was a group of writers who represented a vibrant cross-section of the literary culture of wartime Britain. From anti-imperial Indian nationalists and democratic socialists to Anglophilic high modernists, a broad literary coalition united themselves around the notion that Britain was a political entity worth defending and preserving, if only in the short term and not in its interwar form.[4] This widespread participation in mass-mediated cultural and political programming indicates that the disdain some writers had felt for radio in the 1920s and 1930s had largely evaporated by the war.[5] As the medium left its adolescence and took up a central place in the lived experience of the British populace, it became increasingly difficult to imagine a public existence as a writer without some engagement with radio. The existential threat that Nazi Germany posed to Britain – and to the tenets of liberal humanism and artistic freedom that subtended much of its literary culture – compounded the urgency of this intermedial imperative. In addressing the contributions of several of these writers to the wartime BBC, this study sounds the broadcast forms through which they sought to communicate with the radio public: J. B. Priestley became a celebrity by urging a new form of political and cultural democracy over the air; James Hanley struggled to maintain his grim and idiosyncratic vision within a Features Department shaped by aesthetic and political constraints; Louis MacNeice repurposed poetic technique in the service of rebuilding the nation both physically and psychologically; Denis Johnston confronted the limits of political and journalistic neutrality as an Irish-born war correspondent within the Corporation; and Una Marson transformed a vehicle of imperial interpellation into a hub for black intellectual activity around the Atlantic world.

To say that the BBC served as a central node in the mediation of possible futures for Britain and its Empire is not to minimise the role played by other media and forms of cultural communication during the war. Indeed, most of the writers discussed in this study spent the war years juggling projects in media as diverse as documentary film (Priestley, Johnston and Marson), journalism and essay-writing (Priestley and MacNeice), theatre (Priestley and Johnston) and military handbooks (MacNeice). But the wireless offered writers access to an unprecedented public sphere; it reached into the homes of British citizens and, through the Overseas Service, into homes around the world, to offer simultaneous collective participation in the processes of upheaval and renewal tendered by the war.[6] Furthermore, the intimate acoustics of radio, which brought these conversations into the domestic realm, were crucial in determining the limits of acceptable 'Britishness' on the airwaves and beyond: from Churchill's august oratory to Priestley's demotic burr and Marson's Jamaican lilt, it was the sounds as much as the ideas of British broadcasting that informed distinctions of official nation and organic community, highbrow and lowbrow, coloniser and colonised. Policing the soundscape could be a way of policing the polity, but as the sonic palette of the BBC expanded, so did the parameters of national belonging. For those listeners conventionally excluded from the national imagination for reasons of race, class, gender or region, hearing oneself represented on the airwaves signalled entry into a more robust world of public, civic participation.

Arguments about the tenacity of the social fiction known as the nation risk running against the grain of the current transnational turn in modernist studies, all the more so because an analysis of radio at a time of global war must clearly confront border crossings of all kinds.[7] That several of the writers examined in this study (namely, Johnston, MacNeice and Marson) were born outside of the island of Britain reinforces the transnational nature of British literary and broadcast culture in the period. But if the people, events and representations of the war regularly exceeded the boundaries of Britain as a political and geographical entity, the BBC remained an organ of national self-promotion, and its propagandists consistently converted transnational pressures into opportunities for articulations of British and imperial identity in relation to the wider world. As Michele Hilmes notes in her recent study of the interwoven histories of American and British broadcasting, *Network Nations*, the national and the transnational enjoy a dynamic relation. Nations and national identity remain central constructions for both individuals and collectives, but 'the nation always exists in tension with the transnational and [. . .] these forces have enormous constitutive and productive power, particularly in the cultural field' (2012: 11). Thus while this study concerns itself with the varieties of British political and cultural identity articulated through the radio, it takes as given the importance of transnational 'others' in shaping that identity, whether those others be Irish, West Indian, American or German.

That the versions of British political and cultural identity thus put forth could not be disentangled from the semi-governmental institution that mediated them does not so much render those identities subordinate to a political authority as it reveals the interpenetration of political and cultural spheres normally held to be distinguishable. As literature had once defined itself against both politics and new media like radio, it began to define itself *through* those politics and those new media; participation in a total war against a Nazi government hostile to much cultural production made the convergence of political and aesthetic goals all but unavoidable. In order to address a public eager for quality entertainment, accurate information and a minimum of overt propaganda, writers found they had to blend the literary with the radiogenic.[8] They deployed aesthetic techniques, elaborated in decades of writing for print publication, over the radio and adapted them as necessary to the demands of an acoustic medium. Priestley found that the plainspoken essay proved a viable model for radio 'talks' that embodied an ethics of reciprocal exchange, for example, while MacNeice's experience with the disciplined forms of lyric and dramatic verse facilitated the creation of compelling sonic worlds. Other formal lessons were harder to learn: Hanley's impressionistic prose proved resistant to the shaping influences of the BBC Features Department, while Johnston grew increasingly sceptical of the front-line journalist's mantra of objectivity in a war in which truths seemed plural. Whether they flourished or not, these writers found in the wartime radio public an unprecedented audience for their work. In the crowded media ecology of wartime Britain, radio afforded writers the chance to propagandise on behalf of themselves, their art and their nation.

Radio and its publics

The privileged role writers enjoyed at the wartime BBC reflects the centrality of radio to public life in midcentury Britain and the emphasis the Corporation had placed on Arnoldian notions of 'culture' since its inception.[9] More than the hobby of ham operators, as it had been in the 1910s and early 1920s, radio had become by the end of the 1930s a vast and viable system of public information and entertainment. In Britain, the formation of the private British Broadcasting Company in 1922 – which became a public corporation in 1927 – inaugurated a revolution in the production and consumption of news, music, drama and other cultural content. Between 1923 and 1939 the number of registered wireless sets in the United Kingdom rose from approximately 80,000 to over 9 million, out of a total population of 46.5 million. By the mid-1930s, the BBC had increased its signal strength and expanded coverage of the island to reach 98 per cent of the British population (Briggs 1965: 253; LeMahieu 1988: 230, 273–4). While the poorest households did not own wireless sets, the presence of receivers in pubs, cafés, workplaces and the homes of friends and family members meant that, by 1939, almost all citizens had at least some access to radio programming. The fact that 'nation' and 'audience' became nearly coterminous in this period need not have entailed the involvement of writers with established literary reputations; under the guidance of founding Director-General John Reith, however, the BBC used its monopoly over the British airwaves to pursue a policy of cultural enlightenment through a largely 'highbrow' selection of programmes. Despite the relentlessly elevated tone of the BBC, many intellectuals initially dismissed it as culture for the masses; by the end of the 1930s, however, opinions had shifted sufficiently that broadcasting was seen as a legitimate means by which writers could reach a broad public.

The growing popularity of radio had coincided with the deepening international crises of the 1930s, as the struggle for ideological control of the airwaves over Europe and its dependencies came to inflect all broadcasts with political valences. Before any shots were fired, the Second World War announced its arrival through the rising din of claim and counter-claim, as propagandistic volleys were launched across the world in the form of news bulletins and cultural programming slanted in the interests of the broadcasting nation. Writing in 1936, German media theorist Rudolf Arnheim evoked the eventuality of war in this battle for the ether:

> Each country strengthened its own transmissions so as to drown the disturbance of foreign stations ... whereupon the next country did the same thing and so it came to be a wireless war in which it was no one's fault but everyone's together; voices sounded, as they do wherever there is rivalry and no question of arbitration, not softly and in order, but loudly and on top of one another. What we hear to-day from the loudspeaker is an artistically forceful symbol of war in peace ... a chaos concretised in discord and as such directly perceptible to the human ear. ([1936] 1986: 237–8)

Even in the mid-1930s, this radio war extended beyond the borders of Europe, as German and Italian stations reached British colonies with news propaganda in English and local languages. As its foreign services expanded following the Nazi rise to power in 1933, the German national broadcaster, the *Reichsrundfunkgesellschaft*, actively began soliciting listener opinion overseas. The *Daily Telegraph* reported in April 1935 that German Overseas Radio (*Reichssender*) was circulating questionnaires regarding programme preferences and reception in several British colonies and dominions; in 1935 alone, the *Reichssender* received 28,000 letters from listeners abroad (Briggs 1970: 393–4). Amidst the Ethiopian Crisis of 1935, Italy established a station beaming propaganda to Egypt and British colonies in the Middle East, a turn of events that elicited concern from British officials in Cairo and would lead, eventually, to the expansion of the Empire Service and its successor, the Overseas Service (Briggs 1965: 399).

The outbreak of war brought important changes to the structure and schedule of the BBC. Rates of listening increased, especially in the early months of the conflict and for particular programmes like news broadcasts. Output also grew: the BBC entered the war with 4,233 staff and 23 transmitters with a power of 1,620 kw broadcasting 50 hours a day across a variety of wavelengths. By the end of the conflict, it had essentially tripled in size, with 11,417 staff and 138 transmitters with a total power of 5,250 kw broadcasting 150 hours a day (Angus Calder 1969: 359). The structural change most immediately noticeable to listeners was the abandonment of the Regional Programme as part of contingency plans originally drawn up in the shadow of the Munich Crisis in 1938 (Nicholas 1996: 18). Beginning in the late 1920s, the Regional Programme had been designed to complement the UK-wide National Programme with broadcasts originating from multiple studios and transmitters scattered around the country. With programming tailored for their local audiences, stations covering Western England and Wales, Northern England, the Midlands, Scotland and Northern Ireland had helped to restore a degree of regional specificity all too uncommon under the London-centric monopoly of the Corporation. With the outbreak of war, the national/regional structure was replaced by a unified Home Service with a mandate to serve the entire British population with a single programme schedule (Briggs 1970: 62). Administrators hoped that by placing a single national transmission on only two wavelengths, repeated across dozens of transmitters, they would minimise any disruptions to service caused by air raids; if bombs took out one transmitter, listeners would notice only a diminution in signal strength, as the next nearest transmitter continued to broadcast. Furthermore, since all transmitters would be working on the same wavelength, German bombers could not orient themselves by locating regionally specific transmitters (Briggs 1970: 62–3).

Though motivated by defensive strategy, the contraction of the broadcast spectrum also served to consolidate the power of the BBC as an instrument for the mediation of national identity. (That it coincided with the cessation, in September 1939, of broadcasts directed towards Britain from private Continental broadcasters like Radio Luxembourg and Radio Normandy reinforced this consolidation.) Domestic wartime programming became a means of interpellating British listeners into the nation: the BBC could inform and entertain its citizens while maintaining their confidence in the certainty and justness of a British victory. Radio is, as many critics have noted, a particularly effective medium for binding a public together.[10] Whether or not it is part of a concerted propaganda campaign, every programme effects a synchronisation of the listening public; in collapsing distance, radio brings into being a community of listeners whose common bond is the simultaneous experience of sound. Like the newspapers identified in Benedict Anderson's landmark study of nationalism, *Imagined Communities*, radio creates a common 'now' among far-flung communities sharing a language, as listeners consume time-sensitive programming within a particular historical moment (Anderson [1983] 2006: 35).[11] The synchronised ceremony of radio creates an awareness of simultaneous action across space and thereby helps to shape a community defined by a common language and time rather than immediate proximity. To tune in is to bring this bounded community into being, and to place individuals within the collective audience.

Radio scholars have identified a series of collectivising effects – variously described as 'we-feeling', 'sociability' and 'co-presence' – generated by the synchronous experience of the intimate medium of radio within the private space of the home.[12] Though distinct, these terms all reflect the fact that radio listening is a fundamentally social endeavour that hinges on an understanding, however nebulous, that each audience member is sharing an experience with others. In David Hendy's words, simultaneous listening generates an awareness that 'our lives stand in the same temporal relation to other listeners as much as they stand in the same temporal relationship to the programmes we hear' (Hendy 2000: 184). This collective synchronisation is not ethically or affectively neutral, as Kate Lacey argues; rather, awareness of others aids in the formation of relations of mutual obligation and empathy. Lacey rejects the tendency to label listening a passive process, and instead figures it as a state of charged and attentive receptivity to the utterances of others – a 'radical openness' that is 'fundamentally ethical' insofar as it enables empathetic connection across a distance (2013: 8, 14). Rather than a community defined by isolation, Lacey argues, 'the listening public is made up of listeners inhabiting a condition of plurality and intersubjectivity' (2013: 8). The instantaneity and simultaneity of radio thereby provide listeners with a sense of collectivity unavailable through other media; independent of the content of any one broadcast, radio builds ethical connections through the perception of a common culture unfolding in a shared historical present.

The collectivising affordances of radio were given concentrated effect in the British context. Even if the Home Service faced competition from Nazi propaganda and, as of 1940, the BBC's own Forces Programme, the mandate and coverage of the semi-governmental monopoly meant the BBC could credibly claim to speak to 'the nation' in its entirety. Addressing Britain as a whole – and not its constituent English, Scottish,

Welsh and Northern Irish elements individually – was especially important for the elaboration of a cohesive national identity. With the outbreak of war and the closure of the Regional Programme, the BBC encouraged speakers to replace the term 'England' with 'Britain' whenever speaking of the entire national–political entity, although it took some pressure from Scottish listeners to make this policy stick (Hajkowski 2010: 124, 155–8; Nicholas 1996: 231–2).[13] In particular, writers who had dedicated much of their careers to considerations of England and Englishness found it difficult to adjust their address to Britain, which results in some imprecision in the use of the two terms. Priestley, while he managed to refer to 'Britain' for the most part in his Home Service broadcasts, occasionally slipped between 'England' and 'Britain' in his transmissions to America in the series 'Britain Speaks'. George Orwell, whose India Section broadcasts and larger presence in discussions of national culture make him a kind of patron saint of the wartime broadcasting scene, was always more interested in England than in Britain.[14] He sought to justify the persistence of his Anglocentric vision by insisting, in *The Lion and the Unicorn: Socialism and the English Genius* (1941), that when seen from an international perspective the differences between Britain's constituent nations are less significant than their similarities; with a war on, in other words, Britons are more or less the same (Orwell 1998: vol. 12, 397–8). For most writers under consideration in this study, Britain was seen as a political formation with some admirable traits, if also considerable flaws; though they were willing to lend their skills in its defence, these writers often identified more strongly with other geopolitical formations, be they Johnston's commitment to Irish political and cultural independence, Marson's Jamaican upbringing or the Yorkshire of Priestley's youth.

Projecting Britain out of a sense of political necessity, rather than deep affective connection, hints at the limitations on the considerable power radio exerted as an instrument of what Todd Avery has called 'national discipline' (2006: 15). As much as the BBC took seriously the task of addressing Britain as a unified whole, there were fissures at the heart of this broadcast nation. For one thing, the Corporation aired more programme hours to overseas audiences than to domestic ones during the war, in an attempt to inform and persuade listeners in the Middle East, Continental Europe, the Indian Subcontinent, the Americas and the Pacific. The BBC might have had Britain's interests woven into its form and function, but it exported those interests to audiences whose own identities occupied an oblique, if not hostile, position relative to the wartime British state, which resulted in often divergent tactics for domestic and overseas broadcasting. Even within Britain, the consolidation of the listening public through the contraction of wavelengths and the closure of for-profit Continental competition could not mask significant disagreements in British society on topics ranging from postwar social policy to the question of Indian independence and to the kinds of entertainment the BBC should offer its listeners.

There were, in effect, multiple listening publics in wartime Britain and among its listeners overseas, a condition typical of the midcentury soundscape (Lacey 2013: 15–16). If the term 'radio public' is used throughout this study in the singular for the sake of convenience, its monolithic implications should not be taken to outweigh the evidence attesting to audiences diverse in terms of their geographical position, their political orientation, their tastes, their responses to programmes and policies, and their fluid nature over time. Publics are, after all, unitary only in their ideal, imagined states, as Michael Warner argues; they are 'virtual social object[s]' that enable address even if they never quite live up to themselves (2002: 55–6). Warner's theory suggests membership of the radio public is affiliative, actualised only by listeners' willingness to share in the flow of information through, around and about the medium of radio (2002: 72–4). Public-formation is therefore iterative and cyclical: the conjectural notion of a public affects discourse, and that discourse goes on to constitute its public by circulating among individuals who willingly identify themselves as members of a discursive community, regardless of whether they agree with a particular utterance.

The plurality of that circulation indicates that the wartime British radio public was neither a siloed entity nor a silent one; it both catalysed and responded to the circulation of radio discourse through a variety of cultural forms and channels (Warner 2002: 90–6). These discursive networks, though oriented around the BBC, took shape in the editorial pages and radio columns of every major daily newspaper, and played out in novels, films, variety shows, dinner-table conversations and office chatter. Perhaps most importantly, radio discourse extended into the pages of radio-centric periodicals like *The Listener*, *London Calling* and *Radio Times* in a tangible incursion of the ethereal community into the world of print. Debra Rae Cohen has analysed the BBC weekly *The Listener* in particular as 'an exemplary instance of the medial self-consciousness of modernist form', at once an archive of broadcasts deemed worthy of remediation, a venue for thinking about broadcasting and broadcast culture, and an education-oriented justification for the BBC's continued monopoly over broadcasting (2012: 572–81).[15] *The Listener* and related periodicals might drastically alter the medium-specific effects and temporalities of wireless by translating them into print, as Cohen argues, but by representing the protocols, personalities and ideas of the medium in another venue they also contributed to the process by which the radio public recognised itself as such. Similarly, although these periodicals published only a handful of letters in the pages of each issue, in doing so they expanded the network of discourse beyond the notional isolated listener. Thus if radio as a broadcast medium necessarily inhibits the two-way exchange of information – a condition it shares with literature, commercial sound recordings and film – its wartime producers and administrators did not foreclose the possibility of meaningful communication *about* and *with* the medium of radio.

A complete accounting of the plural, dynamic and often fractious radio public (let alone its interwoven relationship with publics formed around the circulation of other media) is beyond the scope of the present volume. But while this study takes as its objects of focus the broadcast and written articulations of cultural producers on the radio, it also assumes that the listening public exerted an influence on those articulations. The policy of sober and factually accurate propaganda pursued by the BBC, for example, reflected a widespread public antipathy towards 'atrocity stories' in the wake of the First World War;[16] public dissatisfaction with the stodgy offerings of the early war period contributed to the formation of the Forces Programme (later known as the Light Programme) in 1940; a desire to meet the exacting standards of listeners conditioned the modes of address of writers in positions as varied as those of Johnston (broadcasting to troops in North Africa as well as civilians in Britain), MacNeice (in his transmissions to a sceptical American audience) and Marson (broadcasting to a heterogeneous West Indian audience). Broadcasters soon learned, if they did not already know, that these complex and multiple listening publics were not passive vessels for the reception of a version of national or imperial identity dictated from on high, but were instead critical and reflexive communities whose engagement with radio spilled over into adjacent media.

Intermedial aesthetics

This book joins a growing body of intermedial scholarship on midcentury cultural production. The argument presented here takes intermediality – the mutual influence and interpenetration of media, in terms of both their formal potentialities and social contours – not as a special case, but rather as the general condition of artistic production within a midcentury media system characterised by mechanical reproduction.[17] Recent scholarship has lingered on the aesthetic and formal affordances of this era of media proliferation: how the limitations of any particular medium (the stillness and indexicality of the photograph, say, or the exclusively sonic profile of radio) determine certain artistic possibilities and social functions.[18] As Julian Murphet has argued, the proliferation of media in the late nineteenth and early twentieth centuries engendered a reassessment of literature *as a medium* among multiple other media. Murphet concerns himself specifically with modernism, which he interprets not as an aesthetic movement guided by a conscious exploration of new expressive possibilities, but as a 'structural adjustment within a given social and historical media ecology' (2009: 10). This media ecology operates according to a logic of 'convergence' and 'differentiation', as media come together in an interactive environment of competition and seek therein to assert their own formal and technical particularities (21–2). In this view, the formal concerns of literary modernism – interiority, textual ambiguity, and visual and auditory interplay, for example – are defensive articulations of the specifically textual qualities that distinguish literature from other media; and yet, these defensive articulations cannot be disentangled from their catalysing media environment. The present account is less interested in so-called 'high' modernism per se because to bracket off the effects of media competition as applying first and foremost to the literary avant-garde is to overlook the pervasiveness of intermediality in the early decades of the century; the effects of media proliferation were everywhere. But if modernism cannot claim exclusive rights to formal self-awareness in the new media system, Murphet's larger point is well taken: in the first half of the twentieth century, literature, like film, radio, recorded sound and photography, had to advocate consistently on its own behalf in order to survive and to thrive.

Scholars have begun to map, in earnest, the intermedial connections between literature and radio as they jostled at midcentury.[19] At stake in discussions of these connections are not only questions of aesthetic convergence between media but also the very question of the 'aesthetic' as distinct from the 'political'. In *Ireland and the Problem of Information: Irish Writing, Radio, Late Modernist Communication*, Damien Keane offers a clear articulation of the play of forces at work in broadcasting at a time of crisis: for Irish writers in the period around the Second World War, the convergence of mass mediation and total war made explicit the prevailing connections between literature and technologies of mass communication, on the one hand, and literature and politics on the other (2014: 7–8). Moving from Pierre Bourdieu's dictum that 'the most disputed frontier of all is the one which separates the field of cultural production and the field of power' (Bourdieu 1993: 43), Keane challenges the autonomy of 'autonomy' itself, whether in the form of Irish political neutrality or artistic disinterestedness. Instead, he argues that literary and political discourses enjoy a 'constitutive imbrication' that is woven into their circulation through a mediated field of relations (Keane 2014: 9, 47).[20] If the role of 'literary artist' is simply one position among many to be taken up in a media environment that is always articulated to larger economic and social concerns, then it becomes exceedingly difficult to map what Orwell calls 'the frontiers of art and propaganda', and never more so than in wartime (Orwell 1998: vol. 12, 483–6). To carry Keane's vocabulary from its Irish context to a British one, the recurring feature of wartime cultural production at the BBC was not its autonomy, but rather its heteronomy – the subjection, willing or otherwise, of writers to pressures outside themselves.[21]

The BBC radio feature *Alexander Nevsky* (1941) offers one illustration of the forces at work in the densely networked and politically charged wartime media ecology. In the summer of 1941, the BBC commissioned Louis MacNeice to draft an hour-long radio adaptation of Sergei Eisenstein's 1938 film of the same name; this adaptation was to be brought to life by veteran film, radio and television producer Dallas Bower. *Alexander Nevsky* was Eisenstein's first completed film to feature sound, and represented a return from the political wilderness following years of official disfavour. For the film's score, composer Sergei Prokofiev had drawn on lessons acquired from the use of audio-visual counterpoint in the films of Walt Disney, whom both he and Eisenstein admired and whom Prokofiev had visited in early 1938 (Merritt 1994: 42). Despite a positive initial reception, Eisenstein's film lost its political currency with the signing of the Molotov–Ribbentrop pact in the summer of 1939 and was pulled from circulation. In its brief window of aesthetic and ideological acclaim, however, a copy of the film had made its way to the BBC, where Bower used it to train camera operators at the Corporation's short-lived experimental television service, which was shut down upon the outbreak of war. By 1941, with the USSR now among the Allies battling Germany, the film could be resurrected as pro-Soviet fodder for the BBC.

Alexander Nevsky's path to British listeners' ears is thus mediated through international and intermedial networks conditioned, at multiple points, by political demands: a Northern Irish poet and an English producer team up to adapt, for radio, a Soviet film collaboration between an avant-garde composer and modernist filmmaker both inspired by Disney; this adaptation is only made possible thanks to the BBC's nascent television facilities at Alexandra Palace, which held on to the film long enough to bridge a brief chasm of political ineffectuality. In these exchanges, political forces were alternately generative and inhibitive of aesthetic production and circulation. Furthermore, as deeper discussion of the broadcast in Chapter 3 reveals, the problems of intermedial translation prompted in MacNeice some creative propagandising on behalf of older traditions of oral literature, as well as of the particular affordances of radio. The broadcast version of *Alexander Nevsky* is thus a cultural object sedimented with the multiple competing forces of the wartime media ecology: literary practices and new forms of mediation; established literary reputation and the collaborative imperatives of radio; and writerly autonomy and its instrumentalisation by official agencies.

Collaboration and compromise

By laying bare the imbrication of the literary and the political through the threat of their complete equation under totalitarian rule, the Second World War forced writers to approach wartime cultural production with a mix of scepticism and resolve. If the interwar years had gradually revealed the contradictions inherent in the official British version of the Great War, by the late 1930s most British intellectuals could no longer deny the threat posed by fascist governments on the Continent. The Italian invasion of Ethiopia, Franco's takeover of Spain and Hitler's methodical rearmament and occupation of the Rhineland, Austria and the Sudetenland made pacifist arguments and strategies of appeasement increasingly untenable. Faced with a choice between rehearsing the dubious propaganda of the Great War and refusing to participate in what began to seem like an inevitable conflict with Germany, many writers staked out a middle ground by pairing an anti-fascist commitment with an ironic disdain for the jingoism of imperial Britain. 'In 1914, war still seemed a romantic, heroic thing,' observed Cecil Day Lewis in an interview for the BBC programme *Ariel in Wartime* in March 1941, 'but today the poets are more like sirens before an air-raid – they strike a warning note ... It is the pity of war rather than its glory which most affects us' (Day Lewis 1941: 2). Lewis captures the resigned determination of this stance in his poem 'Where Are the War Poets?' (1943), written as a riposte to oft-repeated calls that literary artists should participate more fully in the war of words:

> It is the logic of our times,
> No subject for immortal verse–
> That we who lived by honest dreams
> Defend the bad against the worse. ([1943] 1992: 335)

Emerging from the stark polarisations of the interwar period, British writers cast their lot with a politics of consensus whose public manifestations included the cross-party National Government, the appropriation of private property in the name of total war under the Emergency Powers (Defence) Act of 1940 and the atmosphere of collective solidarity represented by the People's War. The enemy made it easy to define what Britain was struggling against; the more difficult issue was what they were struggling for.

The fact that most intellectuals chose to support a government whose initial war aims did not include a devolved Empire, a welfare state or a levelling of class hierarchies indicates that their support was a calculated instance of collaboration. The term 'collaboration', especially in a work about the Second World War, risks invoking the Vichy government and other puppet regimes set up by authoritarian powers. Its use here is not intended to draw a clear equation between historically specific instances of cooperation with an occupying fascist power, on the one hand, and an established imperialist democracy on the other. Rather, 'collaboration' signals the everydayness of political compromise in a fractious and unequal polity. Whether politically right or left – and most fell somewhere between liberalism and democratic socialism – writers who chose to broadcast traded a measure of their independence for a voice in an anti-fascist struggle that they judged to be more significant than other (still significant) ethical and political issues facing Britain. For many, collaboration offered the only means of advocating for alternatives to the worst injustices of interwar Britain and its Empire en route to victory, especially as the collectivising tendencies of rationing, nationalisation of production and cross-class solidarity began to show what Britons could achieve together. 'To be loyal both to Chamberlain's England and to the England of tomorrow might seem an impossibility, if one did not know it to be an everyday phenomenon,' Orwell wrote in autumn 1940. 'Only revolution can save England, that has been obvious for years, but now the revolution has started, and it may proceed quite quickly if only we can keep Hitler out' ([1968] 1970: vol. 1, 591). That Orwell later dismissed as naïve his early assessments of the 'revolution' under way during the war does not alter the fact that the promise of political gain was sufficient to motivate his work, and that of many others, on behalf of the government.

'Collaboration' is also a useful term in the present context because it carries the positive sense of working together for a mutually beneficial output. It is a particularly radio-centric term; assembling a broadcast demands the cooperation of dozens, if not hundreds, of individuals, from the engineers responsible for maintaining and extending infrastructure to the producers who transform scripts into programmes and the actors and musicians whose performances give audible shape to words and notes. Writing shortly after the war, MacNeice articulated the creative benefits of collective cultural production: 'In this age of irreconcilable idioms I have often heard writers hankering for some sort of group life ... we cannot but envy playwrights, actors or musical executants. And here again I for one have found this missing group experience, in a valid form, in radio' ([1946] 1993: 406–7). As Chapter 3 argues, MacNeice and his collaborators used large-scale radio productions to allegorise the process of collective labour for collective gain through features like *Christopher Columbus*. But even writers who broadcast on a more modest scale collaborated on both artistic and political levels: they shared in the process of creation with editors and producers while adjusting their contributions to fit the propaganda and censorship directives of a nation at war.

Collaboration via radio enabled the dissemination of ideas that could be simultaneously anti-Nazi and progressive, as British writers tested the claims of liberal democracy by pushing for greater socio-political rights for the disenfranchised at home and abroad. But collaboration also entailed a complicated relationship to government agencies like the BBC. In his account of the relationship between modernism and war in twentieth-century Britain, Patrick Deer describes British literature in terms of a tension between official war culture – those texts and cultural forms which are explicitly created or promoted by the state – and other, more 'resistant' forms of writing (2009: 4). Official war cultures claim to offer strategic 'oversight' of the conflict, a commanding perspective from which disruptive and chaotic elements can be subsumed into a larger, more coherent version of events. Deer places literary production in an ambivalent position relative to official war culture: as a nominally autonomous and socially privileged site of expression, wartime literature offered a means of narrating the ironic contradictions between the view from on high and 'the view of those living out the tactical realities of the conflict' (2009: 10). Yet official culture proved remarkably adaptable during the Second World War: 'The deeply conservative Churchillian vision of Englishness and Empire jostled alongside other, more radical perspectives. British war culture was flexible enough to combine apparently contradictory elements with ease' (2009: 134). The People's War succeeded, as a mythology, in part because it could expand to encompass both residual and emergent notions of what it meant to be a part of 'the People'.[22] Seen in this light, official British war culture was hegemonic in a Gramscian sense: an elastic form of political control in which concessions to disadvantaged segments of the polity serve to foster cooperation and therefore minimise disruptions to the status quo.[23] This is not to say that social transformations did not occur, simply that such transformations fell short of some of the more radical goals dreamt of by writers like Marson and Priestley, or took longer to realise.

While hegemonic forms of containment obtained in British society at large during the war, they are especially relevant to the situation at the BBC. As the voice of the nation at home and abroad, the BBC was tasked with projecting Britain as a tolerant and democratic nation, if only to provide a stark contrast with the totalitarian enemy. At the same time, the British government could ill afford serious disruptions of the status quo. Any major change – from an outright revolution at home to the breakout of independence movements overseas – risked the fatal weakening of a country that, by June 1940, was the last obstacle preventing total Axis domination of Europe. To ensure the right message of national solidarity alongside democratic vitality, the BBC chose its star performers carefully, often with an eye for intellectuals and writers whose views put them slightly at odds with the government. In a letter to George Woodcock dated 2 December 1942, Orwell was typically straightforward about how the BBC used dissenters:

> As to the ethics of b'casting and in general letting oneself be used by the British governing class. It's of little value to argue [about] it, it is chiefly a question of whether one considers it more important to down the Nazis first or whether one believes doing this is meaningless unless one achieves one's own revolution first. But for heaven's sake don't think I don't see how they are using me. ([1968] 1970: vol. 2, 307)

To varying degrees, all of the writers who broadcast during the war understood and accepted the compromise that Orwell identifies. They recognised that they were lending their names and literary reputations to an organisation with which they could not agree wholeheartedly, but which offered the best means of contributing to the war effort and furthering their own agendas to whatever degree possible. Unable – or unwilling – to reproduce the patriotic zeal with which some writers served the British government's propaganda interests during the First World War, this next generation approached the field of wartime cultural production with a hard-eyed pragmatism that saw no alternatives but to pursue the fight against fascism.

The ethics of this pragmatism were coloured by the fact that the relationship between the BBC and the government was the subject of much debate during the war. Under the plans drawn up following the Munich Crisis in 1938, the BBC faced the possibility of a complete takeover by the Ministry of Information (MoI) upon the declaration of war (Briggs

1970: 32, 85). In the end, close coordination with the MoI, rather than outright domination by it, enabled the BBC to maintain a measure of independence, specifically over script-writing, performers and programme planning. Scannell and Cardiff summarise this relationship as one in which the BBC 'would take advice and guidance from its many official clients on what were the key propaganda issues at any moment and on matters of fact relating to them, but it reserved to itself control of the forms and manner of presentations' (1987: 176). For the figures considered in this study, official guidance most often took the form of broad programming decisions and minor script-level censorship. Louis MacNeice's dramatic feature *Alexander Nevsky*, for example, emerged from a broader BBC initiative in 1941 to welcome the Soviet Union as a new ally in the war, an initiative which clearly catered to government demands. On the other hand, Denis Johnston and Una Marson each had scripts redacted by internal BBC censors because they violated policy or security protocols established in consultation with the MoI and other agencies. More drastic was the BBC's policy, enacted in August 1940, of banning speakers with pacifist, communist or fascist leanings from the microphone. Although rescinded after a few months under pressure from the public, the press and prominent radio figures including Ralph Vaughan Williams and E. M. Forster, the ban foregrounded the potential for direct political interference in broadcasting (Robert Mackay 2006: 499–502).[24] While public outcry re-established the nominal separation of powers between the BBC and the government, such episodes demonstrate that any boundary between political and cultural spheres would be permeable and fiercely contested.

Politics and propaganda

Given the extensive overlap of power and cultural production between 1939 and 1945, 'politics' functions in this study in its most expansive sense: as a discursive field in which matters of collective existence are imagined, debated, legislated, executed and policed. With the exception of J. B. Priestley's involvement with the Common Wealth party from 1941 and his failed bid (as an independent candidate) for the seat of Cambridge University in the General Election of 1945, none of these writers tried their hand at party politics directly. But war has a way of heightening the immanent political content and impact of cultural production in fields that might prefer to claim autonomy; in these circumstances, the writer–broadcasters examined in this study felt compelled to speak on questions of social organisation, long-term planning, citizenship, colonial relations, race and the prosecution of the war itself. To be a public intellectual during the war was to position oneself in the political field. Like most forms of public cultural activity in the war, broadcasting became a means through which these intellectuals could structure public understanding of the terms and consequences of the war.

Writers who broadcast were therefore propagandists to the extent that they saw their war work as a way of orienting listeners in a crowded media environment, a project most of them felt to be ethically defensible. On the domestic front, the BBC largely stuck to what was called 'White' propaganda: sustaining British morale through programming that instilled in listeners not only a sense of what they were fighting for and against, but also a confidence in eventual victory, all without resorting to deliberate untruth.[25] This strategy was typified by the News Division, which in spring 1938 had outlined its plans, should war arrive. In the words of Home Service news editor R. T. Clark: 'It seems to me that the only way to strengthen the morale of the people whose morale is worth strengthening, is to tell them the truth, and nothing but the truth, even if the truth is horrible' (qtd in Briggs 1965: 656–7). In its overseas broadcasts, the BBC deployed a similar approach: whether speaking to Britain's own forces overseas, to residents of Britain's colonies or to listeners in Axis-occupied countries, the emphasis was on a 'propaganda of truth' through which, it was judged, the struggle to influence opinion and promote British concerns would best be served.[26] As Mark Wollaeger notes, however, one of the lingering effects of the previous war was a public scepticism about official truths, given the British government's record of deploying statistics, tables and reports with deceptive intent:

> The supposed independence of facts, their imperviousness to the assimilative power of systematic knowledge or suasion, made it easier for British officials to declare their fidelity to the veridical while subtly integrating facts into patterns designed to manipulate public opinion. (2006: 22)

Chapter 4 explores in more detail the instrumentalisation of facts, as well as practices of information suppression and 'spin' at the BBC; it is here sufficient to note that British writers were not unaware of the sometimes sinister uses to which truth could be put. E. M. Forster, who was both a listener and a broadcaster during the war, captured in a diary entry of 3 April 1941 the scepticism with which writers treated the BBC's much-touted freedom from cant: 'I know that I am being got at; frankness is used to lull suspicion and make us uncritical of the next lie' (qtd in Lago et al. 2008: 136).

The term 'propaganda' was itself used quite freely within the BBC to refer to all communication with persuasive intent. The Department of Listener Research, responsible for gauging public responses to programming, conducted studies of 'The Audience for Propaganda Features', for example, while officials like Assistant Controller for Overseas Services R. A. Rendall described the Blitz series *The Stones Cry Out* as 'propaganda' directed at an American audience (Silvey 1940; Rendall 1941b). The term nonetheless retained a whiff of disrepute; during the war, some writers tried to distinguish between overtly manipulative propaganda and the subtle persuasion engendered by either forthright communication or literary art. In a broadcast to America in September 1940, Priestley outlined the two scales on which propaganda can be said to operate; while he acknowledged his radio talks might be considered propaganda because they advocated for the prosecution of war against Germany, he claimed that, unlike Nazi propaganda, his broadcasts were not part of a coherent and concerted attempt to sway listeners (1940a: 231-2). While Priestley's claim was disingenuous – he was being paid handsomely by the MoI to promote the British cause to America – it remains true that British writers were freer to say what they wished than were their German counterparts. MacNeice, writing shortly before he joined the BBC, took a different tack by arguing that the best propaganda might not be propaganda at all:

> It is nonsense to say, as many say nowadays, that all great poetry is propaganda ... [T]he fact that a poem in which a belief is implicit may convert some whom direct propaganda does not touch, far from proving that that poem is propaganda, only proves that propaganda *can* be beaten on its own ground by something other than itself, so that we can admit that poetry can incidentally have effects like those of propaganda though its proper function is not propagandist. ([1938] 1968: 201–2)

MacNeice seems, in this interwar comment, to be operating under a fairly narrow definition of propaganda: as brute political communication which seeks to persuade through manipulation. When he signed on for broadcasts to America that can only be described as propagandistic, however, he did not shy away from blending the political and the poetic, even if they remain for him distinct poles ideally separable in peacetime.

While acknowledging that 'propaganda' was a contested term during the war, this study follows the broad use the term enjoyed within the BBC, as signifying information deployed with the intent to persuade the recipient of a particular ideology, a political position or a set of values. Jacques Ellul has outlined a similarly expansive theory of persuasion, arguing that propaganda is not simply a tool used by nefarious governments, but is instead the natural outgrowth of all technological societies in which information travels widely and instantaneously. Propaganda offers a means by which individuals can navigate the surfeit of data they encounter on a daily basis; in easing this navigation, propaganda allows individuals to adapt more smoothly to social life (1962: xvii). While this information management takes many forms, the most relevant here is Ellul's notion of 'integration propaganda', a diffuse form of persuasion that operates through many of the political and cultural structures of everyday life, and which produces 'a progressive adaptation to a certain order of things, a certain concept of human relations, which unconsciously moulds individuals and makes them conform to society' (1962: 64). Rather than being dragooned into political obedience, Ellul argues, individuals participate in their own integration because it offers a palliative to the alienation brought on by the semiotic surplus of a media-saturated existence (1962: 118–60).

Building on Ellul's work, Mark Wollaeger positions propaganda and modernist literature as 'proximate information practices' in the first half of the twentieth century; each offers a means of transforming the informational saturation of the media ecology into something legible or assimilable by the population at large (2006: xvi). While propaganda translates the 'negative affect' of informational excess into 'socially "productive" forms, such as myths, stereotypes, and xenophobia', modernism knits it into more private, metaphoric structures whose abstruseness hints at a coherence to be revealed (2006: 12, 22–3). Though often thought of as the opposite of propaganda, Wollaeger argues, modernist literature in fact 'performs its cultural work [within] a kind of psychosocial contact zone defined at one extreme by subjectivity construed as a sanctuary for being, and at the other by propaganda as an encompassing array of manipulative discourses' (2006: 10). This observation – that literature discovers itself shaped by, through or at the borders of its propagandistic 'other' – offers a useful lens for considering the relationship of writerly radio output to larger government objectives during the war. Not incidentally, this lens reveals a dynamic of convergence and differentiation parallel to that encountered at the level of media competition in the early twentieth century. In each case, the markers of textuality and aesthetic autonomy that are said to define 'literature' emerge more sharply articulated following a chastening encounter with an uncannily proximate cultural form, whether mass-cultural, political or both.

Literature and radio laboured under considerable external pressures during the war. Rather than marking the end of meaningful aesthetic production in wartime, however, the heteronomous conditions of war opened up a highly productive set of relations between ostensibly distinct categories, including the individual and the state, the personal and the collective, and art and propaganda. At a historical juncture in which the very idea of artistic autonomy could be, and was, used for propagandistic ends, writers fused the language of literary aesthetics with the affordances of radio to negotiate emergent forms of national identity and political futurity better. Radio allowed them to disseminate, on a wide scale, the terms of literary and cultural debate in order to address the war's substantial socio-cultural shifts and geopolitical upheavals. But radio did more than repeat the modes of a textual culture: its aurality heightened and foregrounded cultural markers that often lay dormant, or crudely approximated, on the page. Accents demarcating class, race and region rose in the mix, as did registers of sophistication and naïveté, and gendered and sexualised vocalities. Understanding the wartime role of radio demands an attention not only to its auditory particularities, but also to its circulation in a media ecology in which literature, though under sustained challenge, retained the power of an *éminence grise*: hoary, beset by doubts and fears about its own obsolescence, but still distinguished enough to shape the parameters of the larger social conversation. As writers adapted themselves to the medium of radio, they brought with them an array of formal and thematic concerns that influenced the newer medium in its aesthetic and political dimensions.

What follows

The chapters to come address the complex of intermedial, institutional, political and historical forces at work at the wartime BBC through a variety of author-centric case studies.[27] While radio was nothing if not collaborative, individual writer–broadcasters serve as useful nodes from which to consider the wartime BBC both because the reception of their broadcasts in large part depended on the reputations they had cultivated outside of the broadcasting booth, and because the pressures of war often reveal themselves more clearly in the case of writers accustomed to a considerable degree of autonomy. This is nowhere truer than in the case of J. B. Priestley, whose demotic broadcasts proved both useful and dangerous to the BBC and the British government. Chapter 1 contextualises Priestley's famously populist broadcasts of 1940–1 within larger debates about the relationship between popular literary forms and cultural authority, and places his broadcasts in conversation with published and unpublished wartime writings. The spirit of social levelling that animates Priestley's broadcasts in the series 'Postscripts' and 'Britain

Speaks' resonates with his literary output both before and during the war; in particular, his broadcasts articulate, at the political level, a commitment to cultural democracy that builds on his engagement in debates about cultural hierarchies in the 1920s and 1930s. In declaring this commitment, Priestley capitalised on his mastery of both radiogenic and literary forms, from the appealing novelty of his Yorkshire accent and his skills as an everyman orator to his talent in the genre of the familiar essay.

Chapters 2 and 3 move from the genre of the 'talk' to that of the 'feature', a quasi-documentary radio form that prospered at the BBC from the 1930s to the 1960s. Beginning in earnest in 1940, the Department of Features and Drama recruited literary talent in the hopes of improving the quality of the BBC's informative and propagandistic broadcasts. Not all writers found the constraints of wartime broadcasting salutary. Chapter 2 offers a brief portrait of the early radio career of proletarian novelist James Hanley, whose impressionistic prose and bleak outlook proved intractable in the face of attempts to shape them towards the ends of the Corporation. In his struggles, however, Hanley reveals the contingent nature of those ends; if the war could not admit of either excessive experimentalism or excessive despair, Hanley's postwar successes on the Third Programme indicate that his failure was a question of timing as much as talent. Hanley's fellow feature-writer, Louis MacNeice, proved far more adept at the formal demands of radio. Chapter 3 examines his landmark radio features *The Stones Cry Out*, *Alexander Nevsky* and *Christopher Columbus*, and traces in their carefully wrought forms a concern with rebuilding that moves from the physical project of post-Blitz recovery to the larger project of postwar planning. If *The Stones Cry Out* put MacNeice's formal skills as a poet to work in building complex, nationally resonant soundscapes, his later plays emphasise the collaborative effort necessary to guide the listening public through similarly dense acoustic environments that function as parables for the war itself.

If familiarity and form are keywords for Priestley and MacNeice, respectively, Denis Johnston put his faith in a threefold neutrality, as Chapter 4 demonstrates. In his work as a BBC war correspondent in North Africa, Italy, France and Germany, Johnston insisted on neutrality not only as the prerogative of Ireland and its citizens (including himself), but also as the guiding principle of both journalism and the technological mediation of war. Equipped with the latest recording technologies at the front, Johnston saw in their perfect reproduction of the sounds of battle a chance for listeners to hear the war speak for itself, free from human interference. As the war went on, however, Johnston realised not only the bias inherent in all representations of the war, but also his complicity as a participant observer of the conflict. His postwar memoir, *Nine Rivers from Jordan* (1953), enacts a metafictional upending of this goal of neutrality, in favour of a plural, but morally invested, version of the facts of war.

The final chapter of this study concerns the formation of transnational communities of colour through BBC programmes such as *Calling the West Indies*. Having arrived in London in the 1930s, host Una Marson transformed a 'message home' programme for Caribbean soldiers stationed in the UK into a literary and cultural forum for writers from across the Black Atlantic. Though barred from advocating openly for independence, Marson used her programme to promote West Indian cultural autonomy by spotlighting emerging Caribbean literary figures and forging connections with activists and intellectuals from the United States, Britain, Africa and elsewhere. These connections swapped the bilateral arrangement of metropole and colony for a multilateral wireless Black Atlantic, and took up radio waves as a midcentury analogue for Paul Gilroy's chronotope of the ship as technology of black internationalism (1993: 12). Beyond building such transatlantic networks, *Calling the West Indies* afforded listeners in the Caribbean the first opportunities to hear literature spoken in the West Indian forms of English which Edward Kamau Brathwaite would go on to call 'nation language' (1984: 5–6). By focusing on Marson's wartime work, this chapter rectifies a persistent tendency, in histories of Caribbean literature and broadcasting, to omit not only the central role played by this progressive feminist intellectual, but also the role of the war itself as catalyst for the postwar literary renaissance in the West Indies.

This study concludes by leaping over the immediate postwar years to the moment of radio's supersession by a not entirely new media competitor. Though initially developed in the interwar years, television did not replace radio as the pre-eminent medium of national self-representation until the 1950s: specifically, with the spectacular coronation of Queen Elizabeth II in 1953. This double coronation of monarch and medium offered the writers who figure in these pages a chance to meditate on their role in addressing the collective formations that took shape during the conflict. While the war represents a particular and ultimately transient moment in the intermedial history of radio and literature, the consequences of the conflict spilled out from the war to shape the Commonwealth and the welfare state that would greet a newly crowned Queen. If not a wholesale revolution, the radio war had nonetheless facilitated, and borne witness to, significant transformations: having entered the war as an imperial nation riven by class and ideology, Britain left it a nation transformed if not united, prepared to embark on the massive social experiment of the multicultural postwar welfare state with a renewed sense of possibility and promise.

Notes

1. On the origins of the phrase 'the People's War', see Angus Calder (1969: 136–9). On the larger myth and its debunking, see Rose (2004) and Angus Calder (1993). Accounts of literary production during the People's War include Deer (2009), Marina MacKay (2007), Mellor (2011), Piette (1995), Plain (2013) and Rawlinson (2000).
2. Damien Keane makes a strong case for the role of radio in the Ethiopian Crisis of 1935–6 (2014: 18–27). While radio (especially international propaganda) did play an important role in that conflict, as it did in the Spanish Civil War, the Second World War represents an immense expansion of that role in terms of geography, programming hours, staff and infrastructure.
3. While the end of the Second World War heralded the beginning of the end of the British Empire, the process of decolonisation has taken decades. India and Pakistan acquired independence in 1947; Burma and Sri Lanka in 1948; Sudan, Ghana and Malaysia in the 1950s; and a majority of Britain's Caribbean and African colonies by the 1960s. To this day, Britain retains possession of fourteen Overseas Territories.
4. A partial list of those who took to the microphone during the war would include Mulk Raj Anand, Elizabeth Bowen, Cecil Day Lewis, Cedric Dover, T. S. Eliot, William Empson, E. M. Forster, Patrick Hamilton, James Hanley, Inez Holden, Denis Johnston, Rose Macaulay, Desmond MacCarthy, Louis MacNeice, Una Marson, George Orwell, J. B. Priestley, V. S. Pritchett, Herbert Read, Dorothy Sayers, Stevie Smith, Stephen Spender, L. A. G. Strong, M. J. Tambimuttu, Dylan Thomas and Rebecca West.
5. For example, Louis MacNeice initially thought radio 'a degrading medium, both vulgar and bureaucratic and not even financially rewarding' (qtd in Coulton 1980: 44); John Middleton Murry declared his 'instinctive aversion to wireless' in 1925 (qtd in LeMahieu 1988: 180); and Wyndham Lewis blamed the radio (along with cinema and the popular press) for 'destroying individuality in the masses' (Carey 1992: 190).
6. For a range of perspectives on British propaganda directed at the United States and elsewhere, see Susan A. Brewer, *To Win the Peace: British Propaganda to the United States during World War II* (1977); Tim Brooks, *British Propaganda to France, 1940–1944: Machinery, Method and Message* (2007); Robert Calder, *Beware the British Serpent: The Role of Writers in British Propaganda in the United States, 1939–1945* (2004); James Chapman, *The British at War: Cinema, State and Propaganda* (1998); Robert Cole, *Propaganda, Censorship and Irish Neutrality in the Second World War* (2006); and Nicholas Cull, *Selling War: The British Propaganda against American 'Neutrality' in World War II* (1995).
7. On the transnational turn in modernist studies, see, for example, Susan

Stanford Friedman, *Planetary Modernism: Provocations on Modernity Across Time* (2015); Pascale Casanova, *The World Republic of Letters* (2004); and Mark Wollaeger and Matthew Eatough (eds), *The Oxford Handbook of Global Modernisms* (2012). On border crossings both geographical and medial in the case of midcentury radio, see Keane (2014: 8).

8. I here follow Emily Bloom's useful distinction of the radiogenic from the radiophonic. For Bloom, the former term identifies radio-specific traits and techniques that range from modes of address (whether intimate or stentorian) to conventions of audio mixing and the deployment of spatio-temporal codes like flashbacks, voice-overs and interior monologues. The term 'radiophonic', on the other hand, tends to privilege a particular form of radio art, often non-verbal or highly experimental in nature, an association stemming from the specific historical case of the BBC Radiophonic Workshop, founded in 1958 (Bloom 2017: 4–5).
9. On the growth of the BBC and its cultural politics in the 1920s and 1930s, see Chapter 1 of the present volume; see also Avery (2006: 1–31) and Scannell and Cardiff (1991: *passim*).
10. See, for example, Douglas (1999), Hendy (2000), Hilmes (1997 and 2012), Loviglio (2005), and Scannell and Cardiff (1991).
11. Anderson's near-silence on the question of radio has puzzled some scholars, given that broadcasting offers a concentrated example of mediated nation-formation. He makes only two brief mentions of radio; one of these, a footnote, states that radio extends processes of nation-formation to illiterate populations ([1983] 2006: 54). For discussions of Anderson's work in relation to radio, see Hilmes (1997: 11–12, 22–3 and 2012: 12) and Chignell (2009b: n.p.).
12. Scannell and Cardiff refer to the generation of a 'we-feeling' necessary to the creation of collective narratives (1991: 277); Hendy and Chignell emphasise the concepts of 'co-presence' (an awareness of the shared experience of listening) and 'sociability' (a positive emotional effect generated by a presumed intimacy between speaker and listeners) (Hendy 2000: 184; Chignell 2009a: n.p.).
13. That 'Britain' did not, in geographical terms, include Northern Ireland does not seem to have bothered the majority of Northern Irish listeners. Thomas Hajkowski notes that BBC Northern Ireland, already substantially Unionist in orientation, became even more so as the Republic of Ireland committed itself to neutrality for the duration of the war (2010: 205).
14. See the final footnote of this chapter for a list of important research on Orwell's broadcasting career. It is only because of the robust body of scholarship on Orwell's broadcasts that he does not feature more prominently in this volume.
15. Cohen's essay '"Strange Collisions": Keywords Toward an Intermedial Periodical Studies' (2015) offers a further application of theories of intermediality to *The Listener*.
16. On the influence of First World War 'atrocity stories' on interwar and Second World War propaganda techniques, see Wollaeger (2006: 14–22, 222–4).
17. The recent surge in intermedial literary studies has significant forerunners.

Keith Williams (1996) and D. L. LeMahieu (1988) remain vital touchstones in intermedial cultural history of the early twentieth century. Irina Rajewsky (2005) offers a useful elaboration of intermediality as it applies to literary studies; for an overview of recent intermedial approaches to literature and radio studies, see Whittington (2014: 641–3).
18. David Trotter, for example, has labelled the interwar years 'the first media age', describing it as the period in which the mass media's hold on the general public became a 'stranglehold' and writers began to imagine their work in the light of multiple alternatives to textuality (2013: 2–3). For Trotter, radio is a hybrid medium, positioned between the representational properties of media like film and the novel, and the communicative efficiencies of the telephone and the wireless; radio offers both a technologically mediated space for reflection and the smooth transmission of information (2013: 8–9, 174–83). See also Goble (2010).
19. Todd Avery insists that the ethical engagement of writers in interwar broadcasting generated new forms of modernism that demand new scholarly apparatus and forms of attention (Avery 2006: 143). Debra Rae Cohen (2009, 2010, 2012 and 2015) has explored the 'strange collisions' of print media and radio in a series of essays. Emily Bloom's *The Wireless Past: Anglo-Irish Writers and the BBC, 1931–1968* (2017) captures the exemplary midcentury condition of being caught between the past and the future. Melissa Dinsman's *Modernism at the Microphone: Radio, Propaganda, and Literary Aesthetics During World War II* (2015) explores the same historical moment as the present volume, but with an attention to the formation of transnational modernist networks in wartime – British, German and American – rather than the elaboration of socio-political futures for Britain and its Empire.
20. To give just one of Keane's examples, Irish novelist Francis Stuart's broadcasts from Germany during the war both advocated for and instantiated claims of writerly autonomy and Irish neutrality; yet the material existence of those broadcasts cannot be separated from either their origins in the Nazi propaganda infrastructure or their transcription by Allied radio monitoring services (2014: 108–21).
21. On heteronomy, see Keane (2014: 73, 75–6, 83).
22. On 'dominant, residual and emergent' aspects of a cultural system, see Raymond Williams (1977: 121–7).
23. On hegemony, see Hall (1980: 332–4) and Raymond Williams (1977: 112–14). LeMahieu has pointed out the potential tautology and classism of such hegemonic arguments: claims that even expressions of dissent are incorporated by the hegemonic state make every exception seem like part of the rule. Only by 'oracular' judgements about when an act or utterance is truly 'counter-hegemonic' can an assessment of social change be made (1988: 15–16). Moreover, the adjudication of what is or is not in the best interests of the public at large – and of the extent to which the public is complicit in its own domination – depends on a presumed superiority on the part of the scholar (1988: 17). These criticisms, while valid, downplay the extent to which the hegemonic view of culture allows for incremental social change. Indeed, despite his reservations, LeMahieu acknowledges that the theory of hegemony represents a subtler middle ground between

more rigid theories of 'strong containment' and more celebratory accounts of the autonomy of the cultural consumer.
24. While the ban was in fact the result of a decision made by a drastically reduced BBC Board of Governors, that decision was taken in a heavy-handed attempt to align BBC hiring policies with broader government objectives, as Robert Mackay argues (2006: 499–502).
25. So-called 'Black' propaganda – which seeks to mask its political origins and intentions – was the domain of the clandestine Political Warfare Executive, whose deceptive output included Axis-aimed broadcasts that, while written and transmitted from Britain, purported to come from within Axis territory.
26. On the 'propaganda of truth', see Wollaeger (2006: 21–2, 223), Robert Calder (2004: 43–4, 206) and Briggs (1970: 6–7).
27. Some familiar names from the emerging canon of wartime broadcasting – including Orwell, Forster, Bowen and Anand – remain in the margins of this study, not because their work at the BBC was any less important to the articulation of British and imperial identity over the radio, but because it has already received considerable scholarly attention. Important contributions to discussions of Orwell's wartime broadcasts include W. J. West (1985 and [1985] 1987), Davison (1998), especially volumes 13–15, Dinsman (2015), Kerr (2002 and 2004), and Fleay and Sanders (1989). Forster's broadcasts have received attention from Lago (1990), Morse (2011) and Fifield (2014). On Bowen's broadcasts, see Hepburn (2010) and Bloom (2017). Anand is the most prominent among several South Asian writers whose contributions to broadcasting are belatedly receiving due attention from scholars including Ranasinha (2007, 2008 and 2010), Bluemel (2004) and Morse (2015).

Chapter 1

Out of the People:
J. B. Priestley's Broadbrow Radicalism

Already a successful novelist, essayist and playwright by 1939, Joseph Boynton (J. B.) Priestley found himself transformed, with the help of what he termed 'some fortunate accidents of voice and manner', into the greatest radio celebrity of the war (1940c: vii). Aspects of his radio career are now firmly established elements of the 'People's War' mythology: over the course of twenty-eight broadcasts in the 'Postscripts' series, aired between June 1940 and March 1941, Priestley captured, on average, a third of the adult listening public in Britain, with his audience peaking at 40.4 per cent in spring 1941 (Baxendale 2007: 14; LR/231).[1] These short, familiar radio talks – part of his larger wartime output of over 200 Home Service and Overseas transmissions – were designed to offer a commentary on the events of the war and the responses of British citizens. Priestley used the forum to extol the courage of average Britons in his decidedly non-metropolitan Yorkshire accent, all the while insisting that the conflict must yield a more equitable society after the war, a position which led to clashes with BBC officials and Conservative members of government. His place in the public imagination of the war, then as now, depends on his relation to other prominent broadcasters inside and outside Britain: if Winston Churchill presented himself as 'the Voice of the Nation', radio historian Siân Nicholas argues, then Priestley was 'the Voice of the People', at once wise, familiar, and sceptical of officialdom (1996: 60). This scepticism allowed Priestley to draw listeners away from illicit broadcasts emanating from the Continent; he offered listeners a hint of the more scandalous counter-narratives offered by pro-Nazi radio propagandists like Lord Haw-Haw, with none of the treason.[2] Priestley excelled, in large part, because his winking at authority was still thoroughly patriotic. He could fill the gaps between stodgy government pronouncements and public opinion with wry optimism rather than defeatism or rancour.

It does Priestley a disservice, however, to posit him as nothing more than a folksy propagandist whose improbable stardom testifies to the eccentricities of wartime cultural appetites. He was at once more clearly in command of his position in the public eye than such narratives suggest, and the beneficiary of a larger cultural florescence whose roots and branches extend far beyond the narrow bracket of 1939–45. Priestley's trajectory from little-known journalist to People's Warrior, via his status as best-selling author, scourge of the literary elite and radio demagogue, parallels the continued maturation of radio as one medium defining itself among many. Priestley's relentless intermediality – his willingness to project himself and his work through multiple channels and in multiple registers – foregrounds the intermediality of wartime cultural production itself, while also tolling a late, if not final, knell for the highbrow writer as national cultural figurehead. It was in spring 1941, after all, that a lengthy debate erupted in the correspondence pages of *The Times* following an anonymous editorial titled 'Eclipse of the Highbrow', which criticised interwar modernists for their 'hasty brilliance', 'habitual clever triviality' and 'pedantic and deliberate obscurity', and celebrated the wartime turn away from such techniques, towards a more accessible form of literary production ('Eclipse of the Highbrow', 1941: 5; Marina MacKay 2007: 118–20). Though two weeks of letter-writing by *Times* readers failed to determine whether any such eclipse was in fact under way, let alone whether it was desirable, the discussion foregrounds the tensions animating the cultural field in the early years of the war. As this chapter demonstrates, these tensions often blurred distinctions between aesthetic form and institutional function, lumping together stylistically unadventurous novels and public agencies like the BBC under the rubric of the 'middlebrow'. Having rejected, in his essays, the vertical logic of high-, middle- and lowbrow in favour of an expansive term of his own coinage – the broadbrow – Priestley was well positioned to capitalise on the reach and affective potential of the medium of radio (Priestley 1927b: 163). Priestley succeeded by translating his broadbrow literary sensibility into a broadbrow political ideal through a carefully calibrated mode of address adapted to the intimate medium of radio.[3]

In his struggles to be heard at the BBC in the early 1930s, and in his eventual wartime success, Priestley maps the slow democratisation of content at the BBC as it opened its airwaves to voices from beyond the tightly bounded circle of white, upper-middle-class, Oxbridge-educated, Southern English broadcasters. It is no coincidence that these questions of access to an elite, yet publicly mandated, cultural institution mirror debates about the role of middlebrow literature – such as Priestley was said to write – as a cultural intermediary between popular and exclusionary forms of writing. Priestley's politics of democratic cultural production and consumption, established over the course of the 1920s and 1930s, had positioned him as a pluralist in debates that often broke down in terms of populism versus elitism. This public stance granted his wartime calls for widespread postwar social reform a deeper history than that afforded by the conflict itself; moreover, it framed democratic political participation as explicitly linked to broad cultural participation. No nation in which class-aligned aesthetic taste is linked so firmly to the right to political agency, he argued, can expect to survive, untransformed, a war that depends on total public mobilisation.

And yet Priestley was not quite the revolutionary he sometimes presented himself to be. Indeed, his wartime success depended on his ability to forge an identity that placed him both inside and outside circles of cultural and political power: he was an established and wildly popular author, and yet he positioned himself against the literary establishment; he commanded, if only for a few months, a radio audience of almost unprecedented size, and yet proclaimed himself outside structures of cultural authority; he accepted multiple commissions, both print and radio, from the Ministry of Information (MoI), and yet disavowed insinuations of propaganda. His wartime career therefore captures not just the increasing democratisation of the BBC from the 1930s into the 1940s, but also the literary attitudes of collaboration and compromise that characterised the war years. Accounting for Priestley's doubled position as both liability and asset to the BBC and to the nation as a whole demands a slightly deeper historical focus; this chapter therefore steps back in order to unpack the relationships between accent, delivery and cultural politics that positioned Priestley within the contested cultural field of the 1930s and that enabled him to serve as a barometer of wartime cultural shifts. In the process, it also seeks to untangle the complex terminology and history of interwar and wartime cultural hierarchies in which Priestley played a central role.

Interwar radio, the middlebrow and the broadbrow

As a national broadcaster devoted to providing listeners with products of high cultural value, the BBC had been a hub of public intellectual life in Britain since its inception. Under the direction of John Reith (later Lord Reith), the BBC had been conceived as an instrument of cultural uplift, bringing the best that had been thought and said to the ears of an under-educated nation with the goal of creating 'an informed and enlightened democracy' (Scannell and Cardiff 1991: 7). Music programming blended the canonical concert repertoire with challenging modernist works from the Continent and from up-and-coming British composers (Baade 2012: 20). In the early years of the Corporation, Sundays were reserved for religious programming and serious music; variety and comedy programmes were, in general, frowned upon. Reith was clear about his paternalistic intentions in his 1949 memoir *Into the Wind*:

> It is not insistent autocracy but wisdom that suggests a policy of broadcasting carefully and persistently on the basis of giving people what one believes they should like *and will come to like* . . . The supply of good things will create the demand for more. (Reith 1949: 133; emphasis in original)

This mission of mass enlightenment, condescending as it may sound today, in many ways worked against class hierarchies by attempting to level the playing field in a manner that spoke to the cultural aspirations of a working- and middle-class listening public, even if it did nothing to address the material inequalities underpinning cultural difference (Cardiff and Scannell [1987] 2009: 202). Reith's vision, as D. L. LeMahieu frames it, was about freedom of access to culture, if perhaps not freedom of choice (1988: 147). It brought its notion of 'culture' in mass quantities to a mass audience.[4]

Precisely because of its mission of cultural outreach, the BBC could not escape charges of meddling with the tastes of its listeners; furthermore, this intermediary status was bound up with the emergent concept of the middlebrow. The *Oxford English Dictionary* (*OED*) cites as its second printed instance of the word 'middlebrow' a quotation from a December 1925 issue of *Punch* magazine: 'The B.B.C. claim to have discovered a new type, the "middlebrow". It consists of people who are hoping that some day they will get used to the stuff they ought to like' ('Middlebrow', *OED Online*). One of the landmark texts for scholars of interwar cultural hierarchies, Virginia Woolf's 'Middlebrow' (1932), deploys the term in similarly radio-centric terms, to refer to those individuals and institutions that serve as cultural intermediaries. In this essay – conceived as a letter to the *New Statesman* but unpublished in her lifetime – Woolf takes particular aim at Priestley, who had recently delivered a broadcast entitled 'To a High-Brow' and had referred to Woolf as 'the High Priestess of Bloomsbury' in a separate review (Priestley 1932a: 11). Without directly naming him, Woolf attacks Priestley as emblematic of middlebrow attempts to transfer the codes of cultural capital from one economic class to another. Middlebrows, she writes, 'are the go-betweens; they are the busybodies [. . .]. They are neither one thing nor the other [. . .]. Their brows are betwixt and between' ([1932] 1942: 115). The BBC, as an agent of cultural education occupying the middlebrow space of knowledge transfer, is for Woolf a mischief-maker:

> If the BBC stood for anything but the Betwixt and Between Company they would use their control of the air not to stir strife between brothers, but to broadcast the fact that highbrows and lowbrows must band together to exterminate a pest which is the bane of all thinking and living. (118)

In Woolf's mind, high- and lowbrows 'cannot exist apart . . . one is the complement and other side of the other' (115), the implication being that it is better for lowbrows to embrace their class-cultural identity than to betray it by striving. In staking out this position, Woolf occludes the economic foundations of such cultural polarisations: the ways in which, in Pierre Bourdieu's words, '[a]rt and cultural consumption are predisposed . . . to fulfil a social function of legitimating social differences' (Bourdieu [1979] 1984: 7).[5]

Priestley was far more sanguine than Woolf about the role radio might play in modern life, in part because he understood the material benefits attendant on such technologies. 'I like the wireless,' he noted in a *Saturday Review* essay of 1927. 'It has made life even more fantastic and ridiculous than it was before' (qtd in Baxendale 2007: 126–7). Priestley saw radio as part of a larger pattern of acceleration of daily life, an acceleration that brought individuals into closer and more complicated relations with each other. In *English Journey* (1934), he documents the 'new England' that he sees emerging:

> This is the England of arterial and by-pass roads, of filling stations and factories that look like exhibition buildings, of giant cinemas and dance-halls and cafés, bungalows with tiny garages, cocktail bars, Woolworths, motor-coaches, wireless, hiking, factory girls looking like actresses, grey-hound racing and dirt tracks, swimming pools, and everything given away for cigarette coupons. (1934: 401)

For all that this list reads like a critique, Priestley insists that this new England is 'essentially democratic. After a social revolution there would, with any luck, be more and not less of it. You need money in this England, but you do not need much money' (1934: 401–2). While the citizens of this modern England occasionally indulged too heartily in a fantasy of cheap consumption, Priestley was heartened by the fact that this traffic in goods and information contributed to the material well-being of a broad swath of people.

When Priestley brought these ideas to the radio – in the broadcast that so rankled Woolf – they emerge in a slightly more confrontational form. 'To a High-Brow' (1932) was part of a longer series in which speakers address a fictionalised, archetypal interlocutor ('To a Day-Dreamer', 'To an Old Man', 'To a Politician'). Priestley wastes no time in branding his target as a 'small but irritating section of the community' (1932b: 2). The highbrow, Priestley claims, 'mustn't share his pleasures with the crowd ... He's simply Low-brow's opposite ... He is just as much the slave of fashion as Low-brow, but it's always the opposite fashion' (1932b: 3). As formerly acclaimed writers become too popular, Priestley remarks, the highbrows abandon them for fear of being tarred with the brush of common taste. This abandonment of the popular writer seems to be a sensitive point for Priestley:

> So-and-so suddenly writes a book that sells more than two or three thousand copies, and what is the result? So-and-so immediately begins to lose prestige with you. The dreadful word *popular* begins to creep in any reference you make to him and his work. Poor old So-and-so is finished now that he's *popular*. Of course it's impossible to read poor So-and-so any more. And you don't seem to realise – you dunderhead! – that all artists want to be popular. (1932b: 4)

As a popular novelist, Priestley struggled with his relationship to the arbiters of modernist literary taste for years. By insisting on the common imperatives of all writing – the need for economic and cultural capital alike, not to mention the emotional effects of artistic success – Priestley attempts an act of levelling between his own derided craft and that of more experimental writers.

Priestley's informal tone and asides ('you dunderhead!') indicate that his attempts at levelling applied to the delivery as much as to the ideas of his broadcast. As Priestley demonstrates in the familiar essays for which he was already famous, informality is a means of bridging the gap between speaker and listener, thereby destabilising the hierarchies between cultural producer and cultural consumer. That this broadcast is directed 'To a High-Brow' means that, along with bridging the divide between speaker and listener, Priestley can simultaneously collapse the distance between the elite literary practitioner and more workmanlike scribes like himself. Priestley closes 'To a High-Brow' with a wink at broadcasting, as if to foreground the broadbrow medium that would define his legacy after 1940: 'I warn you now. If you persist in your high-browism, I shall denounce you in some place where we might possibly be overheard, perhaps actually in public' (1932b: 6). In this ironic final apostrophe, Priestley alludes to radio's illusion of intimacy between speaker and listener and to the conceit of a series based on direct address ('To a ...'); the 'you' being warned is at once the titular highbrow and the listener, who may or may not identify with that label.

At the same time, by invoking the possibility of public audition, he acknowledges the wide cultural reach of the BBC, a reach that mirrors the breadth of appeal Priestley enjoyed as a popular novelist and essayist. 'To a High-Brow' offers a remarkably compact preview of Priestley's wartime ability to engage with a radio public through populist rhetoric, a demotic register and a carefully orchestrated aura of familiarity.

Though Woolf disparaged Priestley as a meddling middlebrow directing readers and listeners towards more refined content, a more accurate charge might be that his tastes were disarmingly broad. A prolific artist who produced novels as well as works for stage, screen, periodicals and the radio, Priestley encouraged a reciprocal breadth of taste in his audience. In his essay 'High, Low, Broad', published first in *Saturday Review* on 20 February 1926, Priestley sought to establish a culturally lush middle ground between the 'equally contemptible' positions of 'Highbrow' and 'Lowbrow' (1927b: 163; capitalisation as in original). Priestley identifies himself as a 'Broadbrow', claiming that this self-positioning reflects a difference 'not merely of degree but of kind' – a move from the vertical hierarchy of high and low to an implicitly democratic horizontal plane of cultural consumption (1927b: 163). Priestley argues that conventional vertical hierarchies disable aesthetic judgement, rendering both highbrows and lowbrows 'the mere slaves of fashion, moving in herds to decry this and praise that' (1927b: 163). Broadbrowism, he contends, leaves one able to define one's own tastes:

> If you can carry with you your sense of values, your appreciation of the human scene, your critical faculty, to Russian dramas, variety shows, football matches, epic poems, grand opera, race meetings, old churches, new town halls, musical comedies, picture galleries, boxing booths, portfolios of etchings, bar parlours, film shows, symphony concerts, billiard matches, dance halls, detective stories, tragedies in blank verse, farces, and even studio teas and literary parties, and enjoy to the full what there is there worth enjoying, giving even the Devil his due, then you are a Broadbrow. In short, you are the salt of the earth, and, of course, one of us. (1927b: 167)

To be a broadbrow, as this breath-taking and comically long list suggests, is to adopt a pluralist vision of cultural production, and one explicitly opposed to the exclusionary operations of aesthetic hierarchies. Such multiform and wide-ranging taste involves entry into a community of its own; the reader, listener or viewer becomes 'one of us' at precisely the moment when they accept the diversity and idiosyncrasy of modern, mass-mediated cultural production.

It is tempting to collapse Priestley's broadbrow aesthetic into the category of the 'middlebrow'. The positions do seem roughly analogous:

both broadbrowism and contemporary middlebrow studies share an interest in how socio-political power manifests itself through aesthetic hierarchies. Drawing on research by Bourdieu and others, middlebrow scholars argue, for instance, that the high/low split was never Manichean. Rather, as Faye Hammill frames it, the early decades of the twentieth century were characterised by fluid processes of exchange across cultural boundaries, with middlebrow cultural producers serving as sophisticated intermediaries 'borrowing from both modernist and mass cultural forms' and thereby 'diminish[ing] the apparent distance between them' (2007: 11). If, as critics including John Carey have argued, modernism was a reactionary formation that emerged in response to the proliferation of print media and an increasingly educated public, the middlebrow stance offered a kind of reaction to the reactionaries (1992: 18). To be a middlebrow writer in the early twentieth century was to adopt a position of knowing scepticism regarding the modernist concern with form and with difficulty for its own sake.

As Caroline Pollentier has pointed out, however, Priestley's broadbrow philosophy is less a vision of the cultural producer as intermediary than it is an expansive ethics of consumption. Priestley's broadbrow aesthetic offers not a negative position – that is, a middlebrow position that is neither 'authentically' demotic nor avant-garde – but a positive one; by combining a critical discernment that resists cultural trends with an inclusive appetite that welcomes art catering to a variety of individual aesthetic needs, the concept of the broadbrow takes on 'a direct ethical dimension' (Pollentier 2012: 45). For Pollentier, the ethical valence of the broadbrow finds an analogue in Priestley's position within interwar literary culture, as a regular purveyor of not just popular novels but also of the 'familiar' essay of interwar mass periodicals. In addition to an informal, unpretentious tone that stressed the common social position of reader and writer, the familiar essay, by its very repeated appearance in the same place and by the same author, encourages 'the creation of a reader–writer bond of friendship' and what Pollentier calls a 'poetics of reciprocity' (2011: 132–3). Taken together, these formal and circulatory attributes contribute to an 'ethics of familiarity' that represents an alternative to the high/low dichotomy (2011: 127). While some cultural critics would take 'familiarity' itself as typical of literature that occupies a subordinate position in a cultural hierarchy, the broadbrow aesthetic explicitly rejects that very hierarchy.

Priestley's attention to the political stakes of the 'brows' plays out in his novels, which often feature villainous or laughably affected snobs. Building on caricatures of highbrows in *The Good Companions* (1929) and *Wonder Hero* (1933), his novel *Let the People Sing* (1939) – a 'novel for radio' whose simultaneous print publication and BBC serialisation coincided with the outbreak of war – features 'a slender, wavy-haired youth of about fifty-five' named Mr Churton Talley, a 'great art critic and expert' with an effete demeanour, a 'mincing' walk and a tendency to hiss his sibilants until he sounds 'like an outraged serpent' (1939: 204–5). Class snobbery likewise distinguishes heroes from villains in *Black-Out in Gretley* (1942) and *Daylight on Saturday* (1943) (see Baxendale 2007: 142–5, 157–60). Priestley's clearest articulation of the problem with 'brows' as a means of categorising art, however, comes in a novel he began in early 1940 and later abandoned; only the first section, entitled 'Birmanpool', is preserved at the Harry Ransom Humanities Research Center (HRC).[6] Protagonist Humphrey Pike is an actor and an archetypal broadbrow; his equal enthusiasm for performing music-hall farce and the plays of Chekhov confuses and disarms his fellow actors in the fictional Midlands city that lends the typescript its title. When a journalist accuses Pike's friend of being a 'highbrow', Pike jumps in to defend him. He objects to the journalistic tactic of labelling those with artistic and intellectual predispositions 'highbrows'; the tactic of pre-emptive brow-baiting, Pike claims, is designed 'to confuse the good with the bad so that the whole thing will be regarded with contempt':

> Tell the people that some affected lily-handed pansy who dabbles in poetry is a highbrow. Then call a poet, a real poet, a chap who's got more vitality and sense and guts than five ordinary men, a highbrow. The trick's done then ... The trick of keeping the people silly and ignorant. (1939–40: 92)

The sexual politics of this passage – turning the collective sights on 'pansies' as a source of cultural decadence and ineffectuality – are unfortunately typical of Priestley's castigation of 'highbrows'. As with many writers of his generation (notably George Orwell), Priestley conflates heterosexual masculinity with creative and interpretive agency. Priestley's prejudices manifest themselves both in the attention to effete intellectuals with hissed sibilants noted earlier and in his appeal at the end of the 1932 broadcast 'To a High-Brow' that his imagined listener should 'Be a man. Be a broad-brow' (1932b: 6).

These dubious invocations of gender identity obscure Priestley's larger point about the connections between discourses of cultural competence and political participation. Debates about high- and lowbrows, Priestley argues, are a means of clouding the cultural and political judgement of the broad public: a means, in the words of Pike's friend Elliot Dunster in 'Birmanpool', of 'taking care they won't have any encouragement to think and feel for themselves' (1939–40: 92). Wandering the deserted streets of Birmanpool at night, and distraught at the lack of vibrant entertainment on offer to its urban residents, Humphrey Pike ponders the links between cultural and economic segregation in Britain:

> Sometimes at that hour, his imagination a bright torment, Humphrey would feel as if he were some insect wandering among the shafts and cogs of a gigantic money-making machine that had been stopped for a little while. He began to wonder if the real life of England began behind high walls built to exclude the mob, if not only the gold but also nearly all the colour, interest, character were drained out of such streets and people as these to enamel and perfume a privileged life elsewhere. (1939–40: 34)

Though he has ensured himself a measure of cultural sophistication through his independent study of theatre, literature and visual art, Pike understands that the exclusionary operations of late 1930s elite culture reserve the pleasures of artistic sophistication for those with the material plenty and leisure time to afford them. In contrast to the 'high walls' of cultural exclusion, Pike takes solace in the aesthetic awakening he witnesses on a visit to a municipal art gallery, where citizens experience a life-affirming connection with something larger than themselves. He hopes to play an analogous role for theatre-goers:

> All that he asked then was to serve such people, but all he could do was to act for them, to work and work until at last they sat in their balconies wearing the same strangely beautiful look they had here, watching another kind of window fly open. (1939–40: 80)

Although Priestley abandoned the novel, the imagery of enclosure and barriers operating in the 'Birmanpool' fragment emerges in his 'Postscripts' of the same period. 'Sometimes', Priestley told his British listeners on 30 June 1940, 'I feel that you and I – all of us ordinary people – are on one side of a high fence, and on the other side of this fence under a buzzing cloud of secretaries, are the official and important personages' (1940c: 19). In a small but important shift, Pike's concerns about cultural democracy (a people deprived of 'colour, interest, [and] character') have morphed into more directly political questions of governance. Power, Priestley claims in the 'Postscript', operates obscurely in wartime; it is only 'now and then' that 'a head appears above the fence and tells us to carry our gas masks, look to our blackouts, do this and attend to that' (1940c: 19). The shift from cultural to political democracy is telling not because it marks a distinction between the two, but because it testifies to their mutual interpenetration. The fence persists as a metaphor for barriers to public participation in culture and government, for both Humphrey Pike and J. B. Priestley.

'A representative Englishman': Priestley's accent and the radio periphery

Removing such fences at the BBC proved a challenge at first. While some critics stigmatised the BBC as being 'vulgar' or middlebrow throughout the 1920s and 1930s, there was considerable pressure from within the Corporation to maintain the high cultural standards established under Reith. Priestley's own experience at the interwar BBC indicates the persistence of a complex of values linking class, audience, literary reputation and accent. While his voice would become a vehicle of national solidarity in wartime, Priestley found that his Yorkshire accent was a liability rather than an asset in his attempts at broadcasting during the late 1920s and 1930s. Early correspondence in Priestley's file at the BBC Written Archive Centre (WAC) suggests that BBC officials initially did not want Priestley to broadcast at all. In autumn 1929, he offered to read a selection from his best-selling novel *The Good Companions* (1929) on the air, but Talks Producer Hilda Matheson recommended against such a proposal in a memo to the Director of Programmes, Roger Eckersley. Writing on 18 November 1929, Matheson notes firstly of all that authors reading from their own works 'are not good programme value' unless they are gifted speakers; secondly, she argues, presenting a work in this way offers 'such a terrific boost' to the author that the BBC should limit such endorsements to works that have not already received the high level of publicity of *The Good Companions*. Finally, Matheson notes that 'Priestley himself has a very unattractive voice on the microphone, and after using him once or twice we have rather ploughed him' (Matheson 1929). Eckersley responded by equivocating, ruling against Priestley's voice but arguing for the merits of authors broadcasting from their works. Others in the Corporation, however, connected Priestley's peripheral accent to a host of values to be excluded from the metropolitan voice of the BBC. On 21 November, Lionel Fielden of the Talks department wrote to Matheson, echoing her dislike of Priestley's voice but going further. While he claims to be in favour of authors reading their own work on the air 'whenever possible and desirable', he balks at Priestley's offer:

> I am pretty sure that Priestly [sic] is unknown to two-thirds of our audience, and that to the remaining third he is *not* in any way an exciting figure; I do not think that 'The Good Companions' (which I have read with great enjoyment) is *at all* suitable for reading [on air]; we know his voice is *extremely* unattractive, and I consider that his suggestion is dictated purely by self-advertisement. There is no end to our troubles if we once create a precedent of this kind. (Fielden 1929)

This brief exchange among Matheson, Eckersley and Fielden typifies the default BBC opinion about Priestley, his voice and his writings over much of the 1930s. The presumed authority of the authorial voice, which Eckersley seeks to harness, collides with a cluster of biases: resistance to Priestley's accent; rejection of his prose on unspecified, though likely formal and stylistic, grounds; a paradoxical resistance to Priestley as a literary figure both too highly praised and not important or widely read enough to justify putting him on the air; and a disdain for any broadcaster motivated by what Fielden calls 'self-advertisement'. Fielden seems to find it hard to imagine that the BBC audience might enjoy Priestley's writings, as he himself claims to have done; Priestley must either be 'unknown' or unexciting to listeners, implying that broadcasting exists to furnish more sophisticated fare to a more sophisticated audience than would normally read Priestley. For Fielden at least, and arguably for Matheson, broadcast value is tied up with the economics of literary production, and the acoustics of authority with those of class.

For listeners throughout the 1920s and 1930s, this complex of cultural and class values conveyed itself through a homogeneity of accent on the air. News announcers and programme presenters tended towards an educated, Southern English pronunciation whose most distilled manifestation was the Oxbridge accent. According to unofficial BBC policy, regional dialects and accents were deemed 'unclear' or 'extreme variants' – as, interestingly, were the more extreme forms of upper-class drawl (Keith Williams 1996: 30–1). In an ostensibly national broadcaster, the favouritism shown to a particular form of educated, upper-middle-class pronunciation could not help but arouse resentment. George Orwell derided the 'BBC Voice' as unlike anything spoken outside of Broadcasting House; dreaming of a popular wartime revolution in his diary on 24 June 1940, Orwell assured himself that 'the first sign that things are really happening in England will be the disappearance of that horrible plummy voice from the radio' (Orwell [1968] 1970: vol. 2, 356). More diplomatically, Asa Briggs notes that the BBC 'never found it easy fully to penetrate the working-class world which provided it with by far the largest part of its audience'. This shortcoming resulted from linguistic differences of 'accent, vocabulary, [and] style' and from the Corporation's highly conscious performance of gentility, typified by the fact that male announcers wore dinner jackets in studio into the 1930s (Briggs 1965: 40). The situation was so widely recognised that the 1936 Ullswater Committee, launched to determine the future direction of the Corporation, criticised the BBC for hiring a disproportionate number of Oxford and Cambridge graduates (LeMahieu 1988: 183).[7] Although partly motivated by a desire for clarity of speech, the choice of accent at the BBC also provided persuasive evidence of an undercurrent of cultural elitism within the Corporation. As Keith Williams notes, 'The BBC did not invent bias against the demotic, it merely perpetuated one with ancient roots in literary convention' (1996: 31).

The BBC did not ban all varieties of non-standard accent and dialect, but it tended to bracket them off from the main. Other varieties of English were subtly branded as the voice of a radio 'other' through such framing devices as documentaries about the working classes, or comical evocations of regional differences in variety and music-hall programming. Pioneering features writer and producer D. G. Bridson, in his memoirs of broadcasting in Manchester and London, recalls that with the limited degree of Regional programming that occurred alongside the National Programme during the 1930s, 'occasional purlings of a genteeler local Doric were permitted,' but only 'out on the perimeter, in Scotland and Wales and Northern Ireland' (Bridson 1971: 53). The inclusion of strongly non-standard accents, especially those voicing political dissidence, often met with disapproval from superiors within the BBC, as when Manchester-based producer E. A. F. Harding interviewed Northern hunger marchers en route to London (Bridson 1971: 39). Such disapproval partly reflected the potential power of documentary portrayals of the working classes; radio programmes, including *S.O.S.* (1933), *Other People's Houses* (1933) and *Time to Spare* (1934), spurred debate in parliament and in the press about the living and housing conditions of Britain's unemployed and working poor (Keith Williams 1996: 28). Despite such attempts to represent the lives of a large band of the population on the air, announcers and presenters – those voices framed as authoritative – remained almost entirely Southern, middle- or upper-middle-class and 'educated' in their intonation (Keith Williams 1996: 160). Even delivery was policed: over the 1930s, the BBC Talks Department sought to reinforce distinctions between 'authoritative' and 'personal' talks by ensuring that the heightened vocabulary and tone of the former contrasted with the slightly informal character of the latter (Nicholas 1995: 251).

Given their reticence about peripheral dialects in the pre-war period, it is unsurprising that, when the BBC did court Priestley, officials sought to focus his radio engagements on regional themes. Over the course of the 1930s, the BBC approached Priestley several times to present talks on various topics relating to regionalism in general, or to the North specifically. In a letter from 11 July 1930, for example, Priestley refuses to participate in a programme called 'Tour Round the North', noting that there is no such thing as the coherent 'Northern point of view' the BBC had requested and that in any case he has not lived in the North for over a decade. He closes by adding:

> I have done nothing for the B.B.C. for a long time, & when I do talk to that vast public of yours, I am not anxious to appear as a North Country man. I am anxious to avoid the charge of being a 'regional' novelist (my new novel [*Angel Pavement*] is all about London). This for your future guidance. (Priestley 1930)

The BBC appears not to have heeded; he was asked again in January 1931 to represent the North, to which he replied curtly, 'I am not – as the BBC seems to imagine I am – an authority on Yorkshire' (Priestley 1931). In refusing to broadcast on regional topics exclusively, Priestley rejected the pigeonhole fate of many broadcasters with non-standard accents. Categorisation as a regional novelist meant exclusion from the ranks of important British writers and intellectuals; until he could be treated as a novelist *tout court*, he would absent himself from a medium whose increasingly widespread influence on British taste was not yet matched by a broad definition of culture.

This widespread exclusion of non-standard accents from the interwar airwaves indicates the ambiguous position of the BBC with regard to the cultural politics of the era. Castigated by elite intellectuals as 'vulgar' and populist, the BBC performed a high-cultural elitism as a defensive manœuvre designed to shore up its own respectability. In keeping Priestley at bay, the BBC was in many ways resisting its own typification as the definitive middlebrow medium; it aped a highbrow posture in order to continue its mission of middlebrow cultural transmission. While this approach held sway well into the 1930s, it could not survive the broader technological and social shifts of that decade. By the time Priestley began his 'Postscripts', those shifts had become hard to ignore.

From Phoney War to People's War

The period later known as the Phoney War – September 1939 to April 1940 – represented a sustained low ebb for British morale and for British broadcasting. While a host of wartime restrictions had materialised in autumn 1939, including the blackout and, for a few weeks, the closure of theatres and cinemas, the conflict itself had largely failed to materialise in such a way as to justify the constraints imposed by government. The BBC shifted to its emergency wartime broadcasting schedule on 1 September, two days before war was officially declared. In addition to the suspension of Regional broadcasting, the new schedule involved the abandonment of a great deal of familiar programming in favour of regular news bulletins, recorded music played on gramophones and seemingly endless hours of Sandy MacPherson at the BBC Organ. This rather unstimulating output led British listeners to seek out entertainment and war information elsewhere (Nicholas 1996: 40; Doherty 2000: 88–9). The success of Nazi propagandists like Lord Haw-Haw in the early months of the war demonstrated that British listeners were sufficiently tired of official pronouncements, blandly delivered, that they would seek out more colloquial assessments of the war wherever they might be found, including the enemy airwaves.

Fear of losing listeners to Haw-Haw and other propagandists prompted the BBC to undergo what Siân Nicholas calls 'the greatest shift in the philosophy of broadcasting in Britain since its inception': the Corporation began listening back to its audience (1996: 41). In doing so, the BBC acknowledged that it could not simply give the public what it *ought* to want at the expense of what it *did* want. This shift resulted in the progressive expansion of the Listener Research Department, which had been formed in 1936 after much resistance from within the Reithian BBC but grew during the war to occupy a central role in evaluating public response to broadcasts. It also led, in January 1940, to the establishment of the Forces Programme. An alternative broadcast wavelength designed to provide light entertainment for British troops stationed on the Continent, the Forces Programme was extremely popular with civilian audiences as well, and was 'demobbed' and renamed the Light Programme in 1945. The slow process of democratising the Home Service during the Phoney War also included the expansion of variety and popular music programming in a bid to increase both listenership and morale (Baade 2012: 3–5, 34–50).

As part of the larger effort to give British listeners a reason to tune out Lord Haw-Haw and other Nazi propagandists, the BBC launched a series of talks under the title 'Onlooker' in early 1940; by March 1940 these broadcasts were known as 'Postscripts' owing to their schedule placement immediately after the nine o'clock evening news. While the news had quickly become essential listening, many listeners had developed the habit of switching over to scandalous and irreverent Nazi stations as soon as the bulletins ended. The aim of 'Postscripts' was to dissuade channel hopping by staging a vigorous defence of what broadcaster and labour activist John Hilton called 'the philosophy and doctrine of the democratic way of living' (qtd in Briggs 1970: 146). Maurice Healey, a well-known barrister, handled most of the Sunday night 'Postscripts' in early 1940, but he failed to connect strongly with listeners. Following a misstep in which he bemoaned the fact that a friend's annual income had declined by £1000 because of the war, the BBC decided that it was looking for what Assistant Director of Talks (and future Controller of the Third Programme) George Barnes called 'a contrast in voice, upbringing and outlook' (qtd in Briggs 1970: 210).

In selecting J. B. Priestley, the producers of 'Postscripts' knew they were getting a popular novelist and essayist raised in Bradford, whose accent placed him outside the conventional acoustic profile of BBC announcers. They could not have predicted the immensity of Priestley's success. The popularity of his broadcasts is indicated by the unprecedented written response they elicited from listeners across Britain and around the world. Between June 1940, when he began his first series, and October the same year, when the series ended, the BBC received 1,700 letters about the broadcasts from listeners, 1,500 of which were positive (Ryan 1940). The press likewise heaped praise on the 'Postscripts'. 'Mr. Priestley's broadcasts are a privilege,' wrote the *Daily Mail* on 2 July 1940; 'The Government ought to appoint Mr. Priestley Director-General of Broadcasting,' enthused the *Nottingham Guardian* on 3 December 1940 (qtd in Briggs 1970: 210, 321).

In addition to praise from the listening public and the press, Priestley personally received dozens of letters from literary celebrities and other public figures. Storm Jameson, writing to him in June 1940, called the broadcasts 'magnificent' and said, 'you get out the poetry of the English'; Rebecca West, H. G. Wells, Ernest Bevin and Desmond McCarthy each wrote to offer their thanks and encouragement. Even George Bernard Shaw offered grudging appreciation: 'The broadcasts are a fearful waste of your time', he wrote, 'but they are very enjoyable.'[8] Other writers praised his 'Postscripts' publicly. Graham Greene, in *The Spectator*, called him 'a leader second in importance only to Mr. Churchill' and noted that 'he gave us what the other leaders have failed to give us – an ideology' (1940: 646). Louis MacNeice, though less adulatory than Greene, noted in the American periodical *Common Sense* in May 1941 that Priestley manifested the potential of radio to return society 'to the conditions of the Greek City State where the man who can hold the people's ear – or most of their ears most of the time – will acquire the most astonishing influence' (1990: 115). By positioning himself as the voice of radical common sense – in touch with the people but possessed of an intellectual autonomy that parallels his broadbrow cultural philosophy – Priestley was perfectly suited to the changing cultural and media landscape of the 'People's War'.

Priestley's independence was, ironically, key to his efficacy as a wartime propagandist. In his broadcasts to the United States and to a domestic audience, Priestley repeatedly claimed that he operated outside of any coordinated propaganda campaign (see, for example, Priestley 1940a: 95, 113, 231). Despite these claims, much of his wartime output was funded, directly or indirectly, by the MoI. Robert Calder, in his study of British writers' involvement in Second World War propaganda directed at the United States, notes that the paucity of documentation surrounding MoI publishing and broadcasting initiatives often makes tracing such patronage difficult; publishing arrangements were often left deliberately vague in order to obscure government involvement, with money funnelled between shell companies and existing American and British publishers (Robert Calder 2004: 157–8). Nonetheless, there is considerable evidence of Priestley's involvement in MoI initiatives. In September 1939, he toured the country for a Ministry-funded series of daily articles in the *News Chronicle* that were modelled on his celebrated 1934 work of social commentary *English Journey* (Judith Cook 1998: 176–8). He also wrote Ministry-supported books with titles like *Britain at War* (1942) and *British Women Go to War* (1943), and narrated the General Post Office (GPO) film unit's propaganda film *Britain at Bay* (1940) on behalf of the government.[9] His literary agent, A. D. Peters, was briefly the Secretary of the Authors' Planning Committee, the MoI agency responsible for coordinating the propaganda contributions of British writers early in the war; while that connection was probably less important than Priestley's substantial fame in helping him to secure MoI contracts, it indicates the dense interconnections between official and unofficial cultural output in wartime (Robert Calder 2004: 47).

His overseas broadcasting was also largely funded by the MoI. Beginning in May 1940, Priestley made two to three broadcasts a week in the series 'Britain Speaks', aimed mainly at American listeners; these broadcasts occasionally repeated themes and entire passages from his 'Postscripts'. It was a lucrative, as well as patriotic, endeavour: the Ministry of Information paid Priestley twenty guineas (plus five guineas for expenses) per fifteen-minute broadcast at first, compared to an initial fee of ten guineas per seven-minute 'Postscript' (Talks Booking Form 1940). The MoI provided the funds through an account known as the 'American Commentators Special Allowance', and Priestley was therefore cautioned that the Ministry might retain copyright over the broadcasts, should he wish to reproduce them ('Britain Speaks' 1940; Boswell 1940). According to correspondence between Priestley and his American publisher, Cass Canfield, the MoI also funded a monthly South American broadcast, which he abandoned around April 1941 to protest against the 'miserable interference' he felt subjected to by the Ministry (Priestley 1941a). This last comment sheds light on the delicate balance Priestley struck during the war: though willing to help out the

Allied effort by propagandising on its behalf, and even more so when it proved so profitable to him personally, Priestley resented anything he perceived as direct influence by government entities.

'Postscripts' and demotic delivery

While the 1930s had seen changes in programme content from London, diversification of the accents of presenters and announcers was slower to arrive. In 1941, Wilfred Pickles, a Yorkshire bricklayer turned radio announcer, became the first Northerner to serve as a regular newsreader, creating what official BBC historian Asa Briggs claims was 'as much of a stir – and almost as much controversy – as a war-time naval engagement' (Briggs 1970: 59). Similarly, John Arlott's cricket commentaries, which began after the war, were immensely popular, not only for his gift of phrasing and knowledge of the game, but also for his regional accent.[10] Before Pickles and Arlott, however, Priestley had used his Sunday night 'Postscripts' to destabilise the reigning linguistic, political and cultural orthodoxies that had, up to this point, defined public discourse on the BBC. Speaking on a BBC Radio Four programme in 1991, Briggs emphasised Priestley's contribution to this transformation:

> [T]here were a lot of problems of verbal communication in England before the war and in the early part of the war which we've now forgotten. We now find it very easy to communicate with each other whatever our accents. People did find a good deal of problem in communicating across the class dividing lines and across the different regional lines and Priestley broke through all those barriers. ('Radio Lives' 1991)

Contemporary audience responses to Priestley's voice support Briggs's interpretation. A Listener Research Report from August 1940 attributed Priestley's success to 'the homeliness of his voice, the quiet confidence of his manner, and the virile commonsense of his matter' (LR/151 1940). The same report cites a Swindon railway clerk, who describes Priestley as '[e]asy to understand, sincere and honest. Not highbrow'; a miner from Staffordshire notes that '[h]is voice and manner appeal to the working man.' In an article in *London Calling*, the overseas journal of the BBC, an unnamed overseas listener sums up Priestley's central role by calling him 'a representative Englishman' and noting that '[h]e truly can speak for England' ('The Men Who Speak for Britain' 1940).

This voice, as recordings convey, does not speak in a Yorkshire dialect that would have been impenetrable to listeners; rather, Priestley's voice is most often described as 'broad', 'mellow' and 'warm', reflecting a measured regional inflection that draws out vowels without altering them beyond the recognition of non-Yorkshire listeners. Commentators describe the voice in terms that veer into the gustatory: biographer John Braine calls it a Yorkshire 'intonation ... or perhaps *flavour*' while radio critic W. E. Williams describes it as a voice 'nicely flavoured with Yorkshire relish' (Braine qtd in Robert Calder 2004: 212; W. E. Williams 1940). For *Time* magazine, it was a voice 'compact as a beer mug' (qtd in Robert Calder 2004: 212). As important as its warmth was its impression of intelligence; Priestley's educated Bradfordian voice invoked wisdom without indulging in pretensions of intellectual sophistication. In a discussion of wartime propaganda films, one of which was narrated by Priestley, Mass Observation's Tom Harrisson claimed that Priestley's voice 'provides a bridge between middle and working classes', at once homely and poised, refreshingly anti-elitist and intelligent (qtd in Baxendale 2007: 146). If Priestley's claims about class relations during his upbringing in Edwardian Bradford are to be believed, the cross-class acceptability of his accent emerged naturally from his home-town roots. '[I]n a city like this in the industrial North there was little of the class demarcation by accent,' he claims; rather, citizens from diverse economic backgrounds sought to downplay divisions by producing an acoustic effect of commonality (Priestley 1970: 97). Priestley's broadcasting success lay in bringing this erasure of class difference, however superficial, to a medium whose acoustics of distinction had begun to breed disaffection in a population being asked to give everything to the cause of total war.

Even Priestley was surprised by the efficacy of his wartime 'Postscripts'. 'I have been hard at it getting through to the public mind, in one way or another, for about twenty years,' he writes in the introduction to the printed edition of *Postscripts*, 'but as a medium of communication this broadcasting makes everything else seem like the method of a secret society' (1940c: vii).[11] During the war, he professed humbly that '[t]he tricks of the writing trade and some fortunate accidents of voice and manner' conspired to make him a success (1940c: vii). Later, however, Priestley would speak of the uncanny effects his aural persona seemed to have exerted over others:

> I found myself tied like a man to a gigantic balloon, to one of those bogus reputations that only the mass media know how to inflate ... Voices cannot be disguised, and if I went into a crowded shop or bar all the people not only had to talk to me but also had to touch me – I had thousands lay hands on me – as if to prove to themselves that I was more than a disembodied voice. (qtd in Angus Calder 1969: 161)

The enduring popularity of these broadcasts, and the waning popularity of his written works after the war, would come to irritate Priestley in later life, when he came to think the 'Postscripts' overrated (Priestley 1962: 220).

Priestley's success lay in his ability to match a demotic tone of voice and a broadbrow cultural politics to yield a populist message of collective effort in the 'People's War'. Matter, manner and medium conspired to lend the first of his 'Postscripts' both immediate appeal and historical endurance; indeed, few transmissions outside of those by Chamberlain, Churchill and the royal family can be said to have shaped discourse about the war as effectively. The only Wednesday 'Postscript' to be broadcast, Priestley's debut aired on 5 June 1940, after the British military had wrapped up the final stages of the Dunkirk evacuation. While Churchill's speech to the House of Commons the day before – parts of which were read out that evening by BBC announcers – had lifted national spirits with its rhetorical loft, Priestley opted for plainer speech. The kernel of the astounding Dunkirk success was, for him, 'the little pleasure-steamers', those small ships that ferried holiday-makers from one seaside town to the next or, at best, attempted a brief crossing of the English Channel (1940c: 2–3). The broadcast begins on a note of nostalgia: Priestley revels in an evocation of what in 1939 was already a disappearing world of 'pierrots and piers, sand castles, ham-and-egg teas, palmists, automatic machines, and crowded sweating promenades' (3). His point is not that this fading world represents some kind of essential England. Rather, he indicates that the past must be abandoned in order to move forward. It is in the movement of these ships from 'that innocent foolish world of theirs . . . to sail into the inferno, to defy bombs, shells, magnetic mines, torpedoes, machine-gun fire' that they enter history (3). Priestley closes by eulogising one such ship, the *Gracie Fields*, lost during the evacuation:

> But now – look – this little steamer, like all her brave and battered sisters, is immortal. She'll go sailing proudly down the years in the epic of Dunkirk. And our great-grandchildren, when they learn how we began this War by snatching glory out of defeat, and then swept on to victory, may also learn how the little holiday steamers made an excursion to hell and came back glorious. (4)

This peroration showcases Priestley's knack for drawing allegory from the everyday; the flotilla of common little ships serves as a shorthand for the banding together of ordinary British citizens under attack. That he chooses to focus on a ship called the *Gracie Fields*, named after the popular Lancashire singer and actress who rose from working-class beginnings to become one of Britain's biggest stars, emphasises that for Priestley the triumph of Dunkirk is a triumph fuelled from below.

More importantly, this closing passage demonstrates the remarkable process by which he and other writers busied themselves transforming events like the Dunkirk evacuation into myth even as they happened. Radio accelerated this process of mythologisation; it gave writers the means by which to cast the present in terms of proleptic nostalgia, instantaneously. A large part of Priestley's effectiveness as a broadcaster lay in his ability to orient listeners in a historical trajectory; this historical orientation illustrates Greene's comment that Priestley gave listeners 'an ideology' in a way few speakers had (Greene 1940). In its broadest sense, ideology can be understood as a lens, a way of seeing oneself in relation to the world and of seeing that present world in relation to the past and the future; in fixing summer 1940 as a moment of transition between England's lost and foolish interwar holiday and its pending victory, Priestley gave listeners such a lens, allowing them to view the conflict as a productive transformation. Throughout the 'Postscripts', Priestley transforms recent traumas – including Dunkirk, the Battle of Britain and the Blitz – into a usable past, a series of successive trials through which the British people continued to prove their worthiness to inherit a brighter future.

Often, the technique of linking the everyday to the broader experience of the war gains specific power by opening a window on Priestley's own emotional experience of the war. Recalling a night spent on watch for German planes, Priestley speaks frankly of the simultaneously tender and violent feelings generated by the increasing conflict:

> I remember wishing then that we could send all our children out of this island, every boy and girl of them across the sea to the wide Dominions, and turn Britain into the greatest fortress the world has known; so that then, with an easy mind, we could fight and fight these Nazis until we broke their black hearts. (1940c: 12)

Such tightly woven emotions of protectiveness and aggression gain much of their subtle meaning from their delivery; with his measured, deliberate and familiar speaking style, Priestley would have inflected such ideas with more pathos than rage. The tragedy of war, he indicates, is not that Britons are threatened with death, but that they are made to wish death upon others.

Priestley could not overtly stress the moral ambivalence of the war effort in broadcasts to the home front; such equivocation would have suited neither the propaganda imperatives of the government nor the mood of a people under Nazi assault and bracing for a possible invasion

(Angus Calder 1969: 145–62). But in his Overseas Service broadcasts on the programme 'Britain Speaks', Priestley felt freer to question certain aspects of the war. On one occasion, Priestley refused to downplay the underlying violence of the conflict, especially the violence visited upon innocent civilians of both sides. Visiting a munitions plant in July 1940, Priestley reports on the impressive increases in productivity the factory, and British industry more generally, had seen in recent months. He contemplates the long line of workers and focuses on one 'spectacled and studious-looking girl' hard at work:

> [T]he little machine she bent over was presenting her, all with an awful regularity and rapidity, with beautifully turned, tiny pieces of metal, and these, it appeared, were the strikers, which somewhere in distant mid-air would be released to detonate the shells. And then perhaps, because of one of these strikers and one of these shells, another girl far away, perhaps spectacled and studious-looking and sentimental like this one, wouldn't be able to see properly the machine she might be bending over, because the shell had done its work, a young life had gone, and she would be suddenly blind with tears and despair. All of which comes of imagining that because you have machine tools you no longer need God. (1940a: 135)

The turn to contemplate the logical result of arms production is sudden and striking, and echoes the meditations on German death and grief in the First World War poetry of Siegfried Sassoon, Wilfred Owen and others.[12] Because Priestley's broadcasts to America formed part of a larger MoI plan to secure support for the British war effort, this frank assessment of the brutality of war might seem ill-advised. But Priestley, for all his patriotism, had never shied away from either sentimentality or a contrarian position. From the lingering resentments about the First World War expressed in *English Journey* and his many volumes of autobiography to his postwar work with the Campaign for Nuclear Disarmament, Priestley had consistently rejected militarism.[13] Violence was for him a necessary evil, not a cornerstone of British identity. This measure of scepticism made his broadcasts, directed as they were to an audience wary of British interventionism, all the more effective.

Priestley's ability to portray an inner world of confusion and vulnerability, as a natural accompaniment to struggle and resistance, lends the best of his broadcasts an emotional sincerity alien to most wartime propaganda. One of Priestley's most moving 'Postscripts', usually overshadowed by the Dunkirk broadcast, aired on 1 September 1940. Looking back on the first year of the war, Priestley details his own experience of 3 September 1939, travelling from the Isle of Wight to Broadcasting House to present the first instalment of *Let the People Sing*. Priestley litters his account of that day with details: the excessive heat, the deserted streets, the conversely crowded platforms at Paddington station. As his train pulls out of Paddington for the return journey to the Isle of Wight, he notices an unusually brilliant sunset, distinguished by a single patch of cloud 'shaped like a dragon'. In a deft move from the intensely personal to the intensely public, he pauses his remembrance to ask the radio audience, 'Do you remember that, any of you? Yes, a rampant dragon, etched in fire' (1940c: 63). Priestley's thoughts enter a distinctly melancholic register as he remembers the deepening sunset:

> The light had grown unbelievably tender. How was it possible to believe that such a sky could spill ruin and death[?] It caught at the heart – that sky; not the heart that is entirely human and can go home and be content, but that other homeless heart we all possess, which even when there's no war, is never at peace, but dimly recognises that long ago it was conscripted for a bitter campaign and nameless battles in the snow. The train gathered speed; the Bowl of Heaven paled and expanded, and the dragon smouldered and then utterly faded. (1940c: 63–4)

Far from the sentimentalism that characterised the middlebrow in the ears of most detractors, this aside builds a bleak intimacy with remarkable concision. Moving from his own personal memories as a public figure, Priestley brings the audience in through a direct question, and then returns them with force to a remarkably sombre place within himself. Few propagandists would extend the metaphor of shared suffering and wartime perseverance to the realm of the existential; that Priestley manages to do so without sounding maudlin is a greater achievement still.

'Ordinary British folk': the invention of the wartime public

Priestley's mythologisation of everyday life in wartime consistently put what he called 'the people' at the centre of history. Speaking on 30 June 1940, Priestley expressed his admiration for 'ordinary British folk' who, not content to serve as passive vessels of larger events, responded to the crisis of the war by taking up 'the responsibility of manning this last great defence of our liberal civilisation' (1940c: 22–3). Tapping into a similar historical consciousness to Churchill, whose 'Finest Hour' speech of 18 June still reverberated in many listeners' ears, Priestley invoked the gratitude of later generations:

> Already the future historians are fastening their gaze upon us, seeing us all in that clear and searching light of the great moments of history. That light

may discover innumerable past follies and weaknesses of policy and national endeavour, but here and now, as the spirit of the people rises to meet the challenge, I believe that it will find no flaw in the sense, courage and endurance of those people. (1940c: 23)

As a motivation to greater effort and perseverance, Priestley's push for historical perspective among ordinary citizens fits with a more widespread sense that Britons were living in world-changing times. But Priestley goes further by insisting that the duty of interpreting those times, not only marking their place in a trajectory but also naming the very trajectory itself, lies with the people. Attempts to frame the Second World War in the nationalist terms of the Great War have failed, he claims:

> The queer thing is that these attempts, which have been deliberate and often well organised, are frustrated by masses of people who could give no explanation of why they shrug their shoulders and turn away. I suspect that the wisest historian resides somewhere in the collective unconscious minds of whole populations . . . He knows that this conflict is not a repetition of the last war. (1940c: 46)

The notion of a diffused historical consciousness represents an apotheosis of the 'People's War' myth; the population understood their historical position and aspirations, even if they could not put that understanding into words. Priestley saw his role in the war as giving voice to the silent majority: 'People may be almost inarticulate in themselves and yet recognise in an instant when something that is at least trying to be real and true is being said to them' (1940c: vii). The line between spokesperson and demagogue can be a fine one, especially through a one-way medium like the radio; one suspects that Priestley's version of the 'wisest historian' of the collective unconscious of Britain might have sounded quite a lot like Priestley himself.

Indeed, just who Priestley thought 'the People' were remains a somewhat open question. Priestley's wartime writings and broadcasts exhibit some slippage between national categories. For most of his literary career, he showed little interest in Britain as a national community; he chose to focus his intellectual energies on England and the English. But the Second World War effected a temporary transformation of Priestley's national horizons, as the word 'Britain' began to supplant 'England' in his works.[14] Though he refers to Britain in his wartime broadcasts and writings, and occasionally mentions Scotland and Wales, Priestley seems to reserve the affective dimensions of nationhood for 'England' while treating 'Britain' as a primarily political affiliation. An excerpt from one of his broadcasts to America in the series 'Britain Speaks' illustrates this complementary form of dual nationalism. Priestley describes the bond he sensed while watching a German raid from a hilltop in the presence of a group of Local Defence Volunteers (later known as the Home Guard):

> I felt up there a very powerful and rewarding sense of community. And with it too a sense of deep continuity. Ploughman or parson, shepherd or author, we were Englishmen, turning out at night, as our forefathers had often done before us, to keep watch and ward over the sleeping English hills and fields and homes. (1940a: 27)

In this tableau, the affective bonds of Englishness provide continuity with traditions in which English men guard a 'sleeping' landscape explicitly rendered as vulnerable and implicitly gendered as feminine. The pastoral role of the men on guard – watching over a landscape peopled with those in need of salvation from the menaces of the war – blends Christian and rural symbolism to produce a version of the nation as if seen through a Church of England lens. The passage glosses the links between national geography and the family by zooming in on successive metonymic layers of 'hills' and 'fields' before arriving at the 'homes' from which the men have reluctantly turned themselves out. At the end of the same broadcast, Priestley contemplates the stresses and deprivations of the war and claims 'we can only live from week to week. That's how it is with us, the British' (1940a: 28). Englishness offers a reservoir of psychic support in times of struggle, but Britishness names only the political collectivity united under common threat.

It is of course quite possible to draw one's identity from two or more overlapping conceptual categories; as Linda Colley notes, 'Identities are not like hats ... human beings can and do put on several at a time' (1992: 6). Nor is the formation of a national identity through a defensive posture particularly novel. Colley has argued that the conversion of existential struggle into national character forms a pattern in post-Reformation Britain; while the enemy might change (represented at various times by Catholic France, colonial 'Others' and Nazi Germany), the narrative of national endurance, even triumph, persists (1996: 28–9). When the Blitz on London began in early September, Priestley joined other public figures in rendering the experience of shared vulnerability as an opportunity to forge the nation:

> [J]ust now we're not really obscure persons tucked away in our offices and factories, villas and back streets; we're the British people being attacked and fighting back; we're in the great battle for the future of our civilisation and so instead of being obscure and tucked away, we're bang in the middle of the

world's stage with all the spotlights focused on us; we're historical personages, and it's possible that future generations will find inspiration, when their time of trouble comes, in the report in their history books of our conduct at this hour. (1940c: 69)

Priestley's rhetoric of (in this instance) Britishness affords listeners the comfort of both a strong national bond formed synchronically, through the common experience of shared suffering during the Blitz, and diachronically, through connection to both a deep past and a proleptically imagined future. This is, as other critics have noted, one of the key distinctions between Priestley and more patrician orators like Churchill; while the latter ground national identity largely in the institutions and events of the past, Priestley enables listeners to project that national identity into the future (Addyman 2014: 164; Hawkes 2008: 18; Baxendale 2007: 141).

When faced with the task of addressing the country as a whole, Priestley had difficulty specifying what exactly constituted 'the British' as a people, aside from membership in a polity. In the rousing pro-planning tract *Out of the People* (1941), Priestley repeats many of his arguments from the 'Postscripts' about the war being waged not for the maintenance of the previous status quo, but so that the British people might enjoy a better quality of life. Britain, he argues, is not an 'assemblage of properties' or a 'stock-trading concern'; it is quite simply 'the home of the British people' (Priestley 1941b: 42–5). As for British identity, Priestley simply states that his intended audience is 'the people', as opposed to those who see themselves as members of a particular class, religion or other subgroup; 'we are all the people,' he argues, 'so long as we are willing to consider ourselves the people' (1941b: 13). This apparent tautology in fact inscribes the affiliative logic of Michael Warner's notion of the public. Membership in any public depends first and foremost on the willingness of a group of strangers to understand themselves as voluntary participants in the circulation of a common discourse (Warner 2002: 74–6); the nation Priestley addresses is one in which individual volition contributes to the common good through the formation of a progressive collectivity. Priestley is not addressing all British citizens as 'the people', but rather an imagined group of individuals willing to set aside class, regional, gender and other distinctions in order to commit themselves to a better life for all those governed by the political entity called 'Britain'. Every time Priestley invokes this inclusive group through such simplistic statements as 'you and I – all of us ordinary people', it is not so much an interpellation as an invitation to participate in a newly democratic public (1940c: 19). Priestley actively constitutes the parameters of his imagined community of listeners with every appeal to 'the people'; British listeners populated that community by tuning in and choosing to recognise themselves in Priestley's descriptions of the wartime radio public.

As the 'Postscripts' went on, the equation between 'the People' and a specific political commitment became increasingly apparent. On 30 June 1940, Priestley told listeners that if he had his way, he would 'tell people to forget their old ordinary life because ultimately, anyhow, we'll have a better life than that, or bust' (1940c: 20). Surveying the seaside community of Margate in July 1940, a town drained of holiday-makers because of the war, Priestley argues that most Britons can accept the temporary loss of such pre-war institutions 'if we know that we can march forward – not merely to recover what has been lost, but to something better than we've ever know before' (1940c: 32–3). But Priestley went beyond generic appeals for 'a better life' for Britons: in his 'Postscript' of 21 July, he claimed that the war was not simply an interruption in an otherwise stable world order. Rather, Priestley invokes an explicitly dialectical view of history by arguing that listeners should 'regard this war as one chapter in a tremendous history, the history of a changing world, the breakdown of one vast system and the building up of another and better one' (1940c: 36). 'We must stop thinking in terms of property and power,' Priestley argues, 'and begin thinking in terms of community and creation' (36–7). As an example of how this transformation might occur, Priestley suggests that homes left unused by absentee landlords should be requisitioned for communal uses like agriculture and billeting (38). In a broadcast to the United States a few days later, on 28 July, Priestley went further, suggesting that since total war had already forced considerable taxation on the British, they should move to a system where all wages are collected by the state, with each individual given a certain allowance for the necessities of life (1940a: 130). This may have been bluster designed to exaggerate British sacrifice for an American audience, but it demonstrates how far Priestley was willing to push socialist ideas in his broadcasts.

The call to abandon the property model of ownership ruffled some feathers within the government, but Priestley's producers held firm against complaints. A broadcast on 6 October 1940, however, proved too much for some listeners. Priestley described Britain as precariously balanced between two stools, one of which is labelled 'Every man for himself, and the devil take the hindmost,' while the other bears a more collectivist message:

> The other stool, on which millions are already perched without knowing it, has some lettering round it that hints that free men could combine, without

losing what's essential to their free development, to see that each gives according to his ability, and receives according to his need. (1940c: 90)

This reference to Marx's 'The Critique of the Gotha Programme' (1875) did not go unnoticed. The BBC received complaints about the broadcast from former Conservative Party Chairman Lord Davidson and Colonel Scorgie of the MoI, and Nazi radio happily reported on Priestley's 'communist' broadcast (Nicholas 1995: 257). Priestley, citing fatigue, willingly stepped down from the 'Postscripts' on this occasion; since May, he had been delivering one 'Postscript' and two Overseas broadcasts on the series 'Britain Speaks' every week, in addition to writing articles for periodicals and continuing to work on book-length projects. Priestley and his producers agreed that this was to be a temporary break from the 'Postscripts' series.

By January 1941, Priestley was back for a new series of 'Postscripts', his fee having increased from an initial 10 guineas per broadcast to 50 guineas (a sum equivalent to over seventy weeks' wages for a conscripted British private, then fourteen shillings per week). Though he initially claimed that this second series would be even more politically strident than the last, only the first of the new 'Postscripts' offered much political bite. Nonetheless, when Priestley stepped down after eight broadcasts in the second series of 'Postscripts', listeners presumed he had been muzzled. It was an impression Priestley seemed keen to reinforce. Priestley complained, in the *Daily Herald* of 26 March, that '[p]owerful influences' were working against him, and he labelled Conservative Central Office a 'political Gestapo' (qtd in Nicholas 1995: 260). The BBC's failure to renew does seem to have reflected a measure of pressure from above. The BBC Home Board Minutes from 21 March 1941 record that 'Priestley series stopped ... on instructions of Minister'; that is, the Minister of Information, Duff Cooper (Briggs 1970: 322n). As Siân Nicholas has documented, the situation was more complex than such narratives of official suppression of dissent suggest. Priestley had been contracted for only six talks in the new series; the seventh and eighth had been added because of the positive reception of those first six. Priestley had seen renewal of this contract as a mere formality but BBC administrators were less sure. In any case, his removal prompted few complaints from within the BBC, despite the potential of such a move to incite criticism of censorship within the Corporation. Nicholas reads this as an indication that many within the BBC had already decided that Priestley felt entitled to dominate on-air debate: 'Priestley wanted the freedom of the air, but to many what he had been granted was [a] unique privilege' (Nicholas 1995: 265). He had become a victim of his own success, a radio celebrity too popular for the BBC's measured preferences.

'Postscripts' and the rise of the welfare state

Priestley's ultimate impact on the politics of wartime and postwar Britain are somewhat difficult to quantify. He was, first of all, not as radical as he sometimes claimed to be. Despite occasionally giving voice to quasi-Marxist principles of wealth redistribution, his political roots lay less in doctrinaire communism than in an English radical tradition that rejected class warfare in favour of building alliances across classes (Baxendale 2007: 41–2). Many of Priestley's wartime works emphasise this political tradition, and link it explicitly with forms of cultural expression. 'In a certain limited sense,' says Professor Kronak, one of the protagonists of *Let the People Sing*, 'all the English may be said to be anarchists' who share a 'limited and natural anarchy of the national soul' (Priestley 1939: 30). The 'inner quality' of the English, the Professor claims, 'is deeper than politics, though possibly it would not exist now if there had not once been revolutions here' (1939: 45). Rather than manifesting itself directly in politics, the 'deep unspoken poetry' of the English expresses itself 'only in instinctive conduct and in your literature' (1939: 45). Less than a year after *Let the People Sing* aired, Priestley returned to this theme in the 'Postscript' of 11 August 1940:

> It's often been said, and too often by our own unrepresentative men, that we Islanders are a cold-hearted and unimaginative folk, and it's a thundering lie, for we have some of the most glorious witnesses to our warmth and heart, and height of imagination, from Shakespeare onwards, that the world can know. Always, when we've spoken or acted, as a people, and not when we've gone to sleep and allowed some Justice Shallow to represent us, that lift of the heart, that touch of the imagination, have been suddenly discovered in our speech and our affairs, giving our history a strange glow, the light that never was on sea or land. (1940c: 52)

Sentimental and mystical as such pronouncements might be, they indicate Priestley's firm belief in the guiding role that imaginative powers can play in collective governance. He draws a clear line between two tendencies in British cultural life: on the one side, the 'property and power' view endorsed by the Justices Shallow of the nation, and on the other side, the alliance of 'community and creation' identified in the 'Postscript' of 21 July.

The material deprivations of the war reinforced Priestley's longstanding commitment to the broadbrow approach to culture, in which individuals must have access to the full spectrum of cultural production in order to feel as though they are participating actively in society. Priestley's celebration of the imaginative characteristics of the British in the 'Postscript' of 11 August 1940 emerges in the context of a visit to a factory, where he notes the enthusiasm of the workers for a slightly hackneyed lunchtime variety show organised by the Entertainments National Service Association (ENSA), one of the many government agencies formed to sustain civilian morale during the war. 'Let us, by all means, have four young women in green silk playing "Oh Johnny, Oh Johnny,"' he says, 'but at the same time let's have the great symphony orchestras peeling out the noblest music, night after night, not for a fortunate and privileged few, but for all the people who long for such music' (1940c: 53). A truly open and vibrant cultural democracy is the only just reward for those struggling through the war: 'We must all have at least a glimpse, while we labour or fight, of those glorious worlds of the imagination from which come fitful gleams to this sad, haunted earth' (53). Three years later, Priestley published a fictionalised account of such a scene in *Daylight on Saturday* (1943), a novel of wartime factory life. The narrator of that novel sees in the workers' clamour for middlebrow or lowbrow entertainment the trace of something almost spiritual:

> [T]here was about it an air of release and innocent happiness; a kind of struggling goodness in it; a mysterious promise, not mentioned, not tried for, not even understood, but there somewhere all the time, of man's ultimate deliverance and freedom, a whisper of his homecoming among the stars. (1943b: 99)

Priestley at first avoided describing, in detail, how his vision of a vibrant cultural democracy might actually be brought about in the postwar period. It seemed enough to declare, as he did in one of his few broadcasts before the 'Postscripts', that 'a nobler framework of life must be constructed' (1940b). Faced with criticisms that his calls for a postwar plan were not matched with constructive suggestions, Priestley responded in a broadcast of 25 August 1940 that it was his job to deliver 'a seven-minute postscript to the Sunday night news bulletin, and not to give a four-hour lecture on all possible political, economic, and social developments' (1940c: 57). He became increasingly frustrated that Churchill and his War Cabinet were unwilling to declare war aims, let alone peace aims, and in 1941 Priestley began to move beyond vague assertions about the need for democratic change. He helped to form the 1941 Committee, a progressive counterpoint to the long-running

Conservative Party lobby group known as the 1922 Committee. The 1941 Committee took postwar planning as one of its main goals, and eventually merged with socialist MP Richard Acland's Forward March movement to form the Common Wealth Party, which won a handful of seats from Conservatives in by-elections (Angus Calder 1969: 253; Baxendale 2007: 155). The 1941 Committee was also responsible for the publication of Priestley's *Out of the People*. Much of the book consists of the same spirited but indefinite attempts to rally 'the People' as are found in his broadcasts. In an appendix to the volume, Priestley lays out his objectives for postwar Britain relatively clearly, though not before cautioning readers that '[t]here must first be a change of values and atmosphere' before detailed plans for reform can be put into play (1941b: 112). Too often, he says, 'What is lacking is the emotional force, the compulsive drive, of a general idea . . . It is in an attempt at least to sketch that idea, to generate a little of that emotional force, that I have written this book' (1941b: 14).

Among the recommendations contained in *Out of the People* are a firm rationing policy, a wages policy that gives 'equal wages for equal work everywhere', and a system of family allowances (115). Unused accommodation should be requisitioned, and workers of all kinds coordinated in a national employment strategy that prioritises the war effort. Most strikingly, Priestley calls for the nationalisation of 'essential services', including 'banking, transport, fuel, and power' (116). Priestley claims that nationalisation is necessary to avoid not just a postwar bust like that of the 1920s, but also a worse fate: 'Big Business backed by the state is not democracy,' he claims, 'but Fascism' (116). Furthermore, Britain needs to align its international policies with the democratic principles for which it claims to be fighting. 'We shall gain more than we shall lose by pursuing a generous policy with India, and indeed with all our colonial possessions' (117).

The extent to which these policies line up with later developments – the Beveridge Report, the Labour Party's postwar nationalisation of industry, the break-up of the British Empire – lends Priestley the aura of a soothsayer, if not an active determinant of public opinion. That he was an enormously popular broadcaster is not in doubt; the question remains whether he reflected the mood of a population already undergoing significant ideological shifts, or whether he actively determined the nature of those shifts. Most scholars agree that Priestley could not have changed the perspective of an entire nation, at least not on his own (Angus Calder 1969: 139; Nicholas 1995: 265), but at the very least, he managed to channel a widespread disaffection with the prewar status quo into a much broader social conversation about just what the postwar world would look like. By November 1940, Mass Observation reported – albeit anecdotally – a shift in thinking about the war, with an increasing number of respondents seeing it as revolutionary or radical (Angus Calder 1969: 135). Other signs that the cultural conversation was changing appeared. On 25 March 1941, *The Times* – no bastion of radicalism – featured the aforementioned editorial on the 'Eclipse of the Highbrow', which prematurely celebrated the fact that war had sounded the death-knell of modernism:

> What changes of taste this war, and the reactions following it, may produce, no one can foresee. But at least it can hardly give rise to arts unintelligible outside a Bloomsbury drawing-room, and completely at variance with those stoic virtues which the whole nation is now called upon to practice. ('Eclipse' 1941)

Whatever Priestley's personal role in such shifts, the times were changing, and rapidly.

Siân Nicholas downplays Priestley's radicalising force. She claims that by voicing complaints and wishes for a better world (in a socialist vein, without advocating outright revolution) Priestley worked to lull listeners into complacency (1995: 262). But if Priestley was a kind of surrogate dissenter for a public uninterested in radical change, the fact remains that he epitomised a crucial shift at the BBC from a risk-averse public forum to one in which debate and disagreement with the status quo could be voiced, within the limits of wartime censorship. Perhaps more importantly, Priestley was one of the first figures of the radio war to become a common cultural icon for the British public. Regardless of what one thought of Priestley and his opinions, he offered listeners an accessible and intelligent framework through which to read the events of the war. Consider this account from the diaries of Conservative MP and eminent highbrow Harold Nicolson, who dined with a retired Major General and his wife one evening early in the Blitz of September 1940:

> Priestley gives a broadcast about the abolition of privilege, while I look at their albums of 1903 and the Delhi Durbar and the Viceroy's train. Priestley speaks of the old order which is dead and of the new order which is to arise from its ashes. These two old people listen without flinching. I find their dignity and patriotism deeply moving. I glance at the pictures of the howdahs and panoply of the past and hear the voice of Priestley and the sound of the guns. (qtd in Hewison 1977: 43–4)

Like the falling bombs and booming anti-aircraft fire, Priestley's voice – once spurned, now celebrated – sounded the changes visited upon wartime Britain. While postwar transformations did not amount to a revolution, they did bring a measurable improvement to the lives of many of Britain's less privileged subjects. Priestley had discovered in the radio an opportunity for fusing cultural politics and progressive politics through an intimate medium of address; in the process, he helped to shape the popular conception not only of the war, but of Britain's postwar future as well.

Notes

1. Accounts of Priestley's wartime radio career and his conflicts with the BBC and the Conservative Party can be found in Baxendale (2007: 140–65); Briggs (1970: 210–12, 320–2, 618–21); Angus Calder (1993: 195–205 and 1969: 38–9); Buitenhuis (2000: 456–60); and Nicholas (1996: 57–61, 242–5). Nicholas and Baxendale provide the most thorough overviews; frequent references to their work throughout this chapter testify to the foundational nature of their scholarship on Priestley.
2. 'Lord Haw-Haw' was the nickname given to a shifting array of English-language Nazi broadcasters, many with upper-class English accents (whether by birth or imitation), whose irreverent responses to Westminster's official version of the war fascinated British listeners in the early months of the conflict. The name eventually stuck to the former British Union of Fascists propagandist William Joyce, an American-born, Irish-raised Anglophile whose illicit use of a British passport to flee to Germany in 1939 led to his conviction for treason in 1945. Rebecca West's *The Meaning of Treason* (1947) offers a contemporaneous journalistic account of Joyce's trials and execution; Doherty (2000) provides the best scholarly account of Joyce's role within the Nazi propaganda system.
3. In the interest of avoiding excessive punctuation, the terms middlebrow, broadbrow, highbrow and lowbrow will appear without quotation marks for the rest of the chapter, except where treated explicitly as terms being defined. This does not reflect a naturalisation of the categories, which remain constructions embedded in social, economic and gender hierarchies.
4. Indeed, it was only with the splitting of the BBC into the Home Service and the Forces Programme (later the Light Programme) in 1940 that the Corporation abandoned an explicit commitment to cultural homogeneity via the application of a single set of cultural tastes to the entire population of Britain.
5. Beyond his early work on photography as a 'middlebrow' cultural practice, Bourdieu's theorisation of the cultural field has proven valuable to middlebrow literary studies in its emphasis on the social and economic underpinnings of supposedly natural categories of taste and value (Brown and Grover 2012: 14–16; Humble 2001). Some scholars take issue with Bourdieu's tendency to see middlebrow cultural production as only ever aspiring towards the position of more culturally legitimate (that is, 'highbrow') forms of art, and therefore as neither valuable in its own right nor sceptical of the cultural field of which it forms a part (Hammill 2007: 6–7;

Pollentier 2012). This criticism notwithstanding, Bourdieu's clear-sighted dismantling of the social forces that structure class and taste offers a cogent critique of anti-middlebrow positions taken by writers, like Woolf, whose own origins precluded the necessity of striving for cultural knowledge: 'The ideology of natural taste owes its plausibility and its efficacy to the fact that, like all the ideological strategies generated in the everyday class struggle, it *naturalises* real differences, converting differences in the mode of acquisition of culture into differences of nature; it only recognises as legitimate the relation to culture (or language) which least bears the visible marks of its genesis, which has nothing 'academic', 'scholastic', 'bookish', 'affected' or 'studied' about it, but manifests by its ease and naturalness that true culture is nature – a new mystery of immaculate conception' (Bourdieu [1979] 1984: 68).
6. Correspondence between Priestley and his American publisher Cass Canfield (of Harper & Brothers) in March and April 1940 provides the provisional title *These Our Actors* (Priestley Collection, File PRI 13/22, UB). Because no manuscript with this title exists, however, this chapter refers to the extant manuscript as 'Birmanpool', the title given to the ninety-three-page, 30,000–word section preserved at the HRC. According to a note Priestley appended to the manuscript, the novel was to follow the career of actor Humphrey Pike as he goes from obscurity to fame, and finally to a tragic (though unspecified) end.
7. As if to compound the monologism of the Corporation, news announcers remained anonymous until the war. 'In peacetime', Charles Rolo explains in *Radio Goes to War*, 'the BBC announcer had been just a voice – a voice with an exquisitely bored, impeccably impeccable Oxford accent. The possibility that the enemy might "fake" British broadcasts made it vital to enable listeners to recognise instantly the authentic speakers of the BBC. So the voice at the microphone became a personality with a name, and listeners were now told: "This is the news – and this is Alvar Liddell reading it ..."' (1942: 142–3). For the entirety of the 1930s, however, announcers remained anonymous.
8. Correspondence from Jameson, West, Wells, Bevin, McCarthy and Shaw preserved in the J. B. Priestley papers, Ms. [Priestley, J.B.] Recip, Harry Ransom Humanities Research Center, University of Texas at Austin.
9. See Robert Calder (2004: 157–61) for an account of how the MoI administered the publication of works like *Britain at War*. See Baxendale (2007: 146) for a discussion of *Britain at Bay*.
10. Arlott's broadcasts attracted the attention of West Indian listener (and future theorist of 'nation language') Edward Kamau Brathwaite. Brathwaite heard in Arlott's thick Hampshire burr a soft acoustic revolution, one which 'subverted the Establishment with the way and where he spoke' (Brathwaite 1984: 30).
11. *Postscripts* hereafter cited parenthetically in text.
12. See, for example, Sassoon's 'Glory of Women' ([1918] 1996) ('O German mother dreaming by the fire, / While you are knitting socks to send your son / His face is trodden deeper in the mud,' ll. 12–14) and Owen's 'Strange Meeting' ([1919] 1996) ('I am the enemy you killed, my friend,' l. 40).
13. Reminiscing about lost comrades at a reunion of his battalion in *English*

Journey, Priestley blames the death toll of the First World War on a society-wide ethical lapse: 'I have had playmates, I have had companions, but all, all are gone; and they were killed by greed and muddle and monstrous cross-purposes, by old men gobbling and roaring in clubs, by diplomats working underground like monocled moles, by journalists wanting a good story, by hysterical women waving flags, by grumbling debenture-holders, by strong silent be-ribboned asses, by fear or apathy or downright lack of imagination' (1934: 166).

14. The use of the terms 'England,' 'Britain' and their derivatives in the titles of Priestley's works charts a telling course. *The English Comic Characters* (1925), *The English Novel* (1927), *English Humour* (1929) and *English Journey* (1934) all appear pre-war; *Britain Speaks* (1940), *Britain at War* (1942) and *British Women Go to War* (1943) all appeared during the war. *Topside, or The Future of England* (1958) and *The English* (1973) appeared postwar.

Chapter 2

James Hanley and the Shape of the Wartime Features Department

Perhaps no form of radio art emerged from the Second World War more vitalised than the feature. A plural and changeable genre whose roots date back to the experimental dramas of Tyrone Guthrie and Lance Sieveking in the late 1920s, the feature is best understood as a dramatised documentary tailored to the medium of radio. Features were based in fact but could weave music, sound effects, dialogue, verse and fictional re-enactments in order to conjure elaborate sonic worlds for the listener.[1] This composite form allowed the feature to capitalise on the full range of expressive possibilities afforded by radio. Long-time BBC producer Laurence Gilliam considered the feature to be

> the form of statement that broadcasting has evolved for itself, as distinct from those other forms which it has borrowed or adapted from other arts or methods of production. It is pure radio, a new instrument for the creative writer and producer. (Gilliam 1950: 10)

Despite the radiogenic 'purity' of the feature, the BBC did not create a specialised branch for its production until 1936, when the Drama Department, overseen by Val Gielgud, adopted a tripartite structure comprising sections responsible for Drama, Features and the Children's Hour (Briggs 1965: 168).[2] After a string of wartime successes, Features would become its own department in 1945 under Gilliam's direction; it would thrive for two decades before closing in 1965 amid a changing media landscape that then included independent broadcasters, a well-established television culture and pirate broadcasting (Briggs 1970: 347–8; Crisell [1986] 1994: 28; Bridson 1971: 299–304).

That the Second World War witnessed the consolidation of the feature within the hierarchy of the BBC testifies to the central role such productions played in the war effort; the creative treatment of current and historical events lent itself naturally to wartime demands of propaganda. But neither all features nor all feature writers could meet the particular demands of the wartime Features section. Writing for Features was a matter of radio craft as well as a matter of literary expression, and demanded a careful balance of imaginative daring, technical know-how and political astuteness. In comparing the scripts and experiences of two notable wartime contributors to Features – James Hanley and Louis MacNeice – the following two chapters parse the complicated mixture of sensibilities required to meet the needs of the BBC and the publics it addressed. At the same time, these chapters explore the process of writerly recruitment and retention within the wartime Features section, to determine who was valued and why.

Hanley's radio career – indeed, much of his career as a whole – has suffered from critical neglect.[3] The gap in scholarship on his broadcasts of the 1940s is understandable; despite a promising start and the support of Gilliam and other producers within Features, Hanley failed to produce a large body of work during the war. His later and more effective contributions to the BBC Third Programme, however, invite a consideration of his early apprenticeship; he would go on to write dozens of successful radio scripts in the 1950s and 1960s, and collaborate with prominent producers including Douglas Cleverdon (who also produced Dylan Thomas's *Under Milk Wood*) and Donald McWhinnie (who produced many of Samuel Beckett's works for radio). MacNeice, on the other hand, has been celebrated as the most important literary success of the radio war; no other writer of the era made the transition from poet to script-writer and producer seem so effortless or aesthetically fruitful. The disparity in their careers has as much to do with personalities, work habits and philosophical outlook as it has to do with the difficulties of the feature as a genre. Hanley's contributions reflect his tendencies, as a working novelist, to write quickly and with the novel's bulk in mind; by an unfortunate coincidence, Hanley was also reluctant to edit his works despite the entreaties of producers within Features. MacNeice, as Chapter 3 will outline, brought a poet's attention to form and concision to the task of writing propaganda. He also quickly picked up the tricks of the radio trade, both in terms of writing with the microphone in mind and in terms of learning the skills of production itself.

Perhaps the most important distinction, however, was between the two writers' views of what war writing might sound like. The themes that obsessed Hanley throughout his working life – the solitude of human existence, its basis in struggle and frequent failure, the redemption possible through such failure – combined with his insistence on the autonomy of the artist's voice to produce radio works that did not fit the BBC mould, especially in wartime. MacNeice, however sceptical and world-weary his other writings could be, learned quickly to shape themes of destruction and danger into narratives of endurance, transformation and triumph. Most importantly, as the war went on, he paired the theme of endurance with the emerging People's War motif of collective struggle for collective survival. Hanley's commitment to his own idiosyncratic practice, less responsive to the expectations of audience and collaborators, would force him to wait until the postwar Third Programme afforded a venue more receptive to his difficult, iconoclastic radio works.

The growth of the features aesthetic

For all its importance to the landscape of British radio in the 1930s, 1940s and beyond, the feature has a complex and somewhat contradictory genealogy. Radio producer, writer and theorist Lance Sieveking, whose *Kaleidoscope I* (1928) and *Kaleidoscope II* (1929) did much to push the boundaries of radio aesthetics and techniques, saw the feature as a quintessentially wireless genre – what he called 'the stuff of radio' (Sieveking 1934: 26).[4] As opposed to a radio play, Sieveking claims, a feature is 'an arrangement of sounds, which has a theme but no plot', and whose successful orchestration depends on the careful and sensitive operation of the technologies of the studio (1934: 26, 57–8). Central to the success of *Kaleidoscope I*, as with many early radiogenic works, was the skill with which Sieveking 'played' the dramatic control panel, an early mixing board that enabled the producer to control multiple studios housing the various elements of the sonic palette: orchestra, choir, actors, sound effects and gramophones.[5] The seamlessness with which a producer could blend inputs and move rapidly between spatio-temporal settings enabled a liberation from both the stolid genre of the 'talk' and the conventions of the theatre that so many radio plays had adopted relatively unaltered. Radio programmes, whether dramatic or otherwise, now seemed limited only by the imaginations of their producers and the technologies at their disposal.

The feature's promised liberation from the conventions of stage drama contributed to the shape and sound of many wartime features, from *The Shadow of the Swastika*'s examination of the rise of fascism to transatlantic appeals like *Britain to America*, which were able to conjure people and places acoustically in a highly fluid, mobile way. But if such productions echo Sieveking's structurally and technically grounded version of the feature, they also indicate that the genre drew equal inspiration from the documentary aesthetic that had characterised so much British cultural production of the 1930s. Gilliam, who in addition to being a producer was Assistant Director of Features during the war, put it plainly: 'Features deal with fact, Drama with fiction' (qtd in Drakakis 1981: 8). While this distinction would obtain for the duration of the war, with Features responsible for much of the overtly propagandistic material produced by the BBC, the political mobilisation of facts in the feature has roots that extend deeper than the war, and beyond London. Over the course of the 1930s, producers in the North region, based in Manchester, had extended the scope and aims of the genre through the refinement of an explicitly political form of actuality broadcasting.[6] E. A. F. Harding, D. G. Bridson, Olive Shapley, Francis 'Jack' Dillon, Joan Littlewood and other producers in Manchester used the feature to pioneer techniques of mobile recording, the use of regional accents and coverage of pressing social issues. If, as Chapter 1 argues, it was still relatively unusual in the 1930s to hear working-class Britons speaking in their own voices over the air, it was all the more unusual to hear them addressing the spatialised inequalities of a country in which North and South named material as well as geographical differences. Shapley's innovative use of the BBC's lone mobile recording van to capture the voices of rural Northerners for features like *Homeless People* (1938) and *Miners' Wives* (1939) is indicative of the confluence of technical competence, creativity and a broadly democratic impulse necessary for such productions. As the People's War moved the contributions of ordinary Britons into the spotlight, the pioneering features of BBC North served as a template for the accurate, and entertaining, representation of the life, labour, ideas and interests of working- and middle-class citizens from across the country.

The feature thus draws its inheritance from two lineages, which, if not mutually exclusive, are at least motivated by different impulses: the documentary and the radiogenic. Features draw from and have an obligation towards reality, and yet they eschew realism as a dramatic convention, choosing instead to follow the possibilities of the medium. Wartime features, like their precursors during the crisis years of the 1930s, were instruments for the communication of urgent realities. Because of their proclaimed commitment to those realities and their attempts to secure 'actuality' recordings in the field, features could command a truth-value absent from many dramatic productions. And yet their treatment of issues was far more dynamic than that provided by a single speaker in a 'talk'. This dynamism depended upon the feature's aesthetic tendency towards fluidity: its ability to move rapidly between locations and to mix elements based on their potential to evoke an auditory image, rather than their necessary congruity in time and space. For writers and producers at the wartime Features Department, the imperative to tell 'the truth' – itself already a highly mediated and politicised construction – would at times sit uneasily with the need to tell an exciting story.

Although the feature emerged from the war as an important and enduring genre, its role was far from assured at the beginning of the conflict. In the first round of wartime contingency plans drawn up in 1938, BBC administrators deemed the Department of Features and Drama of minimal importance to the impending crisis, the department being generally less informative than news and less cheering than music (Nicholas 1996: 17). The limited scheduling space of the new, nation-wide Home Service necessitated drastic cuts to the time allotted for plays and features. What is more, when war finally arrived with its threat of imminent bombardment, the BBC evacuated several major departments from London. Features and Drama were dispatched to safety in Wood Norton (code-named 'Hogsnorton'), a sleepy estate outside Evesham, while Music and Variety moved to Bristol. For Director of Features and Drama Val Gielgud, being side-lined in both geographical and scheduling terms was incapacitating. In a November 1939 report to the Home Board (the committee responsible for overseeing Home Service programming), Gielgud was blunt:

> Few aspects of broadcasting can have been more seriously handicapped . . . The time limitation of the programme items to half an hour [and] the assumption that the single wavelength programme material automatically excluded anything that could by any stretch of the imagination be labelled 'highbrow' . . . cut at the roots of supply for a department whose listeners had always been a 'minority' audience. (qtd in Briggs 1970: 112)

By the time of this report, however, things had already started to improve from the first, difficult weeks of the war. In mid-November, the department had moved to Manchester – home of the innovative features programming of the BBC's interwar North Region – and they had begun to elaborate a more ambitious and concrete vision of the role they might play in the conflict. Gielgud claimed that Features and Drama was in a unique position to offer 'a contribution to the preservation of civilised culture in time of war' while also providing 'implicit or explicit propagandist contributions to national war-time activity' (Briggs 1970: 113–14). In addition to dramatic staples including Shakespeare, and popular adaptations of Charles Dickens, P. G. Wodehouse and H. G. Wells, the Department of Features and Drama would seek 'to retain the "pure radio" audience's good will with a proportion of definitely intelligent work on experimental lines' (Briggs 1970: 113). In other words, Features and Drama would serve a government anxious to inform and a populace anxious to be entertained, all without abandoning the department's commitment to sophistication and experimentation. Entertaining and informative, propagandistic and intellectual, experimental and popular, the programming produced by Features and Drama crystallised, as if in miniature, the idealised role of the BBC during the war.

James Hanley at the Wartime Features Department

Considering the turn, by some features producers of the 1930s, towards the lives, language and concerns of the working classes, one might think that James Hanley would have offered his works up for adaptation early in his literary career. The son of a sailor, Hanley went to sea in his early teens, served in the First World War, and worked as a railway porter, journalist and racetrack cashier before publishing his first novel (Midkiff 1998: 173). But it was summer 1938 before Hanley submitted his first script to the BBC for its consideration, by which time he was several years into a career as a novelist. His first novel, *Drift*, had appeared in 1930 to critical praise, but it was *Boy* (1931) that had sealed his reputation as a gritty and provocative chronicler of working-class life. *Boy* offers a good example of the hardships and traumas that would form the substance of Hanley's fiction: the novel follows 13-year-old Arthur Fearon, who, after being forced by his family to leave school and clean bilges on ships at port, stows away on a vessel sailing for Alexandria. Over the course of the novel, he is subjected to cruel rites of initiation by his peers and sexual molestation by his superiors. Once in Alexandria, he contracts syphilis from a prostitute who had otherwise provided him with the only experience of beauty and pleasure in his short life. The novel ends with the drunken captain smothering Arthur in order to spare him the slow and painful death that the disease all but guaranteed.

Though controversial, novels like *Boy* earned Hanley some influential supporters. William Faulkner, E. M. Forster and T. E. Lawrence all praised his steady gaze at the violence and tragedy simmering beneath the surface of modern working life; Forster would speak in defence of Hanley when the novel's publisher was charged with obscenity in 1934. Over the course of the 1930s, Hanley continued to explore the difficulties of life at sea and in the hardscrabble ports of interwar England, all the while refining a prose style that could, in his early works, veer erratically between phantasmagoria and a curious flatness. By the outbreak of war his reputation was that of a serious, if uneven, working-class novelist, who refracted his own experiences of seafaring and joblessness in works that tread a line between plain-spoken realism, psychological insight and modernist flourishes.

When Hanley did address his talents to the BBC, in July 1938, he did so through a number of filters. He submitted his first radio play, *We Are the Living*, under the name Seamus O'Hanlon, an apparent Gaelicisation of 'James Hanley'. Within the same month, another letter came in under Hanley's name but signed by his secretary, Paul Wolff.[7] It was three months before the Features and Drama producer Barbara Burnham finally wrote Hanley to decline *We Are the Living*, ostensibly on the grounds of its length. Burnham neglected to tell Hanley that BBC script-readers had found the play 'bulky' and 'turgid' despite what they called its admirable 'culminating effect' (Burnham 1938). The readers' sense that there was simply *too much* of Hanley's play proved prophetic: over the course of the war, Hanley would face repeated requests that he edit, reshape, streamline and soften his works in order to fit them to the demands of wireless propaganda.

Hanley tried, often and unsuccessfully, to interest the BBC in producing new works or adapting stories in 1938 and 1939; he seems to have taken the hint eventually, as there is no record of correspondence between Hanley and the BBC between June 1939 and April 1941. At some point, however, he made a connection with Gilliam; the latter writes to him in April 1941, voicing his enthusiasm for an anticipated Hanley submission to the US-aimed series *Freedom's Ferry*. This series, soon retitled *Freedom Ferry*, aired weekly for several months in 1941, and attempted to represent for an American audience the dangers faced by merchant seamen on the hostile North Atlantic shipping lanes. Hanley's seafaring experience, and his enthusiasm for a medium with the potential to reach millions of listeners eager for stories of the war, made him a natural choice for the programme. On the part of the BBC, there is repeated reference in internal memos to Hanley's stature as a writer; Gilliam, Douglas Cleverdon, Francis Dillon and others all testify to his literary standing and talents. Though they do not say so explicitly, there would have been added value in hiring a working-class novelist like Hanley; his experiences would lend an authenticity to broadcasts that might help persuade American listeners of the erosion of class barriers in Britain as much as the precariousness of Atlantic shipping.

While *Freedom Ferry* presented itself as an exciting, fact-based description of conditions at sea, its function was of course to persuade American listeners that financial support and trade were valued but insufficient contributions to the fight against Nazism, a fight in which ordinary British sailors often lost their lives.[8] Hanley's first contribution to the series, 'Atlantic Convoy', makes a compelling and dramatic case for the dangers of the merchant service. The episode opens on the deck of the SS *Elizabethan*, part of a long line of cargo vessels making its way east across the Atlantic, accompanied by a British Navy escort. The emphasis, for the listener as for the sailors on watch, is on parsing the near-silence of the scene: 'The sea is calm,' the narrator tells us, 'almost soundless. High in the nest, on the fo'c'sle head, on bridge and flying bridge, from poop and house men watch, and they listen for sounds, for sounds that no sea has ever made' (Hanley 1941a: 1). The presence of these alien sounds (whether torpedoes, aircraft or German vessels) renders an already hostile environment even more so.[9] Radio propaganda of the war made a virtue of its monosensory character: listeners with no other option but to listen strain their ears to detect in the broadcast a clue to imminent danger. Navigating the soundscape of a radio feature or play thereby becomes a stand-in for the important act of listening on the home front (Whittington 2015: 50–9).

Although no recording exists, 'Convoy' reads as a gripping narrative, moving efficiently from the calm of the opening tableau to a dramatic German submarine attack, evasive and defensive manœuvres by the convoy and a safe return to British shores. Sonic effects deepen the impression of hectic combat: with the first signs of an explosion on another ship in the convoy, the *Elizabethan* springs into a flurry of action. 'Sound of men streaming out on deck,' the effects cue reads, 'voices, blowing of whistles, sudden clang of bell from nest, a ring on the telegraph' (Hanley 1941a: 2). Despite the relative defencelessness of the merchant vessels, Hanley's narrator represents the scene as full of movement:

> Through and across and around the now breaking lines go two destroyers, shooting past bows, appearing under sterns, veering to port, to starboard, shooting ahead, making the water sing, dropping their deadly loads. The ships are reforming now. But *another* warning has flashed along the lines ... (1941a: 3)

As German planes appear and strafe the convoy, the merchant ships scatter and zigzag their way home, every vessel for itself.

As the first in the *Freedom Ferry* series, 'Convoy' succeeds at placing merchant mariners in a vital intermediary position between soldiers and the home front. Moreover, it dramatises and valorises all ranks of the merchant service. In a move reflective of Hanley's intimate knowledge of the working life aboard a ship like the *Elizabethan*, the programme shifts our attention, around the midway point of the feature, away from the attacking planes towards the stokers in the engine rooms. Hanley knows that the drama that plays out on the surface depends on those below the surface as well:

> NARRATOR: Below deck men work unceasing, in the light of fires, the world of steel shuts out the seascape, the wide arc of sky, the pattern of the hour. The roar of engines dies away against the noise of bombs. Stripped to the waist, they glisten with sweat in the fierce glare. For them escape is the last thought. (1941a: 6)

As in all of his seafaring works, for radio and for print, Hanley understands the successful operation of any large vessel to be an act of unequal cooperation: for every charismatic and decisive captain there are dozens toiling below decks. It is unclear, as John Fordham has noted in his volume on Hanley's writing, whether such representations of the difficulties of working life at sea are meant to challenge the unequal conditions of industrial modernity, or to fold those conditions back into a much longer, romanticised history of seafaring as 'essentially' tragic (2002: 28, 47). For despite their almost superhuman strength, the men working below decks do not think of 'escape' from either the dangers of attack or the strictures of the class system. Whether transcendentalising class suffering or calling for a revolution in class relations, Hanley's emphasis on the stokers implicitly criticises the approach of writers like Joseph Conrad, whose seafaring works Hanley thought were too focused on the officer class: 'What romance, what honour,' Hanley wrote in a 1934 letter to Henry Raymond, his publisher at Chatto and Windus, 'but never for'ard of the bridge, nor aft for that matter' (qtd in Fordham 2002: 46). For the snapshots they provide of the forecastle and engine room, Hanley's contributions to *Freedom Ferry* demonstrate his commitment to rounding out the modern literary vision of working life at sea.

Hanley wrote three more instalments in the series, all of which end with an overt statement of the valuable contribution the merchant navy was making to the war effort.[10] This occasionally meant downplaying the bleaker themes that animated his writings. 'Open Boat' (10 September 1941) offers a particularly instructive example of how adaptation to wartime radio could prompt significant changes in the theme and tone of Hanley's works, changes which he would grow to resist in later radio scripts. 'Open Boat' draws on the plot of Hanley's novel *The Ocean* (1941), one of his most celebrated works and a concentrated expression of his thematic and philosophical interests. Both the radio feature and the novel concentrate on the survival of the crew of a torpedoed vessel at sea. In the radio feature, approximately half a dozen merchant mariners, of a variety of levels of experience, endure a prolonged wait for rescue by adhering to the structures of order that obtain on board a ship. One veteran sailor, Billie, takes charge with the help of a deputy and the support of the other, less experienced, sailors; they dole out rations methodically and without complaint; all men take turns rowing and scanning the horizon. Despite these orderly procedures, the experience of shipwreck is one of mind-bending tedium and uncertainty:

> NARRATOR: Two days drag past. Men begin to look at each other silently. Lips move to speak, but there seems nothing to say, nothing to do but row, towards that horizon line that ever recedes and always mocks them. They wonder about other boats, drifting as hopelessly as theirs; they think of the ship, they think of home. Their leader heartens them, jokes with them and curses them; he makes them hope and keep on hoping – hoping and rowing, rowing and hoping and rowing. And always about them the blue water, and the sun up there shining down on them, warming them but increasing their thirst, dazzling and hurting their eyes. (1941d: 9)

For the sailors of 'Open Boat', the story ends happily and relatively quickly: a British naval vessel appears within a few days and brings them aboard. Within a few days of arriving at port, the narrator informs us, the men will have signed on for another stint aboard a merchant vessel: 'For the ships and the men who sail them will not be *kept* from the sea, while ships and men are wanted to guard the freedom of Freedom Ferry' (1941d: 12, emphasis in original). As with the stokers of 'Atlantic Convoy', the sailors of 'Open Boat' commit themselves bodily to the task of supplying Britain in its time of need; for American listeners, the implication that their nation could do much more would have been hard to ignore.

However evocative this snapshot of life as a shipwrecked sailor may be, it suffers by comparison with *The Ocean*. In this novel, completed just before Hanley began working on *Freedom Ferry* for the BBC, a sailor named Curtain is left in charge of four civilians in a lifeboat following a German torpedo attack on their passenger vessel. Like Billie in 'Open Boat', Curtain takes charge of the boat by organising the rowing schedule and distributing rations of water and food. Despite these similarities, however, the arc of the novel is at once more disheartening and more movingly humanist than the radio broadcast. In the novel, the tiny society of the lifeboat is fractured: only Curtain and his closest supporter, a man named Stone, generally uphold the responsibilities of keeping the boat moving and slowly doling out the rations. One civilian, a priest named Father Michaels, is seriously ill. Other men steal water when Curtain dozes; one man, Gaunt, is caught in a solipsistic world of memories of his wife, now missing from the sunken ship; the youngest man, Benton, slips into hallucinations based on his childhood horror of cockroaches. Above all, the wait for rescue drags on interminably, for days if not weeks. It is not entirely clear, at the impressionistic end of the novel, how many of the shipwrecked men have survived.

For all the hopelessness and disorder in *The Ocean*, however, there are glimpses of the sublime, as when the lifeboat encounters a whale that plays peacefully beside their boat. Benton and the others marvel at a creature that captures the gracefulness and unmeaning beauty of a natural world which had, until this point, treated them with an indifference verging on hostility. As if unlocking the potential for human compassion, this sight immediately precedes the novel's final, complicated moral act: when their lifeboat encounters a similarly stranded but unconscious German airman, Curtain pulls him aboard and gives him the final cup of water from their rations. Giving life to a pilot who may well have strafed their vessel days earlier is a cheek-turning act of charity that might divide the rest of the crew members, were they not all unconscious or otherwise incapacitated from hunger, thirst and exhaustion. As the novel ends, the semi-lucid Father Michaels believes he sees a rock; this rock turns out to be a fishing boat, whose commander appears to Michaels as a religious vision: 'The priest looked out at him, and in his eyes, his was the shape of Christ' (Hanley [1941] 1999: 152).

For all the uncertainties of *The Ocean* – who has survived, whether Gaunt is reunited with his wife, how many more passengers of the sunken liner were rescued – it offers these transcendent images as if to declare that the failure of any one single endeavour does not rob that endeavour of its potential for meaning and beauty. Nor, the novel indicates, can the exigencies of war permanently fracture a human community united in suffering. Indeed, this sense of the persistence of ethics and aesthetics in the midst of failure – indeed, their constitution *through* failure – is what unites Hanley's larger body of work. It is indicative of the constraints placed on wartime propaganda features like *Freedom Ferry* that failure is largely wiped from the broadcast; the BBC needed tales of triumph and survival, not a glorious resignation to defeat, much less one that treated Nazi airmen as charity cases. While BBC broadcasts could not pretend that merchant vessels did not sink, and that sailors were not shipwrecked, they could insist upon the professionalism and confidence of those who served in the merchant service.

Struggles at the BBC

Despite the modest success of these instalments of the *Freedom Ferry* series, Hanley had difficulty getting further work on the air. None of his other scripts would air in 1941, and only two more would be broadcast in 1942: *Return to Danger* in January and *Shadows Before Sunrise* in December. Even these required substantial rewriting by their respective producers, Malcolm Baker-Smith and Brigid Maas. Over the summer and autumn of 1941, Hanley submitted multiple scripts for consideration, on subjects including the South American revolutionary Simón Bolívar, railways, dock workers and the production of coal. Some of these scripts had been commissioned but many were the product of Hanley's initiative; none appears to have been preserved at the BBC Written Archives Centre (WAC), as it was not the policy of the BBC to retain scripts that were not produced. These multiple rejections, often after long delays, irked Hanley: 'I have lots of ideas I would like to see in radio form,' he wrote to Gilliam in October 1941; 'all I ask is something better than weeks of silence. I gave up writing books to do this sort of work, and it has interested me no end' (Hanley 1941e).

For his producers and editors, however, Hanley's work provided its own kind of frustration. Gilliam warned him early on – in comments on *Mute Gods*, Hanley's proposed script about the railways – that his scripts were often too long and shapeless, and needed 'thinning out' (Gilliam 1941b). Such programmes tested the skills of producers; as Gilliam wrote to producer D. G. Bridson, a script like *Mute Gods* 'needs iron control to get a clear impression across' (Gilliam 1941c). Evidently, Gilliam and others within Features decided, more often than not, that the scripts were not worth such exertions. Hanley himself was not enthusiastic about reworking his own material; when producer Baker-Smith sent the script of *Return to Danger* back to Hanley for substantial revisions, the author made only superficial edits. This was especially challenging for Baker-Smith because the inchoate script had already been scheduled for broadcast. 'I venture to hope that this kind of thing will not happen again,' Baker-Smith wrote to Gilliam, 'that an utterly embryonic script be given a date [for broadcast] before being passed to the person responsible for its ultimate success or failure' (Baker-Smith 1941). In other words, producers could not be expected to do their job well when they could not be guaranteed quality scripts; both roles were essential for an effective feature.

Around the same time, Hanley submitted the script for his proposed play on the life of composer Modest Mussorgsky, which would eventually become *Shadows Before Sunrise*. Apparently aware that his work was gaining a reputation for being unwieldy, Hanley declared to Gilliam in the letter accompanying the script that 'Technique is the producer's business, and his only[;] it remains for the writer to give life, drama, colour, urgency, force, atmosphere and truth to his work. That done the rest is the producer's business' (Hanley 1941e). Gilliam, for his part, thought the script had 'force and imagination and real feeling – but so completely disorganized, it makes you weep' (Gilliam 1941g). That *Shadows Before Sunrise* (Hanley and Maas 1942) treats Mussorgsky as a Hanley-surrogate, stubbornly and self-destructively committed to his particular artistic vision despite the condemnation of those around him, adds piquancy to the play's torturous journey towards transmission in December 1942, after Hanley had already returned to Wales to resume writing novels. However gifted he might be as a novelist, Hanley seemed unable to acquire the knack of writing programmes that captured, and sustained, the imaginations of his listeners. The solution, Gilliam thought, was to bring Hanley into the fold as a contracted employee of the Features Department. Up to this point, he had been submitting scripts on an ad hoc basis, but the lack of supervision, and Hanley's ignorance of the job of a producer, led to scripts that were often poorly structured or otherwise unsuitable for a wartime radio audience.

By May 1942, Hanley had accepted a three-month contract. What happened during this stint is not exactly clear, as there is a significant gap in the correspondence at the BBC Archives. In April 1942, he exchanged letters with Brigid Maas about her alterations to *Shadows Before Sunrise* (which were so substantial that she would eventually be credited as co-author); in August, he made plans for a feature about a British 'Everyman' soldier, eventually titled *My Name is Atkins*. But there is little trace of his time within Features, during which he was expected to liaise with producers, to observe the process of radio production and thereby hone his writing skills with an ear for broadcasting. In the end, according to Hanley, he interacted with almost no one, worked alone on scripts and met with little support for his ideas (Hanley 1942b). According to Bridson and Baker-Smith, Hanley had little cause for complaint: if he failed to immerse himself in the culture of radio writing and production while under contract at the BBC, that was his own fault.[11] As for his scripts, producers seem to have felt that they did not show sufficient improvement to justify extending that contract.

It is difficult to be sure what to make of Hanley's failure to blossom at Broadcasting House. John Fordham alleges that Hanley's failures at the BBC were the result of 'the entrenched cultural values and practices of the institution', and that bourgeois producers like Gilliam, Bridson, Maas and Baker-Smith, however sympathetic they might be to a proletarian writer like Hanley, were hampered by a 'characteristic fastidiousness which finds the rawness of the unmediated voice unacceptable' (Fordham 2002: 164). It is true that some of the reaction against Hanley's bleakly existential works resulted from a culture particular to the BBC in its early decades, and that this culture would evolve in later years to enable the inclusion of more 'difficult' productions. But it is also true that Hanley was an unreliable writer with whom to work: though able to generate prodigious quantities of often beautiful prose, he had little sense of what producers often called the 'shape' of a broadcast – the effective interplay of thematic and sonic elements within a balanced narrative structure. If producers within Features were hesitant to put Hanley's work on the air, it had at least as much to do with broadcasting aesthetics as with the politics of acceptable propaganda.

Hanley's final, abandoned feature, *My Name is Atkins*, brings his unstable and ambivalent legacy into focus. He began the feature while still under contract, and when his contract was not renewed he returned to Wales and continued working on it. By October he had submitted the script to the BBC, where it was read by individuals within Features and the War Liaison Office. Because the script was not preserved, the assessments of these readers, together with Hanley's own descriptions, give us our only insights into Hanley's attempt to dramatise the experiences of the titular military Everyman. His correspondence with Gilliam indicates that, from the beginning, Hanley planned a script that would foreground hardship and endurance over glory:

> I am going to put the case for a man who has been left isolated in the backwaters. The man who answered the call, obeyed the orders, asked no questions, and carried them out . . . The man who went to France, advanced & retreated, the man who sat quietly in his camp, weaponless during 1940, who could not fight, because he could not move – yet, who, nevertheless, saw his family bombed, his home smashed. The man who went to Iceland, Libya, Singapore – Russia – Malaya – Burma – India – always advancing – always tragically retreating. All orders carried out, no complaints – pushed time after time to the very rim of despair – yet never faltered – never lost hope – went on believing – stubborn – determined – the common denominator in the war, caught in a vast & ever widening circle of events – the man, whose activities have circled half the earth, the man at the roots, who in the end will I believe decide the final issues. The American forces I suppose will have their own sovereign hour – but I hope that before that time comes the world, & especially America will learn how, but for the common British soldier, millions of people would not even enjoy the privilege of drawing breath. (Hanley 1942a)

Though obviously respectful of the soldier, and offering even a subtle optimism about his ultimate success, Hanley's projected script hardly seems upbeat. Nor does it celebrate survival as some kind of ethical triumph; endurance, in *Atkins*, is not a virtue but a necessity, and one that weighs heaviest on the least powerful soldiers. If, like the stokers in the belly of the SS *Elizabethan*, Atkins does not think of escape, it is not lack of fear but lack of possibility (and perhaps of imagination) that conditions this frame of mind. In a discussion of Hanley's similarly bleak 1943 Blitz novel *No Directions*, whose characters endure a night of bombing while trapped in an apartment building, Patrick Deer stresses that Hanley's claustrophobic setting and impressionistic style prohibit the kind of overview of the war that would render its struggles meaningful in either narrative or historical terms (Deer 2009: 148). *Atkins* presages the resigned subjection to the vicissitudes of war experienced by the civilians of *No Directions*, but in the context of the armed forces; in doing so, it replaces the government's politically instrumental mythology of military heroics with a narrative of isolation, passivity and retreat. That Hanley supposed this might be broadcast as semi-official propaganda on the BBC – an agency central to the production of what Deer calls 'official war culture' (2009: 132–40) – speaks volumes about his commitment to naturalism in all media, regardless of the role he was expected to play.

Response to *Atkins* from the BBC was predictably unenthusiastic. War Liaison Officer R. S. P. Mackarness reminded Hanley that the military's Director of Public Relations has 'for a long time been dead set against all stories dealing with "glorious retreats," and you, by the very nature of your subject, have dealt with almost nothing else' (Mackarness 1942). Within Features itself, the reader assigned to review the script began his assessment with praise, noting that the feature is 'extremely well written' and that 'the numerous effects are necessary and generally succeed in setting the scene and creating the atmosphere.' The result, however, is 'a painfully vivid story of defeat and disaster. Goebells [sic] might have written it' (Hiller 1942). Producer Francis Dillon, reporting the reader's assessment back to Gilliam, takes a remarkably broad view of the situation. Summing up *Atkins*, he concludes:

> Hanley is a pessimistic realist in his writing but not in his politics. He does not adapt himself to the policy requirements of broadcasting, neither is he content to keep just ahead of them. These things might have been set right, as might his technical defects, had he been handled properly during his three months in London ... It is a pity to discard a writer of his calibre, but until the B.B.C. allows writers to use radio as a medium for unedited self-expression, which it cannot possibly do at present, I think we shall have to drop him. (Dillon 1942)

Dillon's letter reveals an awareness not only that proper guidance during Hanley's tenure at Features might have amended the gaps between his strengths as a novelist and the success he sought as a radio writer, but also that broadcasting constraints are always historically contingent. While wartime circumstances might prevent Hanley's 'unedited self-expression', there exist for Dillon possible futures in which Hanley's style would find acceptance and an audience. This would prove to be the case with the launch of the postwar Third Programme, for which Hanley would write many plays, and where he would find sympathetic producers like Douglas Cleverdon and Donald McWhinnie. Through plays like *The Welsh Sonata* (1956), *The Ocean* (1958), *Gobbet* (1959) and *Say Nothing* (1961), he earned a reputation as a vibrant and challenging, if sometimes disturbing, writer for radio.

But if, as Dillon foresaw, the war was not the time for Hanley to present his highly idiosyncratic works, the author could not entirely abandon his interest in radiogenic forms of storytelling. Upon leaving the BBC, he quickly published two novels, *Sailor's Song* (1943) and *No Directions* (1943), in which it is possible to see the influence of his time as a radio writer. Deer has characterised *No Directions* as a radio play *manqué*, given its claustrophobic setting in a blacked-out apartment building during a bombing raid and its abundance of auditory information (Deer 2009: 145). *Sailor's Song*, on the other hand, follows a structure frequently used in radio plays and features: in this novel, an unconscious sailor relives key moments of his life in a feverish dream-state. The motif of a life recollected had been used by radio pioneer Tyrone Guthrie in *The Squirrel's Cage* (1929) and would be used by Louis MacNeice in *He Had a Date* (1944), two features that are regularly cited as important broadcasts of their respective eras. Hanley seemed aware that *Sailor's Song* might be 'the stuff of radio': he proposed a feature based on the novel in November 1943. Although the BBC rejected the idea at the time, the novel would be adapted by Elizabeth Berridge in 1954, by which time Hanley's star had finally begun to rise again.[12] Until then, however, it was time for others to shine.

Notes

1. In the following two chapters, the genre of the feature is uncapitalised, but its institutional embodiments (as department or section) are capitalised and pluralised as Features, following BBC practice. For detailed accounts of the development of the genre, see Scannell and Cardiff (1991: 134–52), Briggs (1965: 167–9) and Bridson (1971: 25–70). For testimonies to the importance of the feature to radio art, see Drakakis (1981: 8–10), Rodger (1982: 86–97), Briggs (1970: 113) and Nicholas (1996: 46). For a critique of experimental features as appealing only to a minority, see Scannell and Cardiff (1991: 137–8).
2. Brother to Sir John Gielgud, Val Gielgud led the BBC Productions Department, later known as the Department of Features and Drama, for

much of the period from 1929 to 1946. His involvement in radio and early television as an administrator, producer, writer and actor exerted a significant and lasting influence on drama in both media in the United Kingdom.
3. For important exceptions detailing Hanley's radio work, see Fordham (2002: 161–5) and Deer (2009: 142–5). For discussions of Hanley's other work and larger career, see Fordham (2002), Rice (2002), Dentith (2003) and Barrett (2007).
4. Though long thought lost, a copy of the script for *Kaleidoscope I* survives among Sieveking's papers at the Lilly Library at the University of Indiana–Bloomington, as was brought to light by David Hendy in 'Painting with Sound: The Kaleidoscopic World of Lance Sieveking' (2013).
5. Sieveking rhapsodises about the dramatic control panel throughout *The Stuff of Radio*; see, for example, pp. 52–3, 102–3 and 397–404. While this panel would be used throughout the 1930s, there is some evidence that by the early 1940s it was considered something of a relic and its use was becoming infrequent. See the 1942 BBC *Engineering Division Training Manuals* section entitled 'Modern Control Rooms and Continuity Working': 'There was a tendency in peacetime for broadcasts to become technically over-elaborate. The use of a number of studios for one production was a growing habit which was catered for to a maximum of 15 channels by a somewhat complicated mixing and control unit known as a "productions panel." With the introduction of local control and the use of larger studios, the multi-studio tendency has largely disappeared and the engineering problems associated with big productions have correspondingly lessened. In any case, the stringencies of wartime broadcasting make such economies essential both as regards accommodation and equipment' (BBC 1942: n.p.). I am grateful to Roger Beckwith for this insight into the fate of the dramatic control panel.
6. Bridson (1971: 25–72) and Scannell and Cardiff (1991: 333–55) offer thorough accounts of the rise of Features at BBC North. Murphy (2016) provides a discussion of Olive Shapley's career in the context of other important female broadcasters at the early BBC.
7. 'Paul Wolff' may be the pseudonym of Douglas Maurice Wolfe, a friend and amanuensis to Hanley who went by the name Paul Sheridan in the small Welsh town where both men were living in 1938 (Fordham 2002: 161, 274 n.2).
8. In the three-month span from March to May 1941 alone, for example, Axis U-boats and airplanes sank a combined 321 merchant ships. See Angus Calder (1969: 231–2) and Churchill (1951: 120–8).
9. Hanley would emphasise the alien quality of mechanised human presence at sea in his 1943 novel *Sailor's Song*, in which a merchant vessel is torpedoed by a submarine '[n]ot like any fish you ever saw . . . This fish was new to a sea, this God's fright, but not to men, being a man's fish, made by men' (1943: 50).
10. His episodes include a 23 July 1941 broadcast on the small ships that guide larger vessels to port ('Pilots'), a closer look at stokers below decks ('Men in Darkness', 6 August 1941) and an account of sailors left adrift in a lifeboat following a torpedo attack ('Open Boat', 10 September 1941).
11. See, for example, Baker-Smith (1942).

12. Though not often mentioned in scholarly accounts of wartime and postwar literature, English novelist and short-story writer Elizabeth Berridge (1919–2009) was a sensitive chronicler of the nuances of social and familial life at midcentury. Gill Plain (2013: 51–3) offers a reading of some of her wartime stories. Berridge made a few forays into broadcasting. In addition to her adaptation of Hanley, her own story 'Lullaby' was adapted for radio by Margaret Ireland in April of 1954. Berridge also broadcast 'A Reconsideration of *Aurora Leigh*' in March of 1979 and a meditation, 'On Becoming Old', in April of 1979.

Chapter 3

To Build the Falling Castle: Louis MacNeice and the Drama of Form

Though the BBC careers of James Hanley and Louis MacNeice would follow different trajectories, they began as part of a single push by Features to draw more writers into the radio fold. Both would move from freelance script-writing to contracted positions with the BBC, but an involvement that for Hanley lasted a little over eighteen months became a decades-long career for MacNeice. He had left Britain early in the war to take a teaching position at Cornell, but returned at the end of 1940 determined to play a role in the conflict. Ruled ineligible for military service on medical grounds, MacNeice instead turned to the BBC, which had approached him in March 1940 about the possibility of bringing his poetic talents to the Department of Features and Drama (Stallworthy 1995: 286–7). In an April 1941 letter to Elizabeth Dodds, a friend from his days teaching Classics at the University of Birmingham and wife to his eventual literary executor E. R. Dodds, MacNeice expressed the mingled excitement and resentment of wartime propaganda work:

> May be going on B.B.C. in the regular way soon if M.I.5 don't turn me down . . . I am beginning to write poems again, so very pleased with myself. But am rather fed up with thinking up ingenuities for the air & then having them chopped about by genteel halfwits; *if* I join the B.B.C. I shall eventually produce my own stuff. When I've learned about the knobs. (MacNeice 1941a)

The 'knobs' in question were the technical controls of the studio, which were to serve as the material link between MacNeice's new occupation as radio artist and his on-going role as poet. Unlike many other writers during the war, Hanley included, MacNeice moved quickly to master the technical aspects of broadcasting, thereby minimising the violent chops dealt to his written works by 'genteel halfwits'. In a field where collaboration and compromise were essential to the creative process,

MacNeice came to exert a greater degree of control over his material than did many other literary broadcasters by virtue of the fact that he could oversee their translation from printed page to produced sounds.

If MacNeice differed from Hanley in the aptitude he showed for the technical aspects of broadcasting, he also brought to his features a much more concerted interest in questions of form. In MacNeice's broadcasts, as in his poetry, architectural metaphors thematise the struggle to impose order on an unwieldy medium. Looking back on his radio beginnings in the long poem *Autumn Sequel* (1954), MacNeice observes:

> To found
> A castle on the air requires a mint
> Of golden intonations and a mound
> Of typescript in the trays. What was in print
> Must take on breath and what was thought be said. ([1954] 2007: 387)

From the delicate, almost insubstantial material of timbre and paper could emerge fantastic structures, 'castles on the air'. If the voice is the currency of radio – its 'mint', the strongest claim it has to immediacy and value – its sonic castles rest on a mountain of paper. Earlier in his career, as he watched the sun set on the 1930s in *Autumn Journal* (1939), MacNeice had used the image of 'castles on the air' to represent the ephemeral political mirages of the Munich pact (MacNeice [1939] 2007: 114), but he had also resorted to architecture as the most resilient metaphor for the project of social and political reconstruction in the face of a war whose first rumblings had already been heard in Ethiopia and Spain.

> Who am I – or I – to demand oblivion?
> I must go out to-morrow as the others do
>   And build the falling castle;
> Which has never fallen, thanks
>   Not to any formula, red tape or institution,
> Nor to any creeds or banks,
>   But to the human animal's endless courage. ([1939] 2007: 104)

Whatever fanciful solutions politicians might have been crafting in 1938, MacNeice argues, the engaged citizen performs the core act of social perpetuation by setting out every day to live life as an inherited, renewable practice. To 'build the falling castle' is to commit oneself to an endeavour less foolish than it may first appear; though ever falling, the castle has 'never fallen', making the project of keeping up civilisation less a question of Sisyphean effort and more one of gradual renovation. MacNeice's vision of the importance of everyday life – and, by extension, work, including the work of poetry and radio – is neither a revolutionary one nor a reactionary one. No 'formula' or 'institution' can bind a society to a past or future vision of itself; rather, the castle remains standing by virtue of its incremental renewal, like a body made new over time by the progressive replacement of cells.

MacNeice's radio works, like his poetry, therefore represent a direct challenge to arguments that the war was just about defeating the Nazis, and not about building something else. 'It's all very well for everyone to go on saying "Destroy Hitlerism,"' he argued in a letter to E. R. Dodds in October 1939, 'but what the hell are they going to construct?' (2010: 160). This construction was to be a collective effort. In applying himself to the task of political persuasion, MacNeice struck an uneasy balance between what he called the 'complex of spiritual intimacies' of lyric poetry and the 'group life' of a collaborative mass medium with a large public ([1946] 1993: 406). The 'typescripts in the trays' in *Autumn Sequel* become not simply the triplicate trace of administrative ritual but the foundation of a new form of art, a form whose broad reach and affective depth promised to unite listeners in defence of a common cultural heritage. From the early features in the *Stones Cry Out* series (1941), through his first verse epic, *Alexander Nevsky* (1941), to the triumphant *Christopher Columbus* (1942), MacNeice built ever more complex soundscapes in which a listening audience might lose themselves, if only to rediscover a sense of collective purpose.[1] As the focus of wartime radio propaganda shifted from the resilience of Britons under fire to their plans for the future, MacNeice's radio parables advocated that these plans be pursued with an urgency and scope to match both the determination of protagonists like Christopher Columbus and ambition of cultural producers like MacNeice and his collaborators. Exemplary instances of the fusion of political and aesthetic imperatives in wartime radio, MacNeice's 'castles on the air' became his means of 'building the falling castle' by manifesting collective radio labour for collective social gain.

The formal potential of radio: collaboration and communication

Louis MacNeice's interest in the formal possibilities of radio grew out of an earlier interest in poetic form. Like many poets of his generation – including W. H. Auden, Stephen Spender, William Empson and Cecil Day Lewis – MacNeice turned to more highly structured verse forms as a means of distancing himself from an earlier generation of modernists.

In Edna Longley's phrase, these poets had individually and collectively 'devoted considerable architectonic effort to the renewal of traditional forms' (Longley 1988: 107). Longley's use of 'architectonic' is apt: throughout MacNeice's critical writings, structural and spatial terms limn the boundary between the Pound era and the Auden generation. MacNeice's most sustained defence of the uses of poetic form, *Modern Poetry* (1938), argues that while free verse had initiated a crucial break with outdated poetic practices, the pendulum ought to swing back. 'The contemplation of a world of fragments becomes boring and Eliot's successors are more interested in tidying up,' he writes, adding, 'There is a chance for poets of today to retain the *élan vital* of Whitman or of Lawrence . . . but to girder it with a structure supplied partly by reason, partly by emotion intelligently canalized to an end, partly by the mere love of form' ([1938] 1968: 13, 17). MacNeice's vocabulary of form, fragments, girders, structure and canals implies a dynamic tension between order and disorder, structure and its intrinsic potential for collapse. This tension would animate MacNeice's poetry, as well as his radio work, throughout his career.

More than any other wartime British writer, MacNeice embraced radio – especially radio drama – as a medium through which artists could explore new, dynamic notions of form. Well before he joined the BBC, he mused in *Modern Poetry* that poets might gain from the experience of writing for different media: 'It is particularly likely that they may find a good medium in radio plays . . . It is very good for the poet that he should employ certain forms which demand collaboration with other craftsmen' ([1938] 1968: 196). In 1946, after several years of radio collaboration, MacNeice reiterated such claims with more authority:

> In this age of irreconcilable idioms I have often heard writers hankering for some sort of group life . . . we cannot but envy playwrights, actors or musical executants. And here again I for one have found this missing group experience, in a valid form, in radio. Radio writers and producers *can* talk shop together because their shop is not, as with poets, a complex of spiritual intimacies but a matter of craftsmanship . . . we are fully entitled to discuss whether dialogue rings true, whether the dramatic climax is dramatic, how well the whole thing works. This is refreshing for a writer. ([1946] 1993: 406–7)

Measured against the 'complex of spiritual intimacies' of lyric poetry, radio offered MacNeice a communal workshop through which dramatic form could be refined. For a poet who valued craft and tradition, if only as a background against which experiment and variation may be measured, this collaborative atmosphere condensed the processes of trial and error through which works of art are revised. In sharing the process of creation, writers must first please their collaborators, who, among other things, stand as ideally informed surrogates for the audience itself. As Hanley had discovered, BBC colleagues could be difficult to please.

Whereas Hanley struggled to master the shape of a broadcast, MacNeice grasped that radio productions could not afford to be overly impressionistic or loosely paced; audiences would sooner switch off than endure boredom or confusion. 'The first virtue of a radio script is construction,' he writes in the introduction to the published edition of *Christopher Columbus* (1944). '[A] radio play or feature must have a dramatic unity; in the jargon of the trade, it must have the proper "builds" and an "overall" shape' ([1944] 1993: 396). This language of radio form emerges in part from early theorisations of radio drama and features at the BBC in the late 1920s and 1930s; Lance Sieveking, in *The Stuff of Radio* (1934), even offers a pictorial representation of the 'shape' of a broadcast, including institutional conventions like announcements and musical lead-ins, but more importantly tracing the rise and fall of narrative and emotional intensity in an archetypal radio production (Sieveking 1934: 408). MacNeice's ability to translate the language of poetic form to the medium of radio serves as a reminder that, as Caroline Levine argues, forms themselves are at once historically situated and portable, persisting across time and medium even as they derive meaning from their particular contexts (Levine 2015: 4, 7). As Levine further argues, the concept of form is operational in the social and political domains as much as the artistic; principles of political organisation, national identification and social hierarchisation follow imperatives of structure analogous to those animating artistic production (2015: 2–9). Through his wartime output, MacNeice not only translates a formal sensibility from the field of poetry to the field of radio, but also he thematises form itself by foregrounding the ways in which the cultural and political structures essential to the anti-fascist struggle are concretised through architecture, as if encoded in the very stones themselves.

The Stones Cry Out: towards an architecture of the nation

Among MacNeice's first features in early 1941 were contributions to *The Stones Cry Out*, a new series which dramatised, for an American audience, the significant architectural and historical losses suffered by London and other cities under German bombing raids.[2] Over the course of thirty-five episodes, each running for fifteen minutes, broadcast between 5 May and 29 December 1941, *The Stones Cry Out* used dramatic sequences, voice-over narration, music and excerpts from literary and historical sources to bring to life the legacy of buildings lost or damaged in the Blitz. These buildings were to be metonyms for larger cultural structures; Assistant Director of Features Laurence Gilliam defined the programme's desired effect as 'a clear and strong statement on the theme [of] traditions and values of this country under fire from the enemy' (1941e). While most of the buildings eulogised in this programme were recognisable symbols of national history and identity, the producers also chose a few less likely edifices: a working-class couple's new flat, for example, or the Café de Paris in central London. MacNeice's contributions were features on Dr Samuel Johnson's house (the first *Stones* broadcast, 5 May 1941), Westminster Abbey (26 May), Madame Tussaud's wax museum (2 June), St Paul's Cathedral (23 June), the House of Commons (7 July), the Temple (1 September), the Royal College of Surgeons (29 September), 'A Belfast Home' (27 October) and the Plymouth Barbican (24 November 1941).

In seeking to attune American audiences to the material and cultural damage caused by the Blitz, *The Stones Cry Out* did not – indeed, could not – report directly from the raids in journalistic style; aside from obvious questions of safety, field recording equipment was too cumbersome to take out during actual bombing raids.[3] Furthermore, British authorities often sought to delay the release of specific information about damaged buildings so as to impede German assessments of the accuracy of their attacks.[4] *Stones* therefore worked retrospectively, at a remove of weeks or months from the bombings themselves, selecting the most culturally and politically significant buildings for commemoration once censorship concerns had abated. More than simply being historical dramatisations, however, the *Stones* broadcasts attempted to link architectural and socio-cultural history in a narrative extending from medieval and early modern England ('Westminster Abbey', 'London's Oldest House') to contemporary wartime society. By housing the political, intellectual, religious and linguistic elements of British culture, buildings become vessels of national identity; their importance resides in the living link they form to the past, rather than their status as historical relics annexed to a vanished national mythology.

As Peter McDonald and Jon Stallworthy have pointed out, MacNeice had a longstanding interest in architectural imagery as a means of thematising personal or collective histories (McDonald 1991: 27 and 2002: 167; Stallworthy 1995: 63, 132). Haunted by the death of his mother while he was still a child, MacNeice turned frequently to spatial and monumental images as a means of staving off that loss, but also as a means of registering it; monuments allow the mourner to transfer the pain of death and mutability into a permanent language of stone. Buildings, as much as monuments, could give a shape to human life and the violence enacted upon it: describing the effects of Falangist bombing in Barcelona in his war-era autobiography *The Strings Are False*, MacNeice relates the 'stinking, berubbled desolation' of the city to the human cost of war: 'The houses were like skulls without eyes, without jaws, there was no more flesh in the world' ([1965] 2007: 184). As buildings crumble, they take on the form of the fragile human bodies they are designed to house and protect.

If bombed buildings stand in for the human lives lost to war, *The Stones Cry Out* suggests that the memorialisation of those buildings might offer a way of redeeming their loss in the interest of a greater national and cultural narrative. It is in this transmutation of threatened heritage into enduring tradition that MacNeice's early features move away from the unsettling potential of the Blitz and into a more triumphant mode. Unlike Hanley – whose *Return to Danger* (Hanley and Baker-Smith 1942), for example, offers a terrifying admonition to irresponsible parents who might bring their children from the safety of rural evacuation back to bomb-plagued London – MacNeice heard in the Blitz the stirrings of a culture determined to rebuild itself. This theme of endurance-as-regeneration emerges clearly in the most successful episodes in the series: MacNeice's twin homages to London's most famous churches. Director of European Services R. A. Rendall singled out both 'Westminster Abbey' (episode 4) and 'St. Paul's' (episode 8) as the best of a series that 'goes from strength to strength' (qtd in Gilliam 1941a). 'Westminster Abbey' was so successful that MacNeice expanded the fifteen-minute *Stones* script to a forty-five-minute broadcast on the Home Service, which aired on 7 September 1941, the anniversary of the first major Blitz of London. In turn, this extended broadcast generated so much interest within England that the BBC commissioned novelist Antonia White to write a companion piece, praising MacNeice's script and the Abbey itself equally, for the benefit of listeners outside Britain through *London Calling*, the Corporation's overseas weekly magazine (White 1941). The strength and popularity of these broadcasts lie in their balance of the familiar and the unfamiliar, as they interweave quotations and recognisable historical imagery with unexpected comparisons, temporal and spatial shifts, and documentary-style sound effects to generate a sonic space unconstrained by the fixity of visual dramatic forms.

Unlike earlier episodes in *The Stones Cry Out* on Samuel Johnson's house or Madame Tussaud's wax museum, which adopt a conversational and familiar tone, 'Westminster Abbey' addresses its subject with a seriousness befitting an icon of national identity. The programme begins with a consideration of sound and silence that will inform its increasingly dense soundscape as the story develops. Following the announcer's introduction, the listener is greeted by a sound not heard for almost two years:

>   *Peal of bells*
> 1st Speaker: The bells that you hear are the bells of Westminster Abbey.
> 2nd Speaker: But they are not ringing today.
> 1st Speaker: You are listening to the bells of peace-time.
> 2nd Speaker: For in Britain today the pealing of bells is forbidden.
> 1st Speaker: And the Westminster bells are silent today[.]
>   *The peal of bells ceases*
> 2nd Speaker: And Westminster Abbey today is the victim of war.
>   *Slight Pause.*
> 1st Speaker: Listen to the silence in the aisles –
>   Like a great stone ship becalmed in the night ... (MacNeice 1941c: 1–2)

The hint of a pause is richly suggestive; while dead air is normally considered anathema to flow-based models of broadcasting, its use here opens an auditory space of reflection. In its earliest years, the BBC had allowed up to fifteen minutes of silence between broadcasts, but this was rare by the war years. Kate Lacey figures this earlier, deliberate carving out of silent time as reflective of the BBC's belief that '[i]n the absence of feedback channels, the broadcasters had a duty to fall silent to let the listeners fill in the gaps' (Lacey 2013: 82–3) War lent broadcast silence further meanings: as a tiny stand-in for the greater silence that haunts the bell towers of Britain, this pause offers listeners the chance to meditate on the sonic absences that characterise the war. This gap in broadcast sound becomes more powerful still when we consider that urban silence is rarely, if ever, total; even the experience of domestic listening may fill a radio silence with the ambient noise of home, street or – in Britain, at least – bombers overhead. Like a small foreshadowing of John Cage's famous *4'33"*, in which the performer appears but plays no notes, the consideration of mute bells allows the listening environment to become the performance, however briefly.

As the broadcast continues, MacNeice follows the meditative solemnity of this tiny silence with verse in a similarly solemn vein. Two narrators begin to set the scene of the Westminster bombing in dialogue that unfolds like an incantation:

> 1st Speaker: On the night of the tenth of May –
>   The German Air Force flew over London.
> 2nd speaker: Fire on the City of London and fire on the City of Westminster.

1st speaker:	Fire on the House of Commons and fire on the Abbey.
2nd speaker:	And the H.E. bombs –
1st Speaker:	A noise to waken the dead.
2nd Speaker:	The dead?
1st Speaker:	The dead who sleep in the Abbey. Knights and statesmen, poets and peers. The famous dead of seven English centuries. (MacNeice 1941c: 2)

In 'Westminster Abbey', as in later dramas, MacNeice deploys a flexible verse whose strength derives from a balance between metrical poise and metrical breakdown. Without a regular metre to structure the line as a whole, the rhythmic centre of these lines emerges from the heavily accented syllables themselves. Further tension arises between balanced, anaphoric lines like 'Fire on the City of London and fire on the City of Westminster', which emphasise the historic places under threat, and grammatically incomplete lines ('And the H.E. bombs –', 'The dead?') whose terseness signals the destructive potential of the threat itself. But the mnemonic nationalism of the Abbey returns to stabilise the verse. Listeners are reminded of 'Knights and statesmen, poets and peers. / The famous dead of seven English centuries.' As these closing lines move from a falling metre to a series of gently rocking iambs, they impart a sense of completeness and dignity to the memory of British nation-builders.

Much of the broadcast relies not on MacNeice's own verse but on excerpts from scripture. As MacNeice admitted in a letter written to E. R. Dodds on 26 May 1941, he composed 'Westminster Abbey' by 'plugging the Bible' (2010: 436). MacNeice's self-deprecation aside, the quotations provide an evocative structure around which he can build his account. As the sound of fire-bells rises up behind them, the narrators invite the audience to listen not only to 'the silence of the aisles' but also to 'the Echoes of English history', of 'great men's funerals' and of 'everyday people praying and singing' (1941c: 3). At this point, the voice of a preacher fades up, reading from Ecclesiasticus 44:

Organ Music.

Preacher:	Let us now praise famous men and our fathers that begat us . . .
1st Speaker:	Who lie under the nave and the transepts and the chapels behind the sanctuary.
Preacher:	Such as did bear rule in their kingdoms –
1st Speaker:	Edward the Confessor, Henry the Third, Edward the First, Edward the Third, Richard the Second, Henry the Fifth, Henry the Sixth and Henry the Seventh;
2nd Speaker:	Edward the Sixth and Mary Tudor, Queen Elizabeth and Mary Queen of Scots.

Preacher:	Men renowned for their power, giving counsel by their understanding –
1st Speaker:	William Pitt, Earl of Chatham; Pitt the Younger and Charles James Fox –
Preacher:	. . . leaders of the people by their counsels –
2nd Speaker:	William Ewart Gladstone and Benjamin Disraeli –
Preacher:	. . . and by their knowledge of learning meat [sic] for the people, wise and eloquent in their instructions.
1st Speaker:	William Wilberforce and Richard Cobden, Sir Isaac Newton and Charles Darwin – (1941c: 3–4)

Though not part of the Protestant or Jewish biblical canons – it was counted among the Apocrypha in the King James Bible – Ecclesiasticus (or the Wisdom of Sirach, as it is known in the Jewish tradition) nonetheless remains a spiritual and cultural touchstone for many American and British worshippers.[5] The insertion of recognisable scripture in the drama therefore plays a threefold structural role: most simply, the citations offer a counterpoint to the words of the two other speakers, thereby alleviating the potential boredom of a back-and-forth dialogue. At the same time, the cadence of the King James Version lends a familiar solemnity to the history enshrined in the stones of the Abbey. Most importantly, the blend of scripture and epic cataloguing of famous personages provides a rhetorical framework through which the American listener can map historical knowledge on to present catastrophe. The two Speakers who complement the Preacher's readings from scripture by naming various 'famous men' – politicians, poets, scientists and thinkers – buried in the Abbey therefore serve as stand-ins for an audience eager to make connections across a millennium of history.

The feature deepens its allusions, quoting from Isaiah 37:11 ('Behold, thou hast heard what the Kings of Assyria have done to all lands by destroying them utterly') to draw connections between Biblical tyrants and their twentieth-century counterparts. As the feature builds to its climax, MacNeice layers scriptural quotations of direct relevance to the plight of besieged Londoners, while the two Speakers connect Biblical disaster with war on the home front:

Preacher:	And they burnt the house of God, and brake down the wall of Jerusalem, and burnt all the palaces thereof with fire, and destroyed all the goodly vessels thereof.
1st Speaker:	They burnt and shattered the monuments of London, the Guildhall, the Temple and the City churches.
Preacher:	Why should my countenance not be sad, when the city, the place of my fathers' sepulchres, lieth waste, and the gates thereof are consumed with fire?

2nd Speaker: Ludgate and Cheapside; Bloomsbury and Soho; St. Paul's Churchyard and Parliament Square.
Preacher: For the dark places of the earth are full of the habitations of cruelty. (1941c: 6–7)[6]

The interweaving of scripture and documentary accounts of bomb damage continues for a further two pages, during which time the frequency and intensity of Blitz-related sound effects increases. Air-raid sirens, anti-aircraft artillery and high-explosive bombs resound successively in the background, as the voices of fire fighters and dispatchers join the Preacher and the two Speakers in framing the attack verbally. The cumulative effect of this barrage of sound is to immerse the listener in a multitemporal, multispatial environment that breaks with Aristotelian unities in order to portray historical depth acoustically. Presented as a modern tragedy in a line of tragedies extending back to the Old Testament, the attack on Westminster Abbey is made at once immediately contemporary and part of a history which consoles by its patterns of suffering and perseverance. This transhistorical sonic environment also emulates, for American listeners, the dense soundscape of wartime London, and captures the dislocation of a city in which material history is literally thrown into the streets with each new bombing raid.[7] Speaking of the forty-five-minute Home Service adaptation of 'Westminster Abbey', which aired in September 1941, *Listener* drama critic Grace Wyndham Goldie praised the programme for its layering of 'the shriek of falling bombs', 'the crash of explosions' and voices that respond 'like a peal of Westminster's own bells'. 'In its setting', she writes, 'this produced the vision-seeing, spine-shivering stir of the imagination which is as real as fear. It was one of those moments which broadcasting and drama exist to create' (Goldie 1941a: 416).

Episode 8 (on St Paul's Cathedral) builds on the dense soundscape of the Westminster episode. 'St. Paul's' opens with the sound of traffic on a modern street and a truncated quotation from Tennyson: 'Here, in streaming London's central roar' (1941d: 1). As this line, from the 'Ode on the Death of the Duke of Wellington', fades away, the sound of traffic is replaced, via cross-fade, by the sounds of Wellington's funeral march almost ninety years previous to the broadcast, in 1852. As cannons salute the dead and the march continues softly in the background, MacNeice interweaves Tennyson's poem with the words of two 1941 narrators – a 'Light Voice' ('LV') and a 'Dark Voice' ('DV') – and a third narrator, the Cockney Voice ('CV'), who emerges from leading the 1852 funeral march to accompany the twentieth-century voices in a tour of Sir Christopher Wren's most famous cathedral. The subtle handling of this shift in time is characteristic of the broadcast as a whole, which, even more than MacNeice's previous *Stones* broadcasts, works to layer historical periods as a means of extrapolating larger political and cultural messages.

For MacNeice, the church embodies the transhistorical value of cultural production by its material endurance. Against the bombs of the *Luftwaffe*, the walls of the building speak up to offer a counter-narrative of cultural survival. Touring the cathedral following its damage by bombs, the three narrators arrive at the Whispering Gallery, the circular base of the cupola above the nave, where whispered words can travel from one side of the cupola to the other in the form of an echo:

> CV: (whispering) St. Paul's Cathedral
> (pause)
> ECHO: St Paul's Cathedral
> LV: is still standing
> ECHO: is still standing
> DV: The walls have mouths
> ECHO: The walls have mouths
> LV: You see? The walls have mouths.
> DV: The stones cry out. (1941d: 7)

The narrators continue to tour the building, ascending to the top of the dome to compare the blitzed landscape with the destruction suffered by the original cathedral during the Great Fire of 1666, and pausing to remember the sermons John Donne held in the original church. As they return to the Whispering Gallery, the broadcast steps further from anything resembling a realistic or documentary feature, as the script notes that 'the 3 voices are no longer to be in character, as they all represent the walls' (1941d: 8).[8] This succession of overlapping dialogue promises that voices have substance, and represent a concrete form of resistance:

> LV: We are the walls of the Whispering Gallery.
> DV: We are the walls of Europe. The Words we repeat are the words of Freedom.
> [...]
> CV: Words against bombs,
> LV: mind against matter,
> DV: truth against lies.
> LV: The words run round and around, a whisper under the dome,
> DV: A whisper under the dome of the sky ... (1941d: 9)

MacNeice's move from realism to the surreal indicates the freedom from dramatic conventions afforded by the radio feature. Human individuals and settings are fluid: characters can become other characters; a guided tour of bomb damage can become a symbolic set piece in the larger debate against fascism; one cathedral can stand in for all of Europe. This fluidity of structure reinforces the message that Nazism poses a generalised threat to the world; the boundaries between characters dissolve as distinct voices become the collective voice of 'the walls' via shared sentences and ideas, emphasising a shared struggle against totalitarian aggression.[9]

At a remove of many decades, such statements of universal humanity in the face of Nazi aggression seem symptoms of their age: earnest if somewhat clunky propaganda manœuvres designed to mobilise American outrage. 'St. Paul's' escapes a possible fate as historical curiosity, however, by transcending its political catalysts and emerging as an example of how to balance formal elements in the construction of emotionally effective radio art. Continuing on from the passage quoted above, 'St. Paul's' links verbal and musical cues from earlier in the broadcast to heighten the effect of its political rhetoric:

> LV: A Whisper that becomes a declaration
> CV: To be cried from the house-tops
> DV: Of the rights of Man; [. . .]
> (*Osanna* passage from Bach, repeat but very distant)
> LV: Here, in streaming London's central roar.
> DV: Here, in darkened London's battered heart,
> CV: We assert the Rights of Man
> DV: and defy the tyranny of man,
> LV: and we say that Freedom must survive,
> CV: and must not perish from the earth,
> and we say that Freedom *shall* survive,
> and shall not perish from the earth.
> (*Osanna* pull up, and fade-out)
> (MacNeice 1941d: 9–10)

In this closing section, MacNeice reintroduces the Tennyson quotation from the beginning of the play, along with a Bach passage that had appeared midway through the programme. In doing so, he connects the message of perseverance in wartime to a broader European cultural endeavour, making the struggle less about England against Germany than Tennyson, Wren and Bach against Hitler. While it might be too much to say that form itself, enacted across a range of creative domains, can palliate the effects of aggressive militarism, 'St. Paul's' at the very least names the stakes of the anti-Nazi struggle as creation versus destruction, order versus disorder. Furthermore, these elements from earlier in the broadcast remind listeners of where they have been in the fifteen minutes since the programme started: from outside the cathedral to the top of the dome, via the Whispering Gallery whose voices now channel the political message of the broadcast. While the rhetorical sweep of the closing statements gives the end of the broadcast a feeling of crescendo, the overlay of familiar elements recast in subtly different forms gives a hint of symmetry to the piece. By, as it were, revisiting the plan of both cathedral and broadcast, it reminds the listeners that they have returned to the place from which they started, only to hear it with new ears, and with a new sense of political determination.

As MacNeice moved from early features like *The Stones Cry Out* towards more elaborate works, his interest in spatiality and form morphed from a thematisation of architecture within the bounds of carefully constructed scripts to an interest in helping the listener to navigate radio soundscapes. As Neil Verma argues in his study of the golden age of American broadcast drama, *Theater of the Mind*, early radio creators were invested in the construction and exploration of sonic space precisely because radio, as a medium, was so closely identified with its ability to collapse distance and transgress geographical frontiers:

> Radio dramatists of the 1930s went out of their way to create dramatic situations in which time and space are featured as the most prominent design elements, depicting distended spaces, Byzantine sets, rapid segues, protean action, and distances that transform abruptly ... encouraging listeners to explore imaginary space just for the sake of doing so. (2012: 19, 25)

Far from being self-guided, listener exploration depended on the creation of specific points of auditory perspective – which Verma calls 'audioposition' – via techniques of microphone placement, effects of acoustic dampening and distance, and modes of vocal delivery, all of which helped the listener to identify with particular characters within the world of the drama (2012: 34–47). While *The Stones Cry Out* used precisely such effects to position its listeners within imperilled buildings, it was with *Alexander Nevsky* and *Christopher Columbus* that MacNeice would direct listener attention towards the vital wartime task of orienting themselves in a saturated sonic environment.

Alexander Nevsky and attentive citizenship

Following his apprenticeship with *The Stones Cry Out* and other propaganda programmes including *Cook's Tour of the London Subways* (a mock-travelogue of the Underground shelters) and an episode of the series *Freedom Ferry*, historical circumstances dictated that MacNeice begin crafting a more ambitious project. On 22 June 1941, Germany broke its pact of non-aggression with the Soviet Union by launching Operation Barbarossa, an all-out assault on Soviet territory that involved over 3 million troops attacking along a 2,900–kilometre front. With the USSR now allied with Britain, it fell to the BBC to produce suitably enthusiastic programming to welcome this new ally in the war against fascism, a task to which they quickly applied every effort. The minutes from a meeting of the Overseas Board of the BBC on 17 July 1941 reported that 'projection of Russia by cultural programmes was in hand' (Briggs 1970: 393n4). In a display of their developing public relations *savoir-faire*, the BBC enlisted their Listener Research Department to determine what role British citizens thought the BBC should play in popularising the USSR among listeners. Some 850 'local correspondents' – regular contributors to Listener Research surveys – were asked to gauge the sensitivities and concerns of their own contacts in the broader listening community.

Though commissioned after *Alexander Nevsky* aired, this survey reinforces some of the challenges the BBC faced as the unofficial mouthpiece of the British government charged with 'projecting' the USSR. Since the Russian Revolution, British public opinion regarding the USSR had been on the whole divided, with the opinions of some Britons liable to sudden change as Soviet economic and military policies offered reason for sentiments ranging from hope and envy to disillusion and dismay. In particular, questions lingered about Soviet plans after the war, their attitudes towards political dissent and religious worship, and their military record in Poland and Finland. Fortunately for the BBC, public opinion of the USSR had surged in the second half of 1941 as a result of Soviet resistance to the Nazi invasion, not least because this resistance drew fire away from Britain at a time when the Blitz had stretched the endurance of many citizens to the limit (Rose 2004: 44–56).

When asked what kinds of programming would help listeners understand their new ally, 79 per cent of respondents wanted more information on the ordinary lives of Soviet citizens, 63 per cent sought to understand the political and social system of the USSR better, and 56 per cent wanted clarification on the nature and extent of British and American aid to the USSR (LR/1175 1942: 1). Only 31 per cent of respondents requested more programmes about 'Russian history, literature and culture' (LR/1175 1942: 3). Despite the half-hearted public interest in Russian and Soviet culture, the BBC pressed on with a programme of cultural diplomacy. Broadcasts included dramas (Pushkin's *Eugene Onegin*, Anton Chekhov's *The Three Sisters* and Valentin Kataev's *Squaring the Circle*), political broadcasts by Soviet ambassador Ivan Maisky and others, and performances of the music of Russian and Soviet composers including Shostakovich, Rachmaninov and Khachaturian (Briggs 1970: 393). Such cultural overtures were helpful at a time when Soviet sensitivities about information control precluded direct BBC broadcasts in Russian and other languages of the USSR; in an internal memorandum from Director of European Services J. A. S. Salt to Controller (Programmes) Basil Nicolls dated 29 July 1941, Salt remarks that Soviet authorities 'are particularly susceptible to the flattery value of our performing their plays, music, etc.' (qtd in Briggs 1970: 397–8).

This surge in cultural propaganda also led to the commissioning of new works and adaptations. In autumn 1941, MacNeice produced a brief portrait of Anton Chekhov (called simply *Dr. Chekhov*), which he would later expand into a play called *Sunbeams in his Hat* (1944), and scripted overt propaganda features with such titles as *Salute to the USSR* (1942) and *The Spirit of Russia* (1942). MacNeice's first major pro-Soviet script, however, was an adaptation of Sergei Eisenstein's 1938 film *Alexander Nevsky*. The film had considerable political currency: created as an anti-Nazi propaganda piece, the story follows the title character, a thirteenth-century Russian prince who defeated an invading army of Teutonic knights in 1242. Only months after its release in November 1938, Germany and the USSR signed the non-aggression pact, and the film was withdrawn from distribution. A copy had made its way to the BBC, however, and was being used to train cameramen in the art of cinematography during the BBC's short-lived pre-war foray into television. The Corporation was apparently untroubled by the problems inherent in adapting for radio a film of such epic scale, especially one whose most compelling element is arguably its cinematography. In Eisenstein's *Nevsky*, dialogue is stripped to its essentials, characters are reduced to types, and landscapes take on thematic and symbolic weight. In minimising psychological depth and verbal narration, the film relies upon Sergei Prokofiev's score and Eduard Tisse's angular cinematography to convey everything from mood and motifs to power relations between characters.

The act of intermedial adaptation would require some adjustments but the radio play retains certain key elements of the original, including the bulk of Prokofiev's score and the general narrative arc of Eisenstein's film. Hearing news of the impending Teutonic invasion, Prince Alexander Nevsky of Novgorod abandons a hard-earned life of pastoral relaxation in order to defend his land and subjects against foreign aggressors. Like the Prince, Russia is slow to anger but difficult to defeat; as Nevsky says in his closing oration,

> We in Russia are children of peace,
> We do not envy any man's goods or country,
> And we do not close our doors to any peaceful visitor. [. . .]
> And I say this to the rest of the world:
> If you will come to us in peace you are welcome,
> But if you come with the sword or the threat of the sword
> Then remember the old saying – [. . .]
> 'Those who take the sword
> By the sword shall they perish.' (MacNeice 1941g: 42)

While emphasising the measured strength of Russian militarism, MacNeice fleshes out the parallels between Nazis and Teutons by depicting the invaders as excessive in their violence and brutal in their repression. Rumours circulate about the approaching horde; Domash, the governor of Novgorod, warns his people that '[t]hey kill the man who talks for his talking. / They kill the silent man for his silence' (2). In a retroactive effacement of the Nazi–Soviet pact, Alexander berates collaborationist merchants in the city of Novgorod, insisting that 'Peace with the Germans means submission . . . / It means taking a vampire to our bosom' (15). Throughout the play, MacNeice emphasises the inhuman characteristics of the Teutonic forces: 'I've never seen such riding,' says the Russian soldier Piotr as the enemy advances. 'You'd think / The men were part of their horses' (26). His compatriot Dimitry responds by describing the Germans as 'Men on iron horses. Well, / It takes more than an iron horse / Or an iron man to conquer Russia' (26). The overwhelming material superiority of the invading forces renders them machine-like without, in the end, granting them victory; as in Eisenstein's film, the final defeat of the Germans is sealed as their heavy armour causes the ice to give way beneath them during the climactic battle on the frozen Lake Peipus (36).

As a means of avoiding potentially difficult comparisons with the filmic source text, MacNeice turned for inspiration not to new technologies of storytelling but to old ones, drawing especially on his knowledge of classical and Norse epic poetry. The verse itself is of a flexible and varied rhythm, in keeping with MacNeice's longer poems like *Autumn Journal*. At times the lines flow casually, with startlingly colloquial dialogue, but at moments of heightened drama the verse bristles with the heavy rhythms of alliterative, four-stress poetry.[10] As Nevsky's forces appear to crumble during the climactic battle scene, the Prokofiev score swells and drops back to highlight patterns of verbal stress and repetition as an observer narrates the collapse with dismay:

> IGOR: This is the end – rout of the Russians,
> Good men all but the weight too great,

> Steel against leather, lance against bill-hook,
> Hoof of their horses over our dead . . . (30)

As the tides of battle turn in favour of Russia, the verse approaches incantation. Repetition and enjambment elicit a grandiose and hypnotic simplicity, which links old forms of storytelling with the new atrocities of a global war:

> IGOR: Still going on, they're still going on, they're
> Knocking the knights from their horses, they're
> Grappling the iron men with their naked hands,
> Tugging them out of the saddle, pulling their
> Helmets off with a wrench, stamping their feet
> On the German faces – spears in their guts, they're
> Still going on, it's a massacre – (32)

Repetition reinforces the overwhelming totality of military violence, not only through the refrain of 'still going on' but also through the abundance of present progressive verbs ending in '-ing', which conveys a dizzying array of violent actions occurring simultaneously. Furthermore, the homophony of 'they're / their' (and the shifting of the possessive 'their' between Teutonic and Russian referents) hinders quick comprehension. When heard aloud, the effect of the battle sequence is disorienting: similar in pacing to a rapidly edited cinematic scene but rooted entirely in the tumble of words from an actor's mouth.

While the alliterative verse of epic poetry proved suitable for conveying many aspects of the narrative, some scenes posed material challenges for radio adaptation; in particular, much of the force of the climactic battle sequence between Russian and Teutonic forces on the frozen ice of Lake Peipus is conveyed wordlessly, through a series of oblique camera angles and off-centre framing. For this extended scene, MacNeice opted to forge a diegetic surrogate for the listener by creating a visually impaired character not present in the original film: Blind Iuri, an elderly man unable to participate in the battle, listens from the side-lines while a young woman named Marya and other characters relate the struggle to him. As an archetypal auditor, Iuri enables the narration of the battle scene in *Nevsky* and, by extension, the audience's vicarious experience of that battle. Like the radio listener, Iuri submits to and occasions the translation of the world into acoustic experience. Furthermore, Iuri's blindness affords him new kinds of perception, oriented towards the future. When things initially seem to be going badly for the Russians, Iuri claims, against Marya's incredulous protests, that they will ultimately triumph: 'That isn't the way I see it / . . . I know

I'm blind. That is just why / I see the way things go' (27). Iuri's second sight is compounded by the fact that, as Marya herself admits, 'I can't see more than you can hear' (27). Though ostensibly speaking to Iuri, Marya simultaneously reassures the radio listener that to attempt to watch this battle would be superfluous; listening is enough. When a soldier who had just been speaking to Iuri and his daughter returns to the distant battlefield, where he appears to suffer a fatal blow, the blind man remarks that 'When he was here just now / I heard the death in his voice' (30). Iuri's auditory acuity straddles the interpretive and the predictive. He not only hears more, and better, than other characters do; he hears into the future. He functions as a Tiresias figure, deprived of sight but gifted with insight. 'I can see nothing with the outward eye,' as Iuri says early in the play, 'But with the eye of the mind I can see only too much' (8).

In using blindness to allegorise the listener's position, MacNeice was tapping into a well-established tradition of visual deprivation in radio drama. The first play written for radio in Britain, Richard Hughes's *A Comedy of Danger* (1924), is set in a darkened coal mine; Dylan Thomas's *Under Milk Wood* (1954) features narration by the blind Captain Cat; and MacNeice's own *The Dark Tower* (1946) includes a visually impaired prophet named Blind Peter.[11] But MacNeice's choice of Blind Iuri as entry point to the battle in *Alexander Nevsky* goes beyond such representations of the 'blindness' of the medium of radio; as with James Hanley's evocation in 'Atlantic Convoy' of sailors straining to hear signs of Nazi German presence on the waves, Iuri channels the specific message that listening is a skill to be learned and honed as a means of participation in the war. Other characters reinforce this lesson for the audience: when a soldier complains that he cannot see the progress of the battle because of the sweat in his eyes, Nevsky advises, 'Then perhaps you can hear . . . / That is the ice ahead; the lake is breaking up. / Halt your men and leave the Germans to it' (36). Nevsky's superior hearing warns him that the failing lake ice will soon swallow the remaining German soldiers, weighted down with iron armour. Just as close listening can attune listeners to the sounds of victory, failure to listen closely carries dangers for characters and, by extension, the radio audience. Early in the play, the 'Grand Master', leader of the Teutonic forces, threatens both the Russian peasantry and British listeners with despotic oratory: 'A deaf people that will not listen to reason / Must listen to fire and sword' (13).

These multiple imperatives assert that passive listening is insufficient; rather, listeners must actively remain open to sonic details if they wish to extract meaning, whether of victory or death, from a work of acoustic art. MacNeice's emphasis on the skill of listening in *Nevsky* is an invocation of what Jonathan Sterne calls 'audile technique'. As sound-reproduction technologies proliferated over the course of the nineteenth and early twentieth centuries, audile technique became the mark of specialist listeners, those possessed of discerning ears. It was initially mobilised in professional situations – medical examination by stethoscope, or the transcription of wireless telegraphy, for example – but became a broader social practice with the popularisation of technologies like the phonograph and the radio (Sterne 2003: 137 and *passim*). Through the privatisation and commodification of acoustic space – the appearance of radios in private homes and the development of individual listening practices – listeners acquire audile technique as a form of techno-cultural currency, a *savoir-écouter* that can then be translated into collective listening practices (Sterne 2003: 159–67).

By representing audile technique as a wartime skill that is both spatial (positioning your enemies and listening to the landscape) and prophetic (turning one's ears towards the future), *Alexander Nevsky* incites the listener to astute aesthetic participation as a form of home-front participation. It takes only a little imagination to hear the repercussions of this metaphor during the pervasively audible Second World War. As audiences were pummelled by propaganda broadcasts night and day, from all sides of the conflict, it took every ounce of discrimination to separate the useful and relatively truthful from the spurious and false. Bombers, sirens and artillery shots further jammed the soundscape. British listeners could not simply close their ears to the barrage of sound; if anything, hearing became more important than ever in the dimly lit wartime environment. As Elizabeth Bowen writes in the preface to her wartime story collection *The Demon Lover* (1945), 'Walking in the darkness of the nights of six years ... one developed new bare alert senses, with their own savage warnings and notations' (1986: 99). Shut in shelters or straggling through blacked-out streets, British citizens had to open their ears the better to navigate their newly dangerous environments. Programmes like *Alexander Nevsky* ask that listeners tune their ears in order to acquire a keener perception of the war despite visual deprivation.

It seems this emphasis on listening over seeing worked for many listeners. Reviews hailed *Alexander Nevsky* as a great success. 'Here in fact is radio conquered at last and used at last for living purposes by a living poet,' wrote Grace Wyndham Goldie in the pages of *The Listener* (Goldie 1941b: 832). Goldie waxed enthusiastic about the translation from screen to speaker:

Here we have Louis MacNeice taking a Russian film and turning it into magnificent radio; here we have the physical excitement which sight gives in the cinema translated into the physical excitement of the rhythm of spoken verse; here we have the sweep of a cavalry charge put over the air . . . until the beat of the words turned into the beat of the hoofs of horses galloping over frozen ground. (Goldie 1941b: 832)

Even listeners not on the BBC payroll agreed; according to the BBC Listener Research report for the play, 15.2 per cent of the adult public of the UK tuned in to hear *Nevsky*, and the play earned a very high 'Appreciation Index' of 83 per cent. One listener cited in the report, identified only as 'Housewife', called the play 'A great triumph for Louis MacNeice . . . Personally I didn't keep calm enough to be highly critical, which is the greatest test of its perfection' (LR/493 1941). MacNeice's use of Blind Iuri to justify the narration of the battle seems largely to have eased the transition from screen to radio. A Listener Research report produced following the rebroadcast of *Nevsky* in April 1942 noted that '[s]everal listeners said they thought the description of the battle on the ice by the blind singer was the outstanding feature of the broadcast, praising it particularly for its realism and dramatic qualities' (LR/882 1942). The comment is telling; while Iuri does not describe the battle, he does enable the description. The slippage between Iuri as auditor and narrator described in this Listener Research report implies that listening may not be so passive after all, and that the radio public has a role to play in the interpretation of battles both fictional and actual.

Transmitted at 9:20 in the evening on 8 December 1941, *Alexander Nevsky* was the culmination of a heady evening of broadcasting. The Japanese Air Force had bombed Pearl Harbor on the morning of 7 December, bringing the United States into the war. As a result, listeners the next day heard statements on the nine o'clock news by both Roosevelt and Churchill, confirming the expansion of the Allied forces, followed by a previously scheduled introduction to *Nevsky* by Soviet Ambassador Ivan Maisky (Holmes 1981: 39). The political impact of MacNeice's lesson in close listening was thus driven home by the appearance, at the microphone, of three voices representing the nations who would unite against Nazi Germany. Given the success of MacNeice's pro-Soviet propaganda epic that night, BBC producers wasted little time in planning a similar welcome for their newest ally, beginning work on *Christopher Columbus* in early 1942 to celebrate both the 450th anniversary of Columbus's arrival in the Americas and the emergence of America as a combatant in the Second World War. This new play would extend *Alexander Nevsky*'s lessons in close listening: while *Nevsky* succeeds at instilling in listeners a sense of the importance of audile technique, *Columbus* directs this technique towards the goals of postwar social reconstruction.

Christopher Columbus: propaganda as collective labour

As a material endeavour, MacNeice's *Columbus* exceeds *Nevsky* by almost every measure, and it stretches the label of 'feature' under which it was produced; it is, essentially, an epic drama with a factual basis.[12] Over two hours long, it features a score by William Walton and production by veteran Dallas Bower, as well as performances by Laurence Olivier, Robert Speaight and Margaret Rawlings. In all, it took over forty actors, a symphony orchestra, two choruses and a small army of technicians to produce the play. MacNeice's initial outline for *Christopher Columbus* indicates that the play was, from the outset, a collaborative endeavour. Sent to Bower in January 1942, MacNeice's detailed, six-page synopsis of *Columbus* included scene breakdowns and notes on characters. He envisioned an epic production in which score and script work together to produce meaning: 'Music throughout will be used, not only for the purpose of linking sequences, but to reinforce and illuminate the dominant themes' (MacNeice 1942). As per MacNeice's plan, the play is comprised of two sections. The first hour documents Columbus's protracted attempts to secure funding and support for his projected voyage across the Atlantic. In addition to the obstruction Columbus encounters from more conservative members of the church and nobility, his plan is frustrated by the Spanish focus on the liberation of Granada from Moorish control (MacNeice [1944] 1993: 37–8).[13] The second hour concerns the assembly of a crew, the doubt-ridden voyage itself, the arrival in the Caribbean and Columbus's triumphant return to the Spanish court at Barcelona. Throughout the play, twin Choruses of Doubt and Faith highlight Columbus's inner struggles as he seeks to convince his patrons, his crew and himself of the validity of his voyage.[14]

Walton's musical passages, developed from MacNeice's guidelines, are crucial to the sonic orientation of the listener. The score provides valuable spatial and social cues; early in the feature, for example, three middle-aged men discuss the recent arrival of Columbus in Lisbon. Referring to the explorer's talk of 'land in the West', one of the men, Alfredo, exclaims, 'You'd have thought / you were listening to a drunken sailor; / That's the kind of talk you hear in the taverns on the quay,' at which point a gently plucked guitar rises up from the background to lead listeners to the tavern (8). Following an exchange among sailors about such rumoured lands as 'Antilia and Zipangu ... / Aye, and

Vineland and Hy Brasil' (9), the guitar stops and the voices of the sailors fade out, repeating the names of places that were to them only fables, but which today resonate with their modern cognates and equivalents (the Antilles, Japan, Newfoundland and Brazil). The listener is brought back to the earlier Lisbon room with its three men as Alfredo echoes his own line: 'The kind of talk you hear from drunken sailors!' (9).

This form of listener guidance through the repetition of phrases and musical motifs serves as a kind of echolocation throughout *Columbus*. The audience, deprived of visual referents, relies on auditory cues to signal scene changes and establish the spatial and sonic environment of each setting. In the example cited above, the guitar music serves to identify the tavern as a place of leisure and entertainment, while the near-repetition of Alfredo's phrase about 'drunken sailors' brackets the tavern scene as a kind of temporary spatial cut; it is not a 'flashback' so much as a flash elsewhere. *Columbus* similarly incorporates plainsong to mark off the scenes taking place at the monastery at La Rábida and 'tribal' drumming in the scenes of contact between indigenous Americans and Columbus. Unlike the repeated demand throughout *Nevsky* that listeners should develop audile technique as a means of orienting themselves in the wartime soundscape, *Columbus* presupposes such technique as a prerequisite to an appreciation of the play.

MacNeice and Walton's most effective use of music to generate a sense of spatial and social location occurs as the vessels are being prepared for departure. As the Prior approaches the ships to bless them, the crowd begins to chant the Litany of the Saints (45). Columbus gives the order to weigh anchor, and as the ship pulls away, the litany recedes into the background without disappearing entirely, while the sailors begin to sing an ersatz Iberian shanty:

SOLO: We're bound upon a wild goose chase –
CHORUS: pero yo ya no soy yo
SOLO: To find an empire in the West –
CHORUS: ni mi casa es ya mi casa. (45)[15]

After several verses, the audience's attention is shifted back to shore by the return of the litany to the sonic foreground and the corresponding fading-down of the shanty. Columbus's lover Beatriz has arrived to see off the ships, and predicts that they will never return, 'Not in a year of palsied months, / Not in an age of haunted years ... And all they can do is sing!' (47). At this point, the sound of the sailors, having faded completely from earshot, returns with a new melody joyously out of step with the fatalism of Beatriz's prediction and of their own lyrics:

SOLO:	Out upon the ocean we're flotsam and jetsam,
CHORUS:	Gone away for ever, for ever and a day,
SOLO:	We're ragtag and bobtail, we're lost and we're lonely,
CHORUS:	Gone away for ever, for ever and a day. (47)

The fluid movement between musical registers – land and sea, sacred and secular, refined and coarse, establishment and underclass, individual and collective – at once clearly establishes the social and spiritual conditions of each setting, and emphasises their mutual implication in a common endeavour. With audition split between a stable world on land and a much less certain but much more exciting world at sea, the listener hovers in a privileged space of aural surveillance, with the advantage of hearing more than any one character in the feature. This auditory position, however, is neither total nor totalising. As in James Hanley's 'Atlantic Convoy' episode of *Freedom Ferry*, which shifts the listener from the bridge to the boilers, there is in *Columbus* no single position from which all can be heard, no commanding point of audition that reduces the entirety of the action to a single, knowable arc. The listener instead enjoys a limited mobility and receptive sweep; we hear more than any one character, but we do not hear all.

This logic of aural surveillance depends, furthermore, on the listener's audioposition remaining within plausible hearing range of either ship or shore. In *Columbus*, repeated and fluid shifts from one environment to another tend to occur when these environments are to some degree proximate; there are, for example, no repeated transitions between Spain and the Americas. The scene of encounter between Europeans and Caribbean islanders illustrates how MacNeice, Walton and Bower built listener position into the feature. As Columbus and crew head for shore, the play stages the encounter through ritual music: the crew of Columbus's ships begin to chant the 'Te Deum', which soon mingles with the drumming and chanting of the 'Indian Chorus' on the shore (56). For over a minute, the shipboard music and the music from the shore coexist in the background, competing for the attention of the listener and emphasising in musical terms the enormous collision between civilisations that is under way. The listener is, for a moment, in both places at once, experiencing the tension of unresolved cultural traditions in suspension. Eventually, however, MacNeice directs our attention to the original inhabitants of the island with the help of a narrator figure. 'Here they come now, down to the frills of the surf,' notes the sailor Gutiérrez:

> They're gathering there in their ranks, they're lifting their arms to the sky
> And bowing themselves to the sand; I cannot hear a sound

> But it looks as if they're singing or praying,
> I think they're singing or praying . . . (56)

At this point, the Indian Chorus takes over, and our auditory attention becomes focused on their interpretation of the encounter. As with *Alexander Nevsky*, narration by a character is essential to the audience's experience of invisible events. Crucially, Gutiérrez's comment that he 'cannot hear a sound' was cut from the original broadcast; removing this line allows listeners to imagine that the indigenous songs they hear are somehow transmitted through the aural experience of Gutiérrez and the other sailors (*Christopher Columbus* 1942).

Perhaps predictably, the music and chanting ascribed to the indigenous inhabitants of Guanahani (the original name for the Bahamian island of San Salvador where Columbus landed) is stylised and primitivist. The music itself does not entirely descend into offensive parody; rather, it sounds like a necessarily invented non-European musical tradition as imagined by a modern European composer.[16] Scored for tympani, xylophones, maracas, rumba sticks and violin, the songs of the Indian Chorus and their Leader are restricted to a handful of melodic intervals, unlike the more wide-ranging orchestral sections associated with Columbus. The islanders' diction is likewise limited:

> INDIAN CHORUS: Guanahani! Guanahani!
> LEADER: Who come now to Guanahani?
> CHORUS: Over sea. Over sea.
> LEADER: The gods are come from over sea. [. . .]
> INDIAN CHORUS: Guanahani! Guanahani!
> LEADER: Stepping through the silver foam
> CHORUS: On the sands of Guanahani
> LEADER: Come the shining sons of Heaven
> CHORUS: To our land of Guanahani. (56–7)

As Columbus and his crew step ashore, they quickly claim the island for Christianity and for Spain. Throughout the encounter, from the first sighting of people onshore to the eventual departure of Columbus for Spain (an expanse of time contracted into a few minutes of airtime), the singers of Guanahani weave in and out of the soundscape, indicating their continued presence behind Columbus's proclamations of ownership of the islands.

Script and score alone do not bring a radio production to fruition; juggling two choruses, an orchestra and over three dozen actors requires a competent producer. The scale of this project was not lost on Bower, whose views as producer are more amply represented in the correspondence record than are MacNeice's. As if to display his own radio fortitude, Bower continually insists on the difficulties the broadcast posed to the musicians and to him as a producer. He calls the script 'a pretty tough proposition from my point of view' in a letter to Sir Adrian Boult, who would conduct the Orchestra and Choruses (Bower 1942d). Similarly, in a letter to William Walton following the broadcast, Bower references Debussy and Stravinsky, calling *Columbus* 'as tricky for a producer as, say, *La Mer* or the *Sacre* is for a conductor' (Bower 1942c). Bower had reason to be anxious: BBC orchestras were stretched to the limit by the public demand for entertainment and diversion during the war. In an interview with Carol Rosen, aired between acts of the 1992 restaging of *Christopher Columbus* by BBC Radio 3, Bower recounted the remarkable conditions under which the Orchestra operated: following an evening performance of Elgar's Second Symphony and a brand new piece by Alan Rawsthorne on the Home Service, which the Orchestra had to repeat live at 8:00 for the Overseas Service, the musicians encountered Walton's score for the first time. They rehearsed once in the morning and once in the afternoon, and performed that evening. Walton's comment, upon hearing a recording of the rather epic performance, was 'Not too bad, really' ('Not too bad, really/Bower' 1992).

Under such working conditions, distractions had to be kept to a minimum. When asked if a small audience could attend the live performance for promotional reasons, Bower claims in internal correspondence that the 'technically complicated' nature of *Columbus* made the presence of guests unfeasible. The actors alone, he argues, find the presence of an audience visually distracting (Bower 1942a). Having secured Laurence Olivier for the title role, a producer might be excused for not wanting to aggravate his actors. Even without irritants, Olivier's performance – preserved in a recording at the National Sound Archive at the British Library in London – is excessive in all of the right ways. His Columbus, captivating and charismatic, is fixated on the goal of finding land in the West, to the detriment of all personal relationships. Olivier exploits the dynamic range of the studio and microphone to great effect; he spends much of the play ranting at the monarchs and clergymen who initially refuse to finance his quest, shouting down their conservative beliefs and, once his voyage has been assured, demanding for himself a series of hyperbolic titles, including Admiral of the Western Ocean and Governor-General over all the islands he would discover (MacNeice [1944] 1993: 37).

At other times, Olivier capitalises on the ability of the microphone to generate a sense of intimacy: in his final, stirring oration to the crowds gathered to welcome him back to the court at Barcelona, Olivier slowly builds the intensity of his address without ever shouting. While all other noises fall away, he lists the spiritual and economic resources of the Western hemisphere that now lie in the hands of Spain, until dropping the volume of his voice while slowing his delivery to intone, 'Behold, I bring you a new world!'[17] Though it is difficult to diagnose an actor's blocking in retrospect, the sudden increase in audible detail at this point of the recording seems to indicate that he approached the microphone while reducing his voice to a whisper. Every word of Olivier's final sentence is rasped out in a finely pebbled timbre that expresses the personal and spiritual ecstasy of a fulfilled quest.

Olivier's mastery of voice and microphone combines with MacNeice's script to make Columbus an emblematic radio hero; he ranges over the acoustic space of the broadcast without settling. As a thematic figure, he is movable and dynamic, simultaneously the historical Columbus and an agent of timeless dedication and vision. As a protagonist he is pompous and grandiose, but also a figure without a fixed place in the world of the play or of the broadcast. Early in the play, as Columbus roams Spain and Portugal seeking support for his quest, characters quiz him about his origins, to which he offers vague answers: 'I am a man from nowhere,' he says (11); 'I am a native of the Kingdom of God' (11); 'My country, my Lord, is the future' (26). These remarks characterise Columbus as a messianic figure, possessed of a single unshakeable goal, but they also uproot him from his particular historical moment and make his ambitions applicable to other epochs. As much as *Columbus* is a re-enactment of past exploits, it offers a model of future-oriented dedication and discipline.

Indeed, the lesson of *Christopher Columbus* is that while skills of close listening are vital to making sense of events, whether dramatic or historical, those skills must be guided in order to yield the desired political effect. In scripting Columbus's return to Spain, MacNeice indulges in a final, anachronistic gesture of directed listening. Our first exposure to the returned explorer is through the voice of the 'Onlooker', a narrator-surrogate whose style of speech mimics that of a radio or newsreel commentator:

> ONLOOKER: Here they come now, here they come now [. . .]
> Have a good look, ladies and gentlemen, never again
> Will this city of Seville see such a wild to-do.
> Look at the shining soldiers bearing coffers of gold,
> Look at the tattered banners bleached with the brine,
> Look at the red savages crowned with feathers [. . .] . (62)

The Onlooker's repeated injunctions to 'Look' encourage the listener to conjure a mental image of triumphant return, while the rapid-fire delivery mimics familiar forms from the wartime media ecology. The intrusion of twentieth-century media into the dramatised world invites the listener to read the events of the play as analogous to events in the world beyond the broadcast, lending a parabolic intensity to the broadcast. Columbus's journey and return are paradoxically made immediate through this anachronistic mediation; the voyage circulates in the very register of contemporaneity – 'news' – through which the wartime radio public most often constituted itself as a community of listeners.

The parable of Columbus's voyage takes on a clearer political valence when read alongside the promotional materials produced to guide listener engagement with the play. The script lacks the most overt indicators of political propaganda: it does not translate Columbus's fifteenth-century enemies into representations of Axis figures, nor does MacNeice insert allegorical markers that offer a clear transposition of events from Columbus's life to the wartime experience of Britons. Instead, Columbus himself offers a model of dedication on which Britain might base its own process of national defence and planning for the postwar world. A notice in *The Listener* of 8 October 1942, titled 'On, Sail On!', lays out this subtext:

> Columbus had faith – faith when he was pleading before the grandees, faith when he succeeded eventually in persuading the Spanish queen to grant him a ship, faith when he set out with his gaol-bird crews, faith when he faced their incipient mutiny. All the way through, his faith never faltered, and in the end it triumphed. [. . .] It is in some quarters the fashion to deride those who think and plan ahead: and certain it is that until victory has been won all our plans for a better world will remain but aspirations. But to know, even in the most general terms, the kind of world we are fighting for, is the first step towards that feeling of determination which is necessary to achieve it. And determination is the right arm of faith. ('On! Sail On!' 1942: 456)

This promotional notice does considerable work to translate the monomaniacal and charismatic Columbus from an almost authoritarian figure into a leader suitable for the People's War. Columbus is here cast as a model of visionary foresight, an individual capable of seeing beyond the immediate challenge to the promise of riches and new life in undiscovered new worlds beyond. Though in 1940 the topic of postwar planning had been sufficiently controversial to occasion J. B. Priestley's notorious exit, pursued by a Tory huff, from the 'Postscripts' series, by 1942 the BBC felt itself independent enough of official government reticence about the postwar future to venture a statement in defence of planning, however guarded that statement might be.[18] Furthermore, the generally progressive tone of *The Listener*'s call for a clear vision of 'the kind of world we are fighting for' implies that currents of social change given fuller voice by the Beveridge Report in December 1942 were already in popular circulation.[19]

Indeed, if Priestley's 'Postscripts' had driven the question of postwar planning to the fore in the summer and autumn of 1940, questions about the British government's commitment to social change following the war continued to circulate throughout 1941 and beyond. A special issue of *Picture Post* in January 1941, titled 'A Plan for Britain', engendered much debate. The editors' 'Foreword' noted that 'Our plan for a new Britain is not something outside the war, or something *after* the war. It is an essential part of our war aims. It is, indeed, our most positive war aim' ('Foreword' 1941: 4). MacNeice had picked up on this atmosphere in spring 1941 in his periodic 'London Letters' to *Common Sense*, a leftist American monthly:

> It has dawned on some people [...] that a clearer consciousness of aims and ends will promote the solution of some practical problems which have been falsely divorced from ideology. [...] A clear statement of intended social changes – *if* they were the right changes (i.e. in the direction of an intelligently planned economy and the levelling out of the social castes) – would enhance the national war effort and heighten, high though it is, the popular morale. (MacNeice 1990: 112–13)

Columbus's vision of perseverance guided by a desire for a new and better world thus builds on a larger cultural conversation to which the writer was already attuned. The 'New World' of *Columbus* is not just the land of plenty and promise opened up to Europeans in 1492, nor is it only a metaphor for the optimism made possible by the entry of the US into the war. MacNeice's new world represents the promise of a better collective life realised through shared endeavour.

This notion of a new world made possible through long struggle is echoed, in subtle ways, throughout the broadcast. For example, though Queen Isabella is willing to underwrite the journey to America, she insists that it cannot take place until Spanish forces have defeated the Moors at Granada. When this moment comes, the Chorus greets the event with chants that echo the promise of a new England postwar:

> CHORUS: The Old Age was iron; the New Age is golden;
> The Gold Age is coming – oh see where it comes!
> Granada has fallen. The long days of torment
> And bloodshed are over; the battle is done
> And we are the victors. Granada has fallen
> And Spain's resurrection today has begun. (MacNeice [1944] 1993: 34)

Guided by paratextual material including the *Listener* editorial and a similar promotional essay in the *Radio Times*, listeners were encouraged to hear deeper implications in the choral celebrations of the court at Barcelona; like the Spanish kingdom, Britain was bound for a 'resurrection', however postponed it may be by immediate military imperatives (Bower 1942b). As MacNeice knew well, given his two visits to the war-torn country in the 1930s, the fact that Spain itself was under fascist rule by 1942 lent further significance to this passage (MacNeice [1965] 2007: 158–94). For the British listener in 1942, Granada was at once the city liberated from the Moors in 1491, a city currently under fascist control, and a promise of a more general liberation from war in the unwritten future.

Beyond its layers of historical referents, however, *Christopher Columbus* offers a model of collective labour that serves as a corollary to the effort of millions of British citizens and soldiers serving in factories, in the military, in the civil service and in volunteer positions across the country. By its very grandeur and spectacularity, *Christopher Columbus* lends aesthetic labour a material shape, simultaneously vindicating cultural production as a legitimate contribution to the war effort and rewarding tired listeners for their daytime work by offering them entertainment on a scale not previously enjoyed. Olivier's excessive performance embodies the physical work of acting and the psychological intensity of a man gripped by a single idea. The sheer number of instrumentalists and singers entailed a massive mobilisation of artistic talent, a mobilisation that was not lost on listeners inside or outside the organisation. Anthony Craxton, an employee of the BBC Presentation Department who described himself as 'a very critical and conscientious listener', claimed that in eight years of employment at the BBC he had not heard a programme 'which reached the standard of this production'. For Craxton, it was the synthesis of artistic elements that was most important: 'The music I thought superb – the script very fine – but first and foremost, I felt that one was an integral part of the other – a perfect piece of co-operation in fact' (Craxton 1942). Leonard Cottrell of the Features and Drama Department added that it was 'a great subject nobly handled', and 'one of the most moving examples of radio drama which I have heard in ten years of listening' (Cottrell 1942).

The play's reception outside of the BBC was slightly more complex. Like *Alexander Nevsky*, *Christopher Columbus* was rated highly by listeners, earning an 'Appreciation Index' of 82 and attracting just under 13 per cent of the available audience. There are signs, however, that the dense soundscape of *Christopher Columbus* proved challenging to navigate for some listeners. Some thought the subject 'too immense' for a radio play; one unidentified listener quoted in the Listener Research report for *Columbus* thought the play 'took too much time and concentration for a weekday evening', while another complained that '[s]ome important information was conveyed in choral singing – a mistake, as the words are seldom audible' (LR/1264 1942). While Listener Research received few such complaints about *Columbus*, these remarks, preserved in the BBC WAC, reminds us that attention, audition and comprehension are among the many facets of listener experience that vary greatly among members of the radio public. These granular details are prone to escape even the finest of textual nets; while the BBC archives preserve ample evidence of enthusiasm for both productions from inside the BBC, there are only a few sources of information about audience reactions, and no record of the impact these propaganda broadcasts had on listener attitudes about the war. The choral section touting the resurrection of Spain, for example, might be easily interpreted on the page (or with repeated listening) as part of a broader initiative in favour of postwar planning, but its historical effects remain difficult to quantify. By combining close readings of the imagined environments of radio drama with paratextual information about the intentions of cultural producers and the reception of cultural products by the audience, however, we can at least begin to triangulate the absent experience of listening.

Tailored to an audience he hoped would listen, MacNeice's radio works simultaneously imagine and service a public curious about, if not hungry for, the 'community creed' he had lamented as lacking in British culture (MacNeice 1987: 93). Throughout, he managed for the most part to avoid writing either up or down to his audience; rather than pandering to the presumed interests of an imagined community of listeners, he sought to balance intellectual rigour and verbal prowess with propulsive narratives and immersive soundscapes. Central to this balancing act was the form of the radio feature, which enabled MacNeice to build the flexible and dynamic soundscapes necessary to the communication of this collective goal. By allowing subtle elisions of time and space, MacNeice's incorporation of studio techniques into his radio works permits the auditory perception of other worlds, whether of a deep historical past for British buildings or of the multiple worlds in collision on the Russian steppes or the Caribbean Sea. The vast networks of the BBC allowed this multispatial, multitemporal rendering of the world to be diffused globally.

As MacNeice moved from reluctant propagandist in early 1941 to become the most celebrated features and drama writer of the war, he sought to bring the listening public – British and overseas – into a keener state of auditory awareness. His parables of close listening in a time of war are more than hollow pieces of political rhetoric; they form a guide to surviving cacophonous times. They asked a neutral audience to listen to the silence of Britain's bell towers and to imagine the physical and cultural toll of destroyed buildings. They invite British listeners to lose themselves in the history and suffering sedimented beneath their Russian ally's stand against Nazi invasion and, like Blind Iuri, to hear, proleptically, a victory not yet materialised. Most importantly, MacNeice's broadcasts ask that listeners endure the hardship and privation of total war so that they might glimpse a New World at the other side of their long collective journey.

Notes

1. For a fuller treatment of the political repercussions of audition in *Alexander Nevsky* and *Christopher Columbus*, see Whittington (2015: 44–61).
2. The broadcasts were typically recorded live and transmitted on the Eastern Service (to Asia, including the Subcontinent) at 14:15 Greenwich Mean Time (GMT) on a Monday, and rebroadcast (from the recording) on the North American service at 02:30 GMT the next day. Rebroadcasts would take place the following Sunday (18:45 GMT) and Monday (06:45 GMT) on the African service and the Pacific service, respectively. Though these broadcasts were heard around the world, internal memoranda indicate that the primary intended audience was American. In a memo to the BBC's Controller (Programmes) dated 30 September 1941, Lawrence Gilliam described *Stones* as designed 'to capture for propaganda reasons the almost pathological American interest in true bombing stories' (Gilliam 1941f).
3. See Chapter 4, on Denis Johnston's work as a front-line war correspondent, for an overview of the development of portable recording technologies during the war.
4. For example, in an unsigned carbon copy of a letter from the Features Department (possibly, though not certainly, from Gilliam) to Sir John Forsdyke of the British Museum, a BBC official asked whether the latter's refusal to cooperate in producing a *Stones* broadcast about damage to the museum was due to 'the reluctance of the Ministry of Home Security to release the news that the Museum has been damaged' (BBC Features 1941).
5. MacNeice's American contemporaries James Agee and Walker Evans, for example, reference the work in the title of their 1941 volume of photographic and prose documentary, *Let Us Now Praise Famous Men*.
6. The Preacher's words in this passage quote 2 Chronicles 36:19, Nehemiah 2:3 and Psalm 74:20, in that order.
7. As the Blitz waned in summer 1941, the Features Department thought it wise to reduce the use of such sound effects. In a memo to *Stones* producers Glyn-Jones, Dillon and Bridson, Gilliam asked that they alter or remove any 'references which give the impression that we are suffering from air raids at the moment. In general, play down the use of sirens and air raid

effects and if used suggest that they are reflections of experience in the past, possibly of the future, but not of the present' (Gilliam 1941d).

8. As with the time-travelling Cockney, it is unclear from the typescript how this shift was to be conveyed to the audience, aside from clues in the dialogue itself. Given the often-difficult listening conditions created by transatlantic shortwave broadcasting, some of the subtleties of MacNeice's script may have fallen prey to atmospheric interference.

9. Emily Bloom has recently situated this scene from 'St. Paul's' in the context of MacNeice's larger concern with 'echoes' as sonic effects that mediate between the past and the present; she argues that the echoes here testify to the potential for radio to remediate principles of liberal humanism as a counter to fascist broadcasting (Bloom 2017: 80–1).

10. The use of modern dialogue jarred with some listeners. The Listener Research report for the April 1942 rebroadcast of *Nevsky* records several complaints about this perceived anachronism. 'No student', wrote one listener, 'could fail to be shocked to some degree to hear these mediaeval Russians *thinking* and talking like twentieth century Englishmen' (LR/882 1942). The retransmission of *Nevsky* in April 1942 and June 1944 indicates that such concerns did not seriously detract from the popularity of the programme.

11. In a sadly ironic variation on this theme, MacNeice contracted the pneumonia that would kill him while recording cave effects in Wales for his play *Persons from Porlock* (1963), which ends with an artist's retreat underground.

12. Produced under the auspices of the Features section of the Department of Features and Drama, *Christopher Columbus* conforms – barely – to wartime definitions of that particular type of broadcast: it was based in fact and created with informational and propagandistic intent. The use of the terms 'play' and 'drama' in this section is not in any way polemical; it reflects in part the fact that MacNeice's script strays far from the documentary roots of the 'feature', and in part the fact that, heard and read at a remove from its wartime origins, the production strikes modern audiences as *dramatic* more than anything else.

13. Quotations from *Christopher Columbus* hereafter cited in text. For reasons of readerly access, this chapter cites the 1993 republication, in Alan Heuser and Peter McDonald's *Selected Plays of Louis MacNeice*, of the 1944 Faber edition of the play. Although there are some differences between the BBC production script and these published versions – mostly consisting of cuts from MacNeice's draft script which were largely restored, post-broadcast, for the print publication – any relevant discrepancies are discussed herein.

14. Melissa Dinsman points out the parallels between Columbus's journey and MacNeice's own transatlantic crossings in the 1930s and 1940s, which allowed the Northern Irish writer to reflect on his own relationship with England, as well as on political shifts under way within Britain. Read this way, the Choruses make convenient mouthpieces not only for questions of personal commitment but also for the political struggles between isolationists and interventionists within US politics before Pearl Harbor (Dinsman 2015: 79, 89).

15. MacNeice lifts the refrain of 'pero yo ya no soy yo [. . .] ni mi casa es ya mi

casa' ('but I am not I [. . .] nor is my home now my home') without attribution from 'Romance Sonámbulo' (1928), a poem by Federico García Lorca, who was assassinated by Spanish Nationalist forces in August 1936. This appropriation would likely have gone unnoticed by most BBC listeners, but serves to reinforce the complex historical layering, discussed below, at work in *Christopher Columbus*.
16. In her analysis of the score for *Christopher Columbus*, Zelda Lawrence-Curran argues that Walton's 'Indian Chorus' must have been based on existing indigenous music because Walton had taken pains to make the plainsong sections of *Columbus* authentic, and because he had visited America in 1939 'and it is not inconceivable that he would have heard examples of native music at that time. It was not in Walton's character merely to invent "native" music' (Lawrence-Curran 1999: 169). Similarly, she cites as evidence Walton's inclusion of African melodies in a piece composed for a South African audience (169). Lacking a specific piece with which to compare the 'Indian Chorus', Lawrence-Curran's assertion of its 'authenticity' appears too thinly defended. Otherwise, her chapter on *Christopher Columbus* remains the most thorough and detailed musical analysis of the feature.
17. As Dinsman points out, the play as performed here diverges from the play as scripted and published. Columbus was originally to have said, 'Behold, I have brought you a new world!' (Dinsman 2015: 90; MacNeice [1944] 1993: 65).
18. On Priestley's exit from the 'Postscripts' series, see Chapter 1 in this volume, as well as Nicholas (1996: 240–5) and Angus Calder (1993: 196–204).
19. On the contexts and consequences of the Beveridge report, see Angus Calder (1969: 525–36).

Chapter 4

Versions of Neutrality: Denis Johnston's War Reports

On 17 January 1956, more than two years after the publication of *Nine Rivers from Jordan*, a monumental memoir of his years as a war correspondent, Denis Johnston received an unexpected souvenir from the past. His journal records the incident:

> I was taking part in a panel discussion about something in the Belfast BBC Studios, when an Announcer came in and placed a heavy automatic pistol and a few rounds of ammunition on the table before me, and then left with a relieved and somewhat cynical smile.
> 'This is yours, I believe,' he said.
> The incident caused some mixed reactions amongst the other members of the panel, so in some embarrassment I took the weapon hastily & shoved it under the table until the broadcast was over, explaining that it was something left behind since the war days. (Johnston [n.d.], MS 3751)[1]

Picked up from a pile of discarded arms outside the gates of Buchenwald in April 1945, the pistol was more than a reminder of the wartime travels that had brought Johnston from Egypt, across North Africa, north through Italy and into Germany. It indexed a further journey: from a commitment to a multiform neutrality – encompassing journalistic objectivity, technological immediacy and political non-alignment – to a conviction that neutrality represents an ideal incommensurate with the traumas of the Second World War. An examination of his wartime broadcasts, journals and memoirs reveals the pistol to be a loaded correlative of Johnston's lost and found commitment to a moral universe of rights and wrongs. In arming himself at the end of the war, he had finally taken a side.

The belated recovery of the weapon makes for a tidy anecdote about the return of the wartime repressed; indeed, in its elegant and compact symbolism, the scene is typical of Johnston's highly mediated autobiographical writings. Johnston was a prodigious chronicler of his own life:

during the war, he recorded day-by-day observations about life as a correspondent in what he called his 'War Field Books'. While the 'War Field Books' form only one part of Johnston's agglomeration of unpublished life writing, they represent the most substantial and detailed account therein of his experience of the war.[2] Revised and expanded, these journals (along with correspondence and various forms of printed ephemera) formed the basis for his first attempt at an experimental memoir, *Dionysia*, written between 1945 and 1948 but never published; with further revision, *Dionysia* became *Nine Rivers from Jordan*, first published in 1953. Adding to the textual thicket is the fact that Johnston would return to his own journals to revise and extend them; for example, although it appears within the 'War Field Books', the anecdote of the missing pistol was added to the end of the final notebook of the war years in January 1956 or at some point thereafter, and is itself preceded by an undated but postwar 'Correction' which attempts to revise some of his entries from late in the war. This revisionist impulse seems to have been fuelled as much by Johnston's fascination with contemplating the landmarks of his eventful life as by his desire to leave for future scholars and biographers a record of his evolving views on that life.

In the present context, which seeks to connect Johnston's role as a witness to the conflict to his multiple remediations of that conflict, his practice of reworking first-hand experience presents obvious interpretive problems. Adding to these difficulties is the fact that the diaries, as Johnston's biographer Bernard Adams notes, 'are not invariably reliable on matters of fact', susceptible as they are to bias and failures of memory (Adams 2002: xii). Rather than discount Johnston's autobiographical writings, this chapter proceeds from the understanding that all life writing is mediated and liable to error, and that Johnston's is mostly remarkable for the frankness with which he treats his own retrospective revisions. This approach, however cautiously pursued, gains a measure of reinforcement from the corroboration of Johnston's wartime diaries by other archival sources, most notably the papers of the BBC WAC; Johnston generally was where he said he was, and experienced, at least in broad strokes, the events he claims to have experienced. This chapter also presumes that Johnston's day-to-day reflections in the 'War Field Books' are subject to fewer distortions of fact than *Dionysia* and *Nine Rivers from Jordan*, in which Johnston admits to bending truths to suit his literary ends.[3] While it is not impossible that Johnston fabricated events in his unpublished journals, it seems less plausible that he would have done so for such a limited audience. With these caveats in mind, this chapter treats the totality of Johnston's wartime journals, memoirs and broadcasts as an archive that, although unstable, can still serve as a record of his intellectual and emotional response to the war and to his role within it, even if this record is not 'invariably reliable on matters of fact'. As this chapter argues, it is precisely the neutral 'fact' that is in question: Johnston's iterative approach to life writing offers a critical reminder that what Mary Poovey has called 'the modern fact' is a slippery thing, difficult to disentangle from its implication in theory, argument and persuasion (1998: 94–7).

Johnston's inability to find a publisher for his first attempt at a war memoir, *Dionysia*, did not sway him from circulating it. He had several copies of the work typed up and distributed to various libraries, including Trinity College Dublin, the University of Ulster, Coleraine, the British Library and the Houghton Library at Harvard. The goal of *Dionysia*, as he writes in the opening 'Introit', had initially been to combine autobiography with an impish *j'accuse*,

> in the course of which I was going to have a lot of rather malicious amusement in debunking the official pomposities of war, in issuing my own personal list of awards and defamations, with maybe just a small Papal Bull to round the matter off! I was going to perform an entertaining penance for having played the Censors' game so obediently in my despatches. (Johnston 1947a: 4)

Although itself the product of selection and subjective interpretation, then, the memoir was to provide a corrective to the distortions produced by official accounts of the war, not least those in which the BBC was complicit. What Johnston ended up with, however, was a much more complicated document: 900 typescript pages that blend journalistic memoir, moral enquiry, anti-establishment screed and spiritual reawakening. *Dionysia* would resurface, revised but substantially the same document, as *Nine Rivers from Jordan*, published by Derek Verschoyle in 1953.[4] Both versions blend genres and forms with abandon, as if textual abundance might mitigate wartime disinformation: the prose sections draw on the traditions of autobiography, myth, literary criticism and travelogue, while jostling alongside extracts from Johnston's personal and professional correspondence, passages copied directly from his journals, soldiers' songs, graffiti, philosophical dialogues and fully scripted dramatic scenes of metaphysical judgement.

In order to transform informational overload into a usable narrative, Johnston binds these disparate elements through two interlaced threads of personal development: a liturgical framework of initiation that lends the book chapter and section titles including 'Introit', 'Ordinary', 'Catechism' and 'Epiklesis'; and a prophecy, delivered to the author by an Egyptian dragoman early in the book, that states among other things that Johnston will cross the titular nine rivers as he journeys from a depth to a summit and from one white landscape to another (Johnston 1953: 26–7). Through these structuring devices, Johnston transposes his wartime experiences into the discourse of myth, transformation and ritual. (Given Johnston's reworking of an archetypal journey, it is perhaps unsurprising that, when he left for Egypt in the early summer of 1942, he carried a copy of James Joyce's *Ulysses* with him [Adams 2002: 220].) This mythical transposition also allows Johnston to break from the realm of objective recollection and embrace instead a more fantastic mode of documentation. The culmination of Johnston's turn from the realm of strict fact in *Nine Rivers from Jordan* is the work's bipartite ending: in its final chapters, it offers the reader two mutually incompatible conclusions, representative of competing philosophical approaches to the role of the war correspondent as either detached observer or engaged participant.

In seeking to untangle the knots of Johnston's representations of the war, then, his readers must make a place, as the war correspondent himself did, for myth, for indeterminacy and for reinterpretation. To trace Johnston's journey across the desert and into Europe is to trace the progress not just of the war but of its manifold representations – by Johnston and others – and their relation to fact and immediacy. Part of the story of these representations is about the promise particular media seem to hold for transparency; Johnston's ideal of neutrality, it turns out, was tethered not just to his job as a correspondent and his birth in Ireland, but also to a particular form of objectivity that wartime broadcasting technology seemed to make possible. The BBC's War Reporting Unit, of which Johnston was a part, built its identity around the promise of unmediated access to aural experience that radio held for its practitioners and its audience. Mobile recording vans, front-line dispatches and so-called 'midget' recording units all played a role in Johnston's, and the BBC's, quest to represent the war in as direct and immediate a way as possible. *Nine Rivers from Jordan*, in its turn towards myth, argues for the shortcomings of this goal; but in doing so, it reflects not the total failure of the ideal of immediacy and objectivity, but its insufficiency. There was not, for Johnston, a single way of looking at the Second World War; the pistol he could not help but keep was only one version of the story he left the war wanting to tell.

Antebellum

Denis Johnston came of age in a state of political heterodoxy. He was born in Dublin in 1901 to a Nonconformist Protestant family with strong Ulster ties, but he inherited from his father a belief in the necessity of Home Rule for Ireland. This meant, in effect, that Johnston's particular political and religious profile found few perfect analogues among his schoolmates and contemporaries. As independence took violent hold and settled into its post-Treaty pattern in the 1920s, his scepticism towards the binaristic thinking of Irish independence only deepened. His studies took him from Dublin to public school in Edinburgh, and on to Cambridge, Harvard Law School and London's Inner Temple. Johnston would abandon his early law career for a life as a playwright and director, fields in which his ambivalence about the connections between nation and place found their clearest expression. His two early successes as a dramatist, *The Old Lady Says 'No!'* (1929) and *The Moon in the Yellow River* (1931), attack the most pious versions of Irish nationalism without denying either the movement's justifications or its romantic pull. This tension would persist throughout Johnston's life: although sceptical of the post-independence resurgence of a Celtified nationalism, he would carry a firm conviction of Ireland's independence in geopolitical matters forward into the war years and beyond.

While Johnston would continue to work in the theatre for much of his life, he soon realised that his creative ambitions encompassed other media. In autumn 1936, he joined the Features section of the BBC's Northern Ireland regional station, where he scripted several successful works in a frequently restrictive cultural atmosphere (Adams 2002: 172–6).[5] After almost two years of radio work out of Belfast, he signed on as a television producer at Alexandra Palace, outside London, in August 1938. Johnston embraced the challenges of this pioneering phase of television production but it would not last long; on 1 September 1939, the BBC Television service was shut down as part of broader wartime changes.[6] During the early years of the war, the Corporation placed him with their American Liaison Unit, but Johnston soon moved to a cross-appointment as a staff member of the Department of Features and Drama and as a War Correspondent based out of the Belfast studios.[7] He also reported to his superiors on the implications of BBC efforts to broadcast to or about the Irish Republic during a war whose specific details were the subject of tight domestic control by the Irish government.[8]

While Johnston's interstitial position within Irish society made him invaluable to the BBC, it also raised questions about his allegiances. These questions were significant enough to warrant being addressed during an in-person interview on 27 November 1940 with the Assistant Controller (Administration), who sent a record of the interview to the Controller (Overseas) and Controller (Programmes), seeking to allay their fears: 'He is an Irishman first and foremost, and therefore at present a neutral. He is very pro-British in the sense that his sympathies in the present conflict are entirely with Britain and against Nazi-Germany' (L1/225/1). This assessment of Johnston's stance seems to have been acceptable to senior BBC management, who pursued the matter no further. To expect a greater degree of pro-British zeal from Johnston might have been asking too much; in the early years of the war many liberal Irish intellectuals (including Elizabeth Bowen and Louis MacNeice) held the view that Ireland had no real option other than to remain neutral for reasons both domestic (anti-British sentiment and the threat of Irish Republican Army [IRA] action) and international (fear of invasion or bombing) (Wills 2007: 12, 15–83).

A belief in the necessity of Irish neutrality did not preclude individual involvement, however. As Johnston prepared to leave his multifaceted role on the home front for a role as a war correspondent in North Africa, he framed his departure in terms of his obligations as a public figure: 'It is my belief in Ireland's neutrality that has so largely sent me forth. Only those who are prepared to go into this horrible thing themselves have the right to say that Ireland must stay out' (qtd in Adams 2002: 216). Neutrality might offer clarity of perception to the public intellectual in that, as Clair Wills observes, it 'provided a valuable counterweight to the propaganda of war', but it could also carry the taint of escapism or a kind of 'culpable detachment' (2007: 403, 407). For Johnston, speaking publicly of Ireland's right to neutrality requires a knowledge of what that position might be tempted to ignore: battle, occupation and the death and suffering of both combatants and civilians. In this respect, Johnston echoes what Damien Keane has identified as the often fragile harmony Irish writers and politicians struck between cosmopolitan awareness and defensive retrenchment in the period around the Second World War; far from being the product of insularity and parochialism, Keane notes, 'the specificity of Irish national self-determination takes form only in relation to international, "worldly" engagement' (2014: 6). Johnston would sustain his own delicate balance – neutral but pro-British, uncommitted but engaged – for the majority of the war. After almost three years of handling everything from intelligence reports on Irish broadcasting to features on the bombing of Belfast in 1941, Johnston was appointed to cover the desert campaign in May 1942, and shortly afterwards set out for Cairo via Lagos and Khartoum.

Immediacy as neutrality

The BBC's Cairo office was a small room cluttered with spare broadcasting equipment, one floor below a brothel towards which Johnston and his colleagues often had to direct wayward soldiers. As Johnston describes it, the mood in the city was half-panicked in June 1942, with British officials planning to evacuate to Jerusalem in anticipation of Rommel's imminent push into Egypt (1953: 7–9). Appointed to replace a reporter who had been captured by Nazi troops, Johnston initially worked under the supervision of Richard Dimbleby. Dimbleby was an experienced broadcaster but one who had ingratiated himself with local British military officials to the displeasure of politicians and BBC administrators back home, who sought a correspondent less beholden to local interests and more responsive to commands from London (Nicholas 1996: 202–3; Adams 2002: 217–19). In the first months of Johnston's time in Egypt, he and Dimbleby would swap places roughly every two weeks, with one of them reporting on British troops at the front while the other filed dispatches on official business in Cairo. The correspondents themselves were each paired with an engineer – in Johnston's case, a man named 'Skipper' Arnell – who also served as driver of the vehicle that housed the BBC's bulky recording gear (1953: 14). Although Johnston was not among the very first front-line BBC correspondents – a term that quickly replaced the former label 'observer' – his career nonetheless spans some of the most important transformations in the shape, sound and approach of the Corporation's news teams. Compared with the smooth organisation, portable equipment and overall professionalism of the War Reporting Units launched with the opening of the Second Front on D-Day, Johnston's beginnings were often frustratingly humble.[9]

Even at the outset, Johnston saw his role as inextricably linked to the equipment that enabled recording and transmission on location. Without the ability to capture sounds from the war zone itself – voices, machines, artillery, urban and rural environments – a BBC war correspondent was little different from a print journalist. As a December 1942 report from the Foreign News Committee to the Controller (News) argues, the physical presence of the correspondent abroad was important but insufficient:

> The time is long past when a voice freshly recorded from 'some foreign field' could reap an easy advantage over the printed word and command the attention of mass audiences just because of its novel quality ... [W]e must aim at developing to the full such forms as running commentary on action, with sound pictures of battle, and the interview with the man on the front line. It is in these that we can exploit the qualities of immediacy and reality which make broadcasting unique as a medium for bringing the war to life. (BBC Foreign News Committee 1942)

The precise technological means of achieving this ideal of 'immediacy and reality' through 'sound pictures of battle' would change as the war went on. The recording gear in use when Johnston arrived in Cairo – known as a Type C Disc Recorder, which cut sound directly to disc – consisted of three separate components (an amplifier, a power supply and a recording machine, or 'cutter') and weighed over a hundred pounds. This meant the gear had to be transported in a van or large car, and whatever was to be recorded therefore had to be near an easily traversable road. In addition to bringing to the airwaves the voices of soldiers from outposts in the desert campaign, Johnston used this equipment to interview Winston Churchill when the Prime Minister visited the Eighth Army and the Royal Air Force (RAF) in Egypt, and he obtained some dramatic recordings of battlefield sounds whenever he could get close enough to the front lines to do so.[10] Although the quality of the preserved recordings varies considerably, the best contain sounds that evoke the experience of life in camps, in captured towns and on the roads linking settlements across the vast desert. One recording, made at night at an Allied encampment less than a kilometre from the nearest Nazi troops, features Johnston speaking softly as he interviews soldiers about conditions in the camp; one soldier curtly tells another to put out his cigarette owing to the proximity of the enemy. In a moment of self-referentiality that would reappear occasionally in Johnston's broadcasts, he notes that the soldiers have gathered around their vehicles 'in order to hear the news broadcast from London' (Johnston 1942b). Framed by Johnston's descriptions of the position, the portrait conveys the muted soundscape of the desert far more effectively than could a written account, speaking as it does in the same hushed tones.

Johnston saw radio's promise of sonic immediacy as key to a new relationship between reporters, their subjects and their audiences. In an undated entry in his journal around Christmas 1943, he describes his disdain for those correspondents who repeat the official communiqués issued by the military; his own goal, he writes, is 'the search for the great Piece – the thing of the future that's never been done in the past, that opens a new field of radio reporting' (Johnston 1943–4). With an almost Futurist *frisson*, Johnston thrills at the possibility of bringing the noise of battle to listeners in Britain, as the opening section of *Dionysia* records:

> And bracing myself for my first baptism of fire, I would take my recording gear up into the front line and give the folks at home the thundering music of the conflict – the crash of the shells – the caustic and unflinching comments of the happy warriors themselves as they battled in the blood and the sweat. And through it all, my own burning eye-witness accounts of what was really going on. (1947a: 14–15)

Though here exaggerated for ironic effect, the central impetus for Johnston's war broadcasts would remain essentially unchanged throughout the war. Too many journalists, he believed, were hamstrung by censorship and not creative enough to find other ways of communicating the war to an audience at home; immersion in the sonic environment of the conflict offered one such means of communication. If, for Johnston, objective reporting based on first-hand experience of the war was the duty of the engaged but neutral observer, the surest way of representing the war effectively was to allow the war to speak for itself, as it were. However illusory such claims to unmediated truth appear in retrospect, for Johnston and the wartime BBC, actuality recordings promised to move the listener at least one step closer to the war itself, so that audiences might interpret the conflict for themselves.

To that end, Johnston attempted to bring listeners to places they had never been. In one instance, he and Skipper Arnell packed their gear into a Wellington bomber for a raid over the Tunisian port city of Sousse in January 1943, although the poor quality of this recording meant it was not broadcast; on a later occasion, they loaded their gear on to a skiff in the Italian port of Monopoli on a secret mission to the Dalmatian island of Vis, where the RAF and Yugoslavian Partisans were cooperating in the defence of the coast from Axis attacks (1953: 107–10, 200–6). This last foray resulted in several discs' worth of material, including Partisan songs, conversations with RAF and Partisan commanders, and vivid descriptions of life in a communist military camp filled with soldiers of both genders. Johnston had to sneak the recordings back to London via unofficial channels to dodge what he saw as certain rejection by an over-hasty field censor's office; once in the hands of the BBC, the resulting broadcasts proved hugely successful, and count as one of Johnston's major scoops of the war.[11]

Although he achieved a few successes with earlier, bulkier forms of recording equipment, Johnston – like his fellow correspondents and supervisors – hoped for something far more portable. As the prospect of an Allied landing in France became increasingly likely over the summer and autumn of 1943, officials at the News Division scrambled to find some mode of recording technology that would be portable enough for a lone journalist to bring into an active combat zone – roughly, something small enough to be carried on a correspondent's back. The Corporation investigated several existing options – wire recorders, recording sound on to camera film and an American device called the Heller Recorder – but none proved suitable under strenuous wartime conditions (Hannon 2008: 186–9). The Corporation committed engineering resources to the development of its own prototype, and the eventual result was a device formally called the Riverside Portable, but colloquially known as the 'midget' recorder. Weighing in at 42 pounds and capable of recording up to seventy-two minutes on to discs, the Riverside unit was ready in time for the landings at Normandy and was crucial to the BBC News Division's efforts to bring the war vividly to life before its audience's ears (Hannon 2008: 188–9; Hawkins [1946] 2014: 32).[12] In the Introduction to *War Report*, a 1946 collection of the War Reporting Unit's dispatches from Europe, Desmond Hawkins praised the '"sound photography" of the recording unit, reproducing every noise and every word in a given scene' ([1946] 2014: 24). Beyond hinting at the paucity of adequate descriptors for sonic media, the language of photographic reproduction – Hawkins elsewhere says the BBC used radio as 'a "sound camera" aiming at facsimile reproduction' – testifies to the documentary power of actuality recordings ([1946] 2014: 64). In the minds of the BBC and their listeners, perfect reproduction of reality meant photographic reproduction. The BBC had found the audio equivalent of the Leica camera in the Spanish Civil War: trustworthy, portable, easy to use and central to the project of bringing the overseas war home to a British audience.

If Johnston and the BBC News Division were enthusiastic about their ability to represent the sounds of war in a direct, unmediated and transparent fashion, there were, however, still limits to the on-air fetishisation of acoustic fidelity. In a telegram sent to all BBC war correspondents in early 1944, War Reporting Unit Director Howard Marshall encouraged them to limit references to the technical underpinnings of their dispatches in the broadcasts themselves; evidently some correspondents had begun to discuss their equipment in excessive detail. The time is now come, Marshall writes in cablese, 'when [the] availability [of] recording gear in strange or dangerous locations [is] not repeat not more commentworthy than [a] newspaper man's portable typewriter' (Marshall 1944; original all in capitals). This telegram captures a small but telling shift in the wartime relationship between the social medium of radio and its underlying apparatus: while the primacy given to accurate 'sound photography' generated an early enthusiasm within and without the organisation for the technology itself, the maturation of war reporting as a mediated practice entailed a knowing reticence about those means that had once seemed marvels. As the Corporation and its audience became accustomed to what was possible with new field recording devices, the devices themselves were no longer newsworthy.

This trajectory, from foregrounding to downplaying the mediating apparatus itself, conforms to what David Jay Bolter and Richard Grusin have called 'hypermediacy' and 'immediacy': the complementary tendencies of all media towards self-representation and self-erasure.

'If the logic of immediacy leads one either to erase or to render automatic the act of representation,' write Bolter and Grusin, 'the logic of hypermediacy acknowledges multiple acts of representation and makes them visible' (Bolter and Grusin 2001: 33–4). The tendency towards hypermediacy prompted war correspondents to acknowledge, and even champion, the technology and techniques that were transforming the civilian experience of war; the tendency towards immediacy encouraged those same correspondents to sustain the illusion of a barrierless communication of experience and information. Hawkins, in his Introduction to *War Report*, approaches a theory of immediacy himself: 'If Caen and Arnhem seemed less remote psychologically than were Mons or the Somme thirty years earlier,' he writes, 'it was largely because of the power of broadcasting to act as an immediate link between the battlefront and the home' (Hawkins [1946] 2014: 26). The notion of an 'immediate link' – something that enables connection but disavows mediation – channels some of the tension at work in Bolter and Grusin's taxonomy.

Though hypermediacy and immediacy need not follow a developmental arc, Howard Marshall's command that all war correspondents minimise references to the apparatus demonstrates that, at the wartime BBC at least, collective understanding of the medium evolved over time. The portable recording units having proven their worth, a hypermediate attention to the device itself began to be seen to hamper the medium's incipient 'noiselessness': its potential for the pure transmission of signal and therefore of sonic experience.[13] To bring the listener to a combat zone, one had to downplay the means of communication itself; if correspondents could not fully remove themselves from the process of transporting the listener, then at least the institutional, technological and social machinery required by that process could be masked. The goal of the radio correspondent, then, was to pursue stories at the limits of what the apparatus made possible, while eliding the very apparatus that enabled their job. In that way, neither human nor machinic agency could be heard intervening in the communication of the war to its listeners. The goal, in other words, was neutrality.

The correspondent as neutral observer

This commitment to auditory neutrality parallels Johnston's commitment to an ideal of direct, unvarnished truth in his reporting. On the surface, Johnston's attitude aligned neatly with the BBC's vision of itself as a source for unbiased war news reporting, which had been elaborated in distinction not only to totalitarian forms of propaganda, but also to Britain's own history of wartime misinformation. The interwar years had revealed the extent to which false atrocity stories promoted by the Ministry of Information (MoI) and circulated by news organisations during the First World War had eroded public trust in the media. This war had to be different: 'It seems to me', wrote Home Service News Editor R. T. Clark in April 1938, 'that the only way to strengthen the morale of the people whose morale is worth strengthening, is to tell them the truth, and nothing but the truth, even if the truth is horrible' (Briggs 1965: 656–7).[14] This ideal of unbiased reporting seemed, to Johnston, laudable. 'Knowing what was wanted under our system of free and objective reporting,' he writes in *Nine Rivers*, 'I was not going to concern myself with propaganda. I was going to describe soberly and sensibly exactly what I saw, and give the people at home the Truth, the whole Truth, and nothing but the Truth, whether happy or unfavourable' (1953: 8).

As Johnston was to discover, 'the Truth' – as a series of autonomous observations or 'facts' about the war – could itself be made into a powerful propaganda instrument. Mary Poovey has noted that, since about the seventeenth century, 'the modern fact' has enjoyed a bifurcated existence, as at once a self-contained unit of meaning in and of itself *and* evidence inseparable from the arguments it is mobilised to support (Poovey 1998: 94–7). Never is this truer than in wartime, when facts become all the more persuasive, the less they seem geared to persuade. Building on Poovey's observation, Mark Wollaeger has argued that propaganda 'exploits the internal bifurcation of modern facts by amplifying their rhetorical appeal even while insisting on their value-free neutrality' (2006: 21–2). The MoI's deployment of the rhetoric of disinterested facticity – statistics, tables, witness testimonials – in spurious First World War propaganda publications like the Bryce Report on German atrocities in Belgium led, Wollaeger claims, to an interwar 'epistemological decline of the fact' (2002: 21). Johnston's writings document a gradual awakening to this instrumentalisation of facts as propaganda, as his initial enthusiasm for the autonomy of facts as disinterested units of meaning is replaced by an awareness of the heightened *interestedness* of facts during the war. In an environment of information saturation, Johnston finds that the very plurality of facts undermines their claims to veracity: 'I am going to report this War soberly and objectively. All that I have to do is to give the world the Facts. But the trouble is, there are no facts. Or perhaps more truly, there are far too many of them, and none of them strictly true' (1953: 111).

Johnston's idealised notion of journalistic objectivity as the communication of factual truth began to erode soon after his arrival, as military officials used clumsy circumlocutions to downplay the dire circumstances facing Allied forces in the deserts of Egypt in summer 1942. In a telling instance, a military public relations officer refused to confirm that a German assault had scattered an Allied tank garrison from its desert outpost, known as Knightsbridge. Rather, the officer claimed, 'Developments in the battle have resulted in certain areas losing their former tactical importance. Accordingly, the garrison of Knightsbridge has assumed a mobile role' (1953: 10). Such contortions became routine. In January 1944, by which time Johnston was reporting from Italy, a media liaison officer tried to persuade him that the loss of a ridge held until recently by Canadian troops did not represent a withdrawal. Rather, the officer claimed, 'the Brigade that was up there was relieved by another Brigade which regrouped in a somewhat different area' – an area that happened to be farther back (1953: 182). Without always resorting to outright lies, military press officers would often stretch the truth beyond plausible limits in order to avoid publicising uncomfortable battlefield realities.

Misinformation by officials left Johnston 'baffled', even while other correspondents – including, in his opinion, Richard Dimbleby – seemed content to repeat the lines fed them by military officials in Cairo (Johnston 1942a). Combined with the delays attendant on the gathering and dissemination of front-line news to a home audience, it made the project of accurately representing events to audiences at home and in the desert exceedingly difficult. More frustrating for Johnston was the fact that internal BBC censorship protocols limited the kinds of impression he could relay from the front lines. Specifically, Johnston was at pains to stress the shared humanity of soldiers, as compared to the propagandists from whom he was eager to distinguish himself. 'One stinking fact remains,' he remarked in his War Field Book in July 1942, 'that man is man no matter on what side of the line he stands, & that the common enemy is not the other soldier whom he slaughters, but the mean malignant little rats behind the front who would have us hate as well as kill' (1942a). *Nine Rivers from Jordan* repeatedly emphasises the connections forged between opposing forces through a shared experience of battle: Johnston remarks, for example, that British soldiers seem as amused by Allied as by Axis operational snafus, and he relates several stories in which military and medical personnel of both sides insist on treating the enemy as human beings (1953: 23, 49, 50–1). In one poignant scene, which angered the censor when Johnston tried to include it in a broadcast, he describes a group of British soldiers huddled around a radio listening to 'Lili Marleen' in the desert. Though initially directed at German troops, the nightly broadcast of the song from an

Axis transmitter in Belgrade had quickly become appointment listening for British soldiers, similarly separated from female companionship, for whom singer Lale Andersen's voice offered something at once achingly familiar and exotic (1953: 24).[15] Soldiers are soldiers, according to Johnston: as the tide of the battle turns in the desert and Allied forces begin to encounter in greater quantities the abandoned personal possessions of Axis troops, he observes,

> We were all becoming conscious of the surprising fact that these Germans whom we were fighting were actual people, and not mere symbols represented by so many blue marks on a map, and we were rather interested in our attitude towards them as individuals. (1953: 84)[16]

A similar sense of sympathy underlies another of Johnston's thwarted broadcasts. In February 1945, by which time he had traversed much of North Africa, Italy and France, he encountered a community of some fifty people, mostly displaced German civilians from the local community, who had been sheltering for three months in caves with their livestock and possessions. His journal records a meeting of mutually astonished but tentatively friendly parties: those sheltering in the tunnels show no inclination to beg for food or cigarettes from Johnston and his crew, but once these are proffered, the Germans reciprocate by offering them a freshly baked apple cake. In the context of the Allies' steady advance into German territory, such exchanges were against the rules prohibiting fraternisation between occupiers and occupied. Though Johnston often sought to undermine what he thought of as fundamentally inhumane prohibitions, he knew enough about censorship protocol to omit such details from his broadcast. He recalls the process of internal and external censorship he went through to bring the story to air:

> I knew I mustn't mention giving them anything, but Censor killed the fact also that they gave me anything. Regulations say I mustn't accept their hospitality. So I cut out that I had accepted it, & left it that it was offered. Referred to Howell, Chief Censor, he cut this out too. Said we mustn't show Germans in a favourable light. (Johnston 1944–5: 21 February 1945)

For Johnston, the absurdity of the situation resonates on several levels. These are civilians displaced by a war in which, in his mind, they are more victims than aggressors. Furthermore, he insists on identifying with such non-combatants on the most intimate terms. 'No regulation on earth will stop me giving my own chocolate to small boys who look like my own son,' he writes. But his aversion to branding all Germans as culpable is not simply a matter of extending to strangers the mercy one would show to one's own kin: it reflects deeply felt concerns about his own culpability in the war. 'If these people are responsible for Hitler's actions then I am far more responsible for Churchill's, which God forbid' (Johnston 1944–5: 21 February 1945). That the censor, Howell, would extend guilt to all Germans but deny that a parallel guilt might apply to Johnston, let alone to Howell himself, strikes Johnston as jingoistic and incoherent. The broadcast eventually aired without reference to the exchange of food, although the censor allowed Johnston to describe the tunnel-dwellers as 'Good Germans', 'well conducted' and 'neither hostile nor ingratiating' (Johnston 1945b).

Dilemmas like this reveal the depth of Johnston's reluctance to demonise Germany and the Germans. His sympathies are rooted in a longstanding affinity for Austria and Germany that was forged during travels in the 1920s and 1930s (Adams 2002: 180, 276). But beyond this affection, born of familiarity, he was acutely sensitive to what he perceived as a strong threat of retributive violence against Germany following the war. As he advanced with Allied forces through Europe in late 1944 and early 1945, Johnston became certain that, faced with the choice of redoubling the punitive spirit of the Versailles Treaty or treating Germany as a guilty but redeemable member of the European community, the Allies would choose the former:

> What are we going to do to Germany afterwards? She has got to be punished for causing all this trouble – not the natural, educative punishment that goes with being marched in on, but calculated punishment designed to tide us over the fact that it is not at all clear what this war is about, or even, in some cases, who we would prefer to win it. (1953: 319)

This 'calculated punishment' would reflect, as in a carnival mirror, the cruelties Germany had inflicted upon its own citizens and those of other nations: 'We are going to make a concentration camp of all of Germany' (1953: 437). This stark prediction in *Nine Rivers from Jordan* in fact represents a more measured version of that which appears in *Dionysia*, which follows the 'concentration camp' remark with more graphic details: 'We are going to pillage your homes, and dismantle your industries, to rape your women by the thousand, and hold your men as slave labourers, and starve your children as a matter of deliberate policy' (1947b: 875). This is, it should be emphasised, not Johnston's own view, but rather one that he ascribes to those preaching retributive violence against Germany; the 'we' he uses when outlining such future violence signals his awareness that, however much he may resent the bloody facts of Allied occupation, his dissent emerges from a position firmly within the ranks of the occupiers.

Arms and the correspondent

Johnston's growing awareness that, like the displaced Germans sheltering in the cave, he may bear some responsibility for the violence committed in his name held particular meaning, given his understanding of his role as a reporter. Though attached to a military unit, war correspondents could claim the protections outlined in the Hague (1907) and Geneva (1929) conventions against attack and summary execution only if they went unarmed and avoided combat.[17] For Johnston, the security afforded the non-combatant was a corollary to the journalistic objectivity that shaped his reporting: in one of many articulations of this sentiment, he claims near the outset of *Nine Rivers* that 'I am not in this war as a belligerent, and so long as I remain in my own role and refrain from carrying arms, the war can do me no harm' (1953: 60). Whatever international conventions protected correspondents and restricted their ability to carry arms, Johnston believed himself to be protected under a further covenant, with Providence: 'If one is not in a position to shoot other people, one cannot be shot oneself, without old Nobodaddy losing face' (1953: 220). Though irreverent, this reference to William Blake's inconsequential father-god reflects Johnston's persistent appeal to an organising moral principle that might guide his involvement in the war. If nothing else was clear-cut for Johnston, the separation between combatant and non-combatant was one constant to which he clung for as long as he could.

As the war progressed and Johnston continued to gather innovative front-line reports, however, he began to understand his role differently. In particular, he realised that the pursuit of a newsworthy broadcast could sometimes look uncomfortably like the catalyst of the newsworthy event itself. It was one thing to record Churchill in the desert or capture the ebullience of Yugoslavian partisans at Vis, but it was quite another to participate in events that had immediate consequences for other human lives. If his first trips aboard a bomber, during raids on Benghazi and Sousse in autumn 1942, had offered valuable glimpses into the nightly routines of the RAF over important targets, later raids proved more problematic. Seeking to improve on the recording quality of his early raids, Johnston (accompanied now by an engineer with the resplendent name of Robert Molesworth St Aubyn Wade) joined a Wellington bomber crew on a mission to mine the Danube river, which Axis forces were using to ferry supplies in their struggle with Yugoslavian forces. As soon as the mines had been laid, the planes sought out barges and other ships and machine-gunned them indiscriminately, on what

Johnston not inaccurately called the '*prima facie* assumption that everything in Central Europe is connected with the War and may profitably be attacked' (1953: 218). The recordings, Johnston reports, were satisfactory, whatever he may have thought about the attack itself.

A later recording session would trouble Johnston more deeply, however. As the Allies prepared for their full assault on the European mainland in spring 1944, Johnston joined a bomber crew for a raid on the Italian headquarters of German General Albert Kesselring. Accompanying Johnston were at least two print journalists. Johnston implies that this bombing raid, if not orchestrated purely for the media, was one in which their interests and their role as witnesses to the war in general were strong considerations. Johnston was there to test new equipment and hopefully obtain some viable field recordings. Speaking of this experience in a mock catechism in *Nine Rivers from Jordan*, Johnston claims that the BBC had provided him with 'the latest type of tape recorder, with the object of finding out how it worked under service conditions ... It did not work' (1953: 224). Finding impenetrable clouds blocking their passage, the bomber crew opted instead to bomb Civitavecchia, a port city north of Rome. The pilot's comment immediately before the bombs fall – 'Nice little place that. I wonder where it is?' – captures the kind of wartime insouciance that infuriated Johnston; the plane's navigator, on the other hand, calls the raid a waste of 'time, money, and bombs' (225). Neither man seems overly concerned about the loss of civilian life. Asked by his 'catechist' in the mock catechism of *Nine Rivers* if he made any comment to the bomber crew at the time, Johnston replies: 'There is no permissible comment to be made on the wiping out of cities in such an irrelevant manner' (225).

If he is reluctant to offer more than an oblique condemnation here, however, Johnston was increasingly troubled by the rising toll of civilian casualties in the war. More particularly, the bombing raids that had once seemed to offer opportunities to bring the war home to British listeners began to look alarmingly like staged media events themselves, their victims born of the correspondent's thirst for novel representations of the war. Johnston's reluctance to celebrate civilian deaths mirrors larger debates within the News Division of the BBC. Although a public appetite for retribution against Germany had led the BBC to shift the tone of its reporting on Allied bombing raids during the middle years of the war, from reticence about civilian casualties to open acknowledgement, the News Division remained divided about catering directly to that appetite (McLaine 1979: 160–3). In spring 1944, the News Division engaged in a protracted internal debate about the prospect of broadcasting live from an Allied bomber. Ultimately, Editor-in-Chief

William Haley ruled against such a broadcast, saying 'The BBC's policy regarding the bombing of Germany is that it is a scientific operation, not to be stunted, to be gloated over, or to be dealt with in any other way than the most objective factual reporting' (Haley 1944). Thus while the BBC felt an obligation to do what it could to celebrate Allied victories in the interest of maintaining home front morale, it felt no such obligation to celebrate – much less contribute to – the deaths of German citizens through bombing raids staged for public consumption.

On collective responsibility: Buchenwald and moral commitment

Johnston's sense of guilt for his direct involvement in civilian deaths accretes in the final chapters of *Nine Rivers from Jordan*. As it builds to a close, the book takes on an increasingly heterogeneous form, which includes (in addition to the aforementioned mock catechism) an eighteen-page dramatised scene of judgement called 'The High Court on the Brocken'. In this play-within-a-memoir, Johnston – under the pseudonym 'Faustus'[18] – appears as a witness at a metaphysical trial in which both Hitler and Churchill stand accused of war crimes. Once his Faustian role as radio propagandist emerges, however, Johnston is himself charged in the trial. His cross-examiner, who bears the name of respected *Times* war correspondent Christopher Lumby, asks him whether he ever felt any responsibility for the deaths 'of the people whom you killed in Sousse? [...] Or in Kaiserslautern? Or up and down the Danube? Or in Civitta Vecchia [sic]?' (1953: 408). Johnston-as-Faustus can only reply, 'I was just a passenger' (408).

If this is an insufficient reply in the context of the trial, it is because Johnston has just claimed in the preceding pages to have rediscovered a moral compass oriented towards collective responsibility for actions carried out in the name of the collective. Though it exists outside of historical time, the metaphysical trial of the 'High Court on the Brocken' occupies the pages of *Nine Rivers from Jordan* that immediately follow the account of Johnston's real-life visit to the recently liberated concentration camp at Buchenwald on 16 April 1945. Although he devotes only six pages (out of the 450 pages of the entire work) to his description of the camp, these pages represent a moment of rupture for Johnston, not only within his text, but also within his experience of the war as a whole. Johnston's awakening to the genocide of Jews sharpens the focus of what had been a somewhat picaresque tale; the narrative of his journey across Africa and Europe appears now as the chronicle of a search for meaning that had mired itself in particulars in the belief that any coherent view of the conflict would be false by virtue of being selected and assembled with persuasive intent. The camps insist that it might be necessary to organise the congeries of contradictory facts about the war into a synthesised whole system of knowledge.

The main camp at Buchenwald had been liberated by American troops on 11 April; by the following day, journalists had begun to arrive. When Johnston got there on 16 April, the camp was still in a largely chaotic state: emaciated displaced persons stream out of the camp, an American sentry guards a pile of German weapons at the gates and filthy prisoners squat over open drains to defecate (1953: 392–4). When his taciturn guides, former prisoners, reveal the first of many piles of gaunt corpses heaped under tarpaulins, the sight brings Johnston's sheltered experience of the war to date into sharp focus. 'I used to remark that I had not seen many dead in this war,' he acknowledges; 'graves by the hundred, and impersonal lumps under covers; but the unsheeted dead have been limited to those waxlike figures in the houses of Ortona and a few more here and there by the roadside. This was a sight in full measure, and I did not brood on it for long.' Overwhelmed with revulsion, he steps into his role as a correspondent: 'Cover it up', he tells his guides, 'and tell me how it happened' (1953: 393).

Unlike the first camp he had visited, which Johnston believed to have been dressed up by the French with fabricated evidence of torture and execution, Buchenwald bears the signs of a hasty attempt at a cover-up: whitewashed walls through which bloodstains still show; hooks from which prisoners were once suspended now removed, their holes plastered over; 'a white coat like that of a hospital attendant, half washed of the blood that had once engrimed it' (393). The signs of the dead were perhaps not as shocking to Johnston as the plight of the barely living, still packed densely into overcrowded barracks. His description is worth quoting at length:

> As we entered the long hut the stench hit us in the face, and a queer wailing came to our ears. Along both sides of the shed was tier upon tier of what can only be described as shelves. And lying on these, packed tightly side by side, like knives and forks in a drawer, were living creatures – some of them stirring, some of them stiff and silent, but all of them skeletons, with the skin drawn tight over their bones, with heads bulging and misshapen from emaciation, with burning eyes and sagging jaws. And as we came in, those with the strength to do so turned their heads and gazed at us; and from their lips came that thin, unearthly noise.

> Then I realized what it was. It was meant to be cheering. They were cheering the uniform that I wore. [...] From the shelves the feeble arms rose and waved, like twigs in a breeze. Most of them were branded with numbers.
> – Hoch – Hoch – Viva – Viva! (1953: 395–6)[19]

The uncanniness of this experience, for Johnston, is as much about the distressed sounds of celebration as the sight of the prisoners' ravaged bodies.[20] The voices of the prisoners have been transfigured, rendered almost unrecognisably human, in the same way as their visible bodies have been. Shelved like household utensils and similarly instrumentalised through labour, their skeletal arms reduced to 'twigs in a breeze', the survivors of Buchenwald force Johnston to grapple, for the first time, with the reality of what Nazi persecution had done to the human bodies of Europe: 'This is the intentional flower of a Race Theory,' he admits. 'This is what logic divorced from conscience can bring men to. This is the wilful dehumanisation of the species, and an offence against man himself' (396). As they did for so many wartime journalists, the bodies of Holocaust victims signalled the tangible cost of what Johnston had mistaken for ideological bluster.

The sights and sounds of the camp drive home an unpleasant truth that Johnston had long avoided: that the war no longer represented a clash of belligerents with fundamentally similar worldviews and ethical systems. For Johnston, as for many liberals who had sought to avoid the demonisation of the other side and the possibility of a postwar bloodbath against Germany, this clarity was devastating as much for its effect on his ideological and moral framework as for the actual human cost of the battle. His 'War Field Books' state the problem bluntly: 'God what a sight,' he says of Buchenwald. 'All I ever believed or hoped is buggered up' (1945–61: 16 April 1945). The strict neutrality in Johnston's political position, his commitment to a fundamentally humanitarian outcome to the war and his belief in the relative equivalence of Nazi and British geopolitical claims begin to collapse under the weight of the evidence he had strained to ignore:

> Oh, I have tried so long to fight against this conclusion, but now – at the thirteenth stroke of a crazy clock – all previous pronouncements become suspect too. Everything else falls into place, and acquires a new meaning in the hideous light of Buchenwald. The words of Winston Burdett – the million shoes of Lublin – that camp in Alsace that I laughed at, because I did not want to believe such things of men – because they were not true of men as I had known them.
>
> Cruelty I have known, and sadism, and the rascalities of red-hot anger. But mass dehumanisation as a matter of planned policy has not so far come my way.

> Worse for me is the fact that we have been made fools of. Appeals to reason were just a cover-up for this! Our good will has been used as a means to betray us; and that is as great a crime as the degradation of humanity, for it means that good will is a mistake – that destruction is our only means of preservation.
> How did I ever doubt that there is not an Absolute in Good and Evil? (1953: 396–7)[21]

The Nazis' absolutist pursuit of Continental domination and racial extermination demanded, Johnston now believes, a similarly unequivocal response: 'Unconditional surrender is the only answer' (1953: 396). Thus moved, he chooses to contravene a key rule of journalistic neutrality: stopping outside the gates of the camp, and at the suggestion of his guides, he picks up a pistol from the heap of discarded weapons while the American sentry looks away. This decision will structure the closing events of *Nine Rivers from Jordan* and Johnston's evolving views on the conflict.

Johnston's distress at the crimes committed at Buchenwald goes beyond his sense that Germany had betrayed the good will of other European nations. He comes to believe that the abandonment of religion by a generation of European liberal intellectuals, and its replacement by a secular logic of utilitarian instrumentality built around results rather than ethical certainties, has led directly to bloodshed on a Continental scale. His own moral relativism about Germany's right to preserve itself is, he realises, a symptom of a larger pattern of obfuscation and denial. 'Buchenwald was the result of that doubt of the existence of an Absolute in Good and Evil,' he admits. 'But it does exist, however maliciously successful Life may be in confusing us as to which is which' (1953: 426). Political and moral neutrality were not simply inadequate to the horrors now facing the European conscience; they had enabled them. But if, in picking up a weapon outside the camp gates, Johnston provides himself with an objective correlative for his rediscovery of a moral position in the war, he does not pursue the remainder of the war with any retributive intent. Instead, he directs a great deal of his literary energy towards interrogating himself, and others, about their relative implication in the horrors of the conflict. Immediately following the Buchenwald episode and his self-accusation in 'The High Court on the Brocken', the narrative of *Nine Rivers from Jordan* returns to his experiences in occupied Germany. Billeted at a civilian home, he confronts the schoolteacher with whom he is staying, who is complaining to him about the damage done to her home by American soldiers. Johnston answers the question of responsibility for the damage to her home by referring to what he has witnessed at Buchenwald and elsewhere, and asks her who is responsible for the havoc wrought by Nazi Germany. 'Maybe we are both guilty in a sense,' he reflects to himself as much as to the schoolteacher. 'Neither spectacle is edifying. But I will tell you one thing, Fraulein. I would rather be on my side than on yours' (1953: 424–5).

The BBC, the Holocaust and the crisis of representation

Buchenwald removed the final obstacles to Johnston's clear understanding of the war, and Germany's actions within it; it undid his commitment to an impossible ideal of total neutrality in the conflict; and it forced him to accept not only his own guilt in the conflict but also the necessity of postwar punishment for Germany and its people. For all that his firsthand witnessing of the Holocaust changed Johnston, however, there is no evidence that he broadcast anything from or about Buchenwald or any other camp. Johnston admits as much under examination in the fictional 'High Court on the Brocken':

> FAUSTUS
> My intention has always been to mitigate the horrors of war as far as the Censors allow me by trying to tell the whole truth. Look at my files! You'll find that I have always avoided horror stories.
> LUMBY
> Even when they were true?
> FAUSTUS
> What do you mean?
> LUMBY
> You admit, don't you, that such stories are sometimes part of the whole truth? Did you report Buchenwald, for instance?
> FAUSTUS
> [*mumbling*]
> Aren't things bad enough as they are? (1953: 408)

None of Johnston's dispatches were broadcast until five days after his 16 April visit to Buchenwald (Home News Bulletin Index).[22] The next recording that made it to air mentions nothing about Buchenwald or the powerful effect it had on the correspondent. Instead, he describes the more general atmosphere of Germany as it comes under increasing Allied occupation. 'It's such a fantastic mixture of Gala Night and horror', he says, that it 'baffles one's powers of description.' The landscape has become populated with so many of the displaced that 'it assumes the air of a hilarious international convention, where every language under the sun is spoken, and national differences become as commonplace and unimportant as parochial ones at home' (Johnston 1945c: 21 April

1945). Although he stops short of mentioning Buchenwald, there are echoes of the camps in his descriptions of the vast array of liberated people moving through the German landscape:

> By one of those inversions of war, all the former marks of bondage become badges of honour, and now give the wearer a sense of security. The worn-out uniforms of forgotten armies, the hideous, striped habits of internees; the numbers and letters tattooed or branded on an arm or a wrist, as title deeds to food, shelter, and transportation. (1945c)

There are a few possible explanations for Johnston's failure to document his experiences at Buchenwald. Such a broadcast might have seemed superfluous, as a handful of BBC and American correspondents had broadcast from various camps between 14 and 19 April (Cesarani 1996: 610). Having missed the chance of a 'scoop', Johnston may have thought it better to focus on other aspects of the European front, but he seems also to have quickly become cynical about correspondents 'thirsting for Concentration Camp horrors' (Johnston 1945d: 2 May 1945). With mild scorn, he notes on 3 May 1945 the journey of two colleagues, engineer Laurie Hayhurst and broadcaster Ian Wilson, 'back to Dachau. The latter seems fascinated by the corpses. Hope they don't bring back any lice' (Johnston 1945d). This macabre assessment does not do justice to Wilson's motivations or effectiveness as a correspondent. His broadcast from Dachau on 1 May 1945 catalogues images that have become central to later generations' collective memory of the Holocaust: railway cars stacked with bodies; ditches filled with the summarily executed; crematoria decorated, absurdly, with murals and appeals to cleanliness; and the apparently endless ranks of what seemed like living corpses (Hawkins [1946] 2014: 449–51).

There are further elements of Johnston's relation to the events of the Holocaust, however, that resonate uncomfortably for readers separated from the conflict by decades. At a May 1945 press conference in which Allied commanders paraded the captured Hermann Göring to answer journalists' questions, Johnston was the only correspondent who stood to salute the architect of the *Gestapo* and long-time Commander-in-Chief of the *Luftwaffe*. Johnston omits this episode, which took place after he had visited Buchenwald, from the closing chapters of *Nine Rivers from Jordan* (Johnston 1945d: 11 May 1945). However, his journal records the event with a sympathy that seems at odds with all that Johnston, and the broader public, knew by May 1945. 'I feel that the Germans are a great people in many ways,' he writes immediately following the press conference with Göring. 'They live in a difficult geographical situation with hardly any natural frontiers. If they hadn't been a strong military nation there would have been no Germany at all' (1945d). It is possible to read this as merely Clausewitzian realism about global warfare being an extension of global politics by other means. After all, Johnston's political formation during the struggles for Irish independence had taught him that the consolidation of a national identity will always involve confrontations at its physical and discursive margins. Pious home-front pundits might rail that British troops in Germany should not 'be allowed to shake hands with murderers', he argues in *Nine Rivers from Jordan*, but in doing so they ignore the blood on the hands of countless others. 'God dammit I've been shaking hands with murderers all my life and if I'm not to be allowed to do that now I'll have bloody few left to shake hands with' (1953: 153). It was 'the Black and Tans', he argues, who legitimated torture as a tool of twentieth-century politics. 'If that's not murder what is? ... Oh there won't be much shaking hands after all this if we don't shake hands with murderers' (1953: 153). The business of war, like the business of politics, had been bloody for a long time; what mattered to Johnston was making the postwar world less so.

And yet Johnston's reluctance to condemn Nazi leaders like Göring goes beyond this. From a postwar perspective, Johnston appears to have chosen to ignore clear signs of the genocidal violence of the Nazi regime. Indeed, one of the remarkable things about his memoirs is their willingness to document the less creditable stages of his slow awakening to the extent and severity of Nazi persecutions of Jews and others. Partly, this slowness is sign of a more general scepticism of atrocity stories (1953: 114–16); partly, as previously mentioned, it reflects a fear for the postwar fate of Germany and its citizens (1953: 320). But these lenses of scepticism and apprehension blind Johnston even to incontrovertible evidence. On his first trip to a liberated concentration camp in France, for example, he observes 'the alleged torture chamber, gassing room, and cremation oven, all of which showed no signs whatever of having been used for such purposes' (342). Johnston rejects the offer, by a British captain accompanying him, to see the pickled evidence of Nazi experimentation on the bodies of prisoners, on the grounds that 'it wouldn't prove anything' (342). The real mental obstacle for Johnston, however, is that evidence of such crimes would contradict the powerful emotional bias he has in favour of the German people:

> I certainly don't want to have it proved that the human race is different from my own experience of it. Hitler tells us that the Jews are monsters, and I don't believe him. Nor do I believe you when you try to prove that the Germans are monsters. I've met Germans. (342)

Although Johnston here claims not to believe Hitler's anti-Semitic ideology, a pair of statements in his journals indicates that his attitudes towards Jews were complex and not entirely positive. On a visit to Austria in summer 1938, following the *Anschluss*, he records, in his diary, his alarm at the abundance of swastikas and copies of *Mein Kampf*, and states plainly his distaste for Nazism: 'it is all a lie this thing. The anti-Jewish myth is a lie.' Yet his entry continues:

> I don't like Jews in the mass myself. Individuals are different . . . [T]oo many Jews can create a problem that must be faced. They are so damned defensive and exclusive. Still – because we may not be able to stomach a ghetto around the corner, it does not make it any the less monstrous to invent a race-myth that drives me to persecute Einstein and Freud. (qtd in Adams 2002: 180)

The depersonalising language of distaste through which Johnston communicates his feelings about Jews ('in the mass', 'stomach') is complicated by a logic of the particular over the general. Johnston's distrust of Jews and his dislike of their repression operate along inverted axes: he likes individual Jews but dislikes Jewish collectivities; he reserves the right to personal prejudice against Jewish ghettos, while disliking society-wide religious and cultural persecution. In both cases, the personal, individual and local trump the collective and general; private anti-Semitism is acceptable even if a pogrom is not. If such a position is not necessarily incoherent, it takes a measure of self-deception for Johnston to ignore the connections between personal and society-wide forms of intolerance. If large-scale persecution of an ethnic group requires the spark of a particular demagogue, it also needs the fuel of a public comfortable in their prejudices.

An even uglier side of Johnston's complicated attitude towards the Jewish community emerges in his wartime journals on a visit to Jerusalem in September 1942. He arrived in Palestine in the hopes of arranging a BBC recording on board a Liberator bomber raid over North Africa but delays drew out his stay by weeks. His entry for 17 September notes:

> Tormented by itch in blood & very hot. Morning – breakfast on nice balcony but more ants, & woman shaking dirty rags from balcony above. Intolerable Jews – the scum of Europe – Arabs at least decently open about their dirt. [. . .] No more Jewish Paradise for me. (1942a: 17 September)

It is difficult to know what to make of this vicious, isolated outburst. Johnston does not tend to take this tone while speaking about Jews, although his journal does not often speak of them either individually or collectively; they are, in fact, conspicuous by their absence. A charitable reading of this passage would note that, given Johnston's acerbic sense of humour, it is conceivable that he is here parroting Nazi anti-Semitism in ironic form. Seen less charitably, this entry captures a moment in which the casual anti-Semitism at play in his comments made in Austria following the *Anschluss* – an ethnic discomfort Johnston freely admits, in order to position it in distinction to persecutorial hatred – flares up in a moment of frustration and ill temper. However he might keep this discomfort under wraps, it is difficult not to connect Johnston's mistrust of Jews 'in the mass', as he put it in 1938, with his reluctance to believe Germany capable of murderous repression once the war had begun in earnest. If Johnston were predisposed to doubt the intentions of a persecuted minority – one he saw as 'damned defensive and exclusive' – this might lend further weight to his existing biases in favour of Germany and the Germans.

In this, Johnston was not unlike a great many individuals within the BBC and the British public; such subtle, sub-surface assessments of the veracity of Jewish claims about the unfolding Holocaust would condition the troubling, indeed baffling, incongruity between what was known, and what was believed, during the war. In recent decades, scholarship on Britain's relationship to the Holocaust has begun to clarify the complex reasons why British politicians, intellectuals and citizens in general could not, or did not, understand the scale of anti-Jewish persecution in Europe, even once evidence had become freely available.[23] In the broader context of the British press, David Cesarani has documented the plentiful evidence of Jewish persecution provided by newspapers including the *Jewish Chronicle* from 1941 onward, much of which was picked up by mainstream newspapers including the *Daily Telegraph* and *The Times* (Cesarani 1996: 606–7). Arthur Koestler's 1943 novel *Arrival and Departure* took as a given the mass murder of Jews, and was greeted with charges of atrocity propaganda when a representative portion was excerpted in *Horizon* that year (Plain 2013: 67–71). Within the BBC itself, Jean Seaton notes, there was a similar surfeit of information; many of the national desks within the BBC's European Service – that is, internal departments directing broadcasts in European languages to European audiences – had access to ample firsthand accounts of Jewish persecution, resistance and extermination from 1942 onward. Nor was this news suppressed, at least in BBC broadcasts to the Continent; in February 1941, Director-General Frederick Ogilvie wrote to the head of the Polish and German service asking for 'constant reiteration of atrocity stories in Poland, without exaggeration and with full statistics' (qtd in Seaton 1987: 164).

Although persecutorial practices including summary executions, ghettoisation and labour camps were clearly documented, genocide was a harder reality to grasp. The Nazis adopted a policy of outright Jewish extermination at the Wansee conference in January 1942, but Allied officials did not confirm this information until some months later. On 17 December 1942, eleven Allied nations signed a Declaration on the Persecution of the Jews, which acknowledged the mounting evidence of systematic murder and pledged to punish Germany for its crimes. And yet, despite a brief flurry of news coverage and public statements about the accelerating atrocities in winter 1942–3, the British public remained strangely unmoved for the bulk of the war. Ian McLaine surmises that news organisations – including the BBC – balked at the scale of the slaughter: 'the language of hate was too exhausted to describe the enormity of what had been done in occupied Europe when it became known' (1979: 166). McLaine acknowledges, however, that the MoI sought to play down the particularity of Jewish suffering, for fear that it might stoke anti-Semitism in Britain (1979: 166–8).

Exhaustion by atrocity and fears of anti-Semitism explain only part of the resistance, by the BBC and other news outlets, to clearly delineating the horrors unfolding in Europe. For Tony Kushner, the story of British understanding of the extermination of Jews can be grasped only in terms of the expectations that framed the delivery and reception of information. There was, in the first instance, a widespread resistance to the horror stories emerging from Europe because they echoed and often outdid the atrocity propaganda fabricated during the First World War. Furthermore, early official reports described concentration camps as prisons rather than death camps, which, when combined with collective scepticism, continued to condition public understanding, even once the picture of Nazi policies became clearer. This twofold conditioning compounded a liberal humanist tendency, widely shared among broadcasting officials, journalists and intellectuals, to avoid singling out the Jews, even as evidence mounted of their particular persecution (Kushner 1994a: 250–4). Similarly, for Seaton, the combination of anti-propagandistic thinking, resistance to atrocity stories, collective disinclination to believe the enormity of the crimes and a lack of centralised news sharing meant that while all of the necessary information was available from December 1942 onwards, the BBC as a whole failed to recognise and publicise the extent of the Holocaust (1987: 167). Collectively, the very attitudes of moderation, caution and sobriety that subtended the self-image of the BBC and the larger British population in the interwar period worked to ensure that even if information about the Holocaust was freely available, it was not internalised and processed in such a way as to mobilise public sentiment, much less prevent further bloodshed.

This intricate network of moderation meant that even front-line reporters like Johnston and Dimbleby, once they became witnesses to the camps, expressed disbelief at their own ignorance of the situation. Dimbleby reported that he had been left unprepared for Bergen-Belsen: 'no one even hinted at what I was to see' (qtd in Seaton 1987: 157). This resulted, for those confronted with first-hand evidence of the massacre of Jews, in a sense of one's own failure to conceive of a tragedy in time: a kind of second-hand trauma. Dominick LaCapra has noted that mass atrocities such as the Holocaust can produce effects less visceral, but still profound, for those who witness but do not endure suffering first-hand:

> Especially for victims, trauma brings about a lapse or rupture in memory that breaks continuity with the past, thereby placing identity in question to the point of shattering it. But it may raise problems of identity for others insofar as it unsettles narcissistic investments and desired self-images, including – especially with respect to the Shoah – the image of Western civilization itself as the bastion of elevated values if not the high point in the evolution of humanity. (LaCapra 1988: 9)

Or in Johnston's words, 'All I ever believed or hoped is buggered up' (1945–61: 16 April 1945). The camps seemed, in the words of one British survivor, 'absolutely out of the world. Everything which happened here was without relation to anything which had ever happened before.'[24] For many witnesses to the camps – prisoners, liberators, civilians who lived nearby, listeners at home – the easiest thing was to relegate their disruptive effect to the realm of the unimaginable or otherworldly.

While this response to the camps is entirely understandable – it is hard to imagine how one might begin to process the collapse of an entire belief system founded on Enlightenment rationality – Johnston, like many other reporters and officials within the BBC, turned quickly away from the camps and towards the project of winding down the war and seeking to rebuild afterwards. Indeed, even in those broadcasts that focus on the camps, there is little emphasis on the fact that most of the victims were Jewish; while mention of Jewish victims did make it into the hundreds of home-front news broadcasts made in the final months of the war, none of the texts that treat the camps in the published version of *War Report* mentions Jewish suffering specifically.[25] Again, as Tony Kushner notes, this erasure of the particular plight of the Jews is attributable to wariness about singling out one ethnic group, out of fear that special attention might inflame resentment among anti-Semitic Britons:

Government passivity due to its lack of faith in the British public, but also the dominance of a monocultural liberal ideology across state and society, ensured that there was little conception of the reality of the Final Solution, let alone an understanding of the impact of the Holocaust on European Jewry as the war came to an end. (Kushner 1994a: 258)

In retrospect, however, such an omission by the BBC looks like a willing ignorance of the aims and effects of the Holocaust.

The facts of narrative proliferation

Denis Johnston's commitment to describing the war as he saw it, with as little distortion and mediation as possible, meant that he had to find some way of representing the sights that had transformed his understanding of the war; hence the brief, but vivid, portions from his journals and memoirs that deal with Buchenwald. This lucid encounter with the camps, however, undermined the precarious aesthetic of neutrality that had brought him to that phase of the war. Whether his failure to broadcast from Buchenwald reflects a belief that the airwaves were already saturated with news of the atrocity, or an unwillingness to confront, on air, the limitations of those values he had cleaved to as a journalist and liberal intellectual, Johnston now faced a problem: how to atone for the failure of an ideology of journalistic and political neutrality, without moving towards a punitive future for Germany and her millions of citizens. In the end, Johnston chose not to choose.

The 'War Field Books' indicate that, on 4 May 1945, Johnston accompanied American forces from the Western European campaign as they moved from Innsbruck up the Brenner Pass, on the border between Italy and Austria; there they planned to meet their Allies from the Italian campaign. The closing chapters of *Nine Rivers from Jordan* contain two different versions of this scene, along with two different, but equally dramatic and stylised, scenes of judgement and penance. In one version of the book's closing act, Johnston encounters a wounded senior Nazi official named Otto Suder in a car parked at the Brenner. Following a long conversation in which Suder defends the actions of the Nazis while Johnston equivocates about the justness of the retributive violence he felt was sure to follow the conclusion of the war, Johnston passes him the gun he had picked up at Buchenwald, thinking that Suder has no option but to commit suicide. Instead, Suder turns the weapon on Johnston and pulls the trigger, killing him. The moral lesson of this version is clear: having taken up arms in violation of the ethical and legal conventions governing impartial observers, Johnston endures a physical death to parallel the moral death attendant on his abandonment of neutrality. 'A Cato untroubled by scruples might have come through unscathed,' he notes following the scene of his death, 'but that is not what I happened to be, any more than the community from which I came' (1953: 439). While the 'community' in question refers first and foremost to the profession of war reporting, a profession whose sober objectivity had proven inadequate to the task of capturing the war, it resonates also with Johnston's status as citizen of a nation officially neutral but friendly to the Allies. For neither community was total neutrality an ethical framework commensurate with the demands the war placed on its observers.

Soon after his symbolic death on the Brenner, however, Johnston directly confronts the metatextual conundrum posed by the death of the author: 'Or would you prefer a different ending?' he asks the reader (1953: 441). In this other version, Johnston passes by the car in which resides, an army public relations officer tells him, the body of a Nazi official – presumably Otto Suder – who has killed himself once he realised he could not cross from Italy to Austria. Johnston chooses not to investigate, and (again, presumably, for this is not narrated to us) returns to Ireland to draft the work we are reading. Between the two versions, however, comes 'The Canon of an Unknown Mass', a fifteen-page dramatisation of a liturgical service in which Johnston, as an 'Acolyte' accompanied by the commentary of a choric 'Antiphon', contemplates his death at the hands of Suder and contends with the complex feelings of simultaneous complicity and powerlessness produced by his involvement in the war. Much of the weight of this scene comes to rest on Johnston's relationship to the Christian God, who appears in the Canon as 'A Voice out of the Silence' and with whom Johnston struggles to reconcile himself. 'Since I have helped to slay the monster that made Buchenwald,' he asks himself, 'How can I serve a God who has made Hell?' (1953: 445). The answer, for Johnston, is learning to denounce the cruelties of an unknowable God, in order that he might forgive them. As the Voice tells him: 'You must first accuse the Lord / Before he will lend his ear. / Speak up, therefore, and confess my sins' (1953: 448). Only when he can forgive a deity capable of atrocities does Johnston achieve the kind of human compassion that can acknowledge the evil of the Holocaust without seeking retributive judgement against Germany. Once Johnston has committed to a belief in a God whose actions appear as inexplicably evil as those of mortals, the Voice commands him:

Fight your own sins wherever you may find them.
Outboast the vain, despise the proud,

Neglect the slothful, and rage at the angry.
These are your own transgressions
And Pity is the Soldier's way to absolution.
But, here is my command.
Avenge all others' sins on me, as you have done this day,
And leave the human race in peace. (1953: 454)

Thus commanded to abstain from judgement of the human race, and to indulge only in pity, Johnston throws his pistol down from the altar.[26] The act is an expression of hope: having tasted of the fruit of the knowledge of good and evil, and having been tempted to judge entire nations for the crimes committed in their names, Johnston moves towards an apparently ideal state of moral knowledge without moral judgement. It is perhaps unexpected, given Johnston's insistence elsewhere in the text on his religious doubts, that he would turn to faith of this kind as a way of resolving the horrors of the Holocaust. But as Gene Barnett points out, the renunciation of vengeance aligns Johnston's persona in *Nine Rivers* with many of his other protagonists, for whom the suspension of vindictive ethics is the only way to sustain community cohesion (1978: 122–3). If the turn towards a particularly Christian faith is unexpected, then, it does provide a theological framework for Johnston's longstanding commitment to an ethics of pity in which judgement is suspended.

Clair Wills, in a concise reading of *Nine Rivers from Jordan* that highlights the connections between Johnston's neutrality and that of Ireland, captures a further difficulty of the work's ending: namely, the question of its formal and stylistic effectiveness. 'The awkwardness of the contrivance', she notes, 'reveals the depths of Johnston's dilemma. Unable to resolve the conundrum of neutrality, atrocity, guilt and moral engagement, he leaves us with a fragmented tale, with a nightmare vision of the split self' (2007: 407). If it is true that the ending of *Nine Rivers* denies the reader a simple resolution to the sprawling narrative, it is also true that the metafictional turn of the work does more than simply leave the reader with a heap of fragments from which to attempt to construe meaning. On a thematic level, it enables the symbolic death of the paragon of neutrality who had, up until then, driven the narrative, and affords the opportunity for a psychic healing such as might be necessary for any number of disillusioned liberal humanists in the wake of the Second World War. But beyond such thematic and symbolic resolutions, the ending of *Nine Rivers* serves as a formal self-performance as text; it shows up its radiogenic subject matter – the facts, objectively told – as incapable of the kinds of branching, self-contradictory, multiple truths of which print is capable, however tenuously. Julian Murphet, in *Multimedia Modernism*, argues that such self-assertions of the formal potential of print media – the manifestations of textual experiment that we call 'modernism' – are the symptoms of the dense and jostling media ecology of the early twentieth century (2009: 10–14). The logic of mechanical reproduction that arose in the wake of the second industrial revolution forced a *convergence* among media (an environment of intermediality) that prompted a compensatory and symptomatic *differentiation* between media (characterised by specialisation and a renewed investment in formal distinctions) (Murphet 2009: 20–1). The investment in multiple forms of textuality on display in *Nine Rivers from Jordan* can therefore be read as a late modernist echo of earlier writers' efforts to foreground the specific traits of their medium within a competitive media ecology. These traits include the non-decision between alternate versions of narrative 'truth'; like the formal capaciousness of Johnston's text itself, with its Canons, drama, dialogues, broadcasts, memos and snippets of song, its ability to suspend narrative resolution between two mutually contradictory endings suggests that print enjoys a flexibility that radio had not, up to that point, explored sufficiently.

This is not to say that radio, or indeed any medium, could never explore the kind of multigeneric, multiformal, narrative open-endedness that *Nine Rivers from Jordan* enjoys. But Johnston's wartime experience with the medium of radio had been constrained by a resistance to just that kind of narrative and formal proliferation; just as attempts by censors and administrators to condense accounts of the war into a single ideological wavelength had resulted in Johnston quashing his more sympathetic portraits of German citizens and soldiers, so too had those constraints made it difficult to tell the multiple, contradictory truths of the war. If he could not use the medium of radio to channel the war's perplexing surfeit of facts, 'none of them strictly true', he would do so through print (1953: 111).

The proliferation of interpretations of the war would go on to haunt Johnston, and would result in multiple rewritings and revisions of his experiences in the decades following the war. Indeed, in his later writings, he reveals that the dual ending of *Nine Rivers* was not simply a symbolic or metatextual game, but the result of his conviction that he had, on some level, experienced both versions of the event. In his 'Correction' to the 'War Field Books', which is undated but probably originated at some point between 1947 and 1956, Johnston claims that he recalls two journeys up the Brenner Pass.[27] In what he calls a 'purely factual' problem, Johnston struggles with a sharp sense that his memories of the Brenner Pass are the result of a blending between two versions of the journey, one real and the other 'a dream of some sort (although a damn queer one in that I feel perfectly well acquainted with the FACTS therein, although I cannot remember any of them visually)' (Johnston [n.d.]). Johnston would pursue this conviction that he had experienced the same events twice in a much later volume, *The Brazen Horn* (published privately in 1968 and again, in a limited edition of 1,050 copies, in 1976). 'Any investigation of what actually occurred in my vicinity on the evening and the following morning of 3/4 May 1945 will confirm that there is not too little information, but too much,' he writes (1976: 4). Johnston appeals to contemporary physics, and its theories of multiple simultaneous presents, in an attempt to resolve his own experience of plurality. Although a full assessment of *The Brazen Horn* is beyond the scope of this chapter, it is enough to note that the results of Johnston's forays into the science and philosophy of time are decidedly mixed; the book comes across as something of a vanity project. However, his commitment to finding a framework through which to understand, and even celebrate, the proliferation of multiple existential narratives testifies to his investment in the plurality of meanings that can be extracted from an experience.

In documenting his experience as a war correspondent, Johnston had set out to thumb his nose at those arbiters of fact – military censors, BBC officials and propagandists – who sought to channel the complex and contradictory nature of the war into a single, easily grasped narrative of right and wrong, good and evil, truth and falsehood. Instead, his memoirs were to allow the war to speak to audiences in its full complexity. Johnston's experiences as a witness to the conflict and its aftermath, however, pointed to a reality at once lopsided and nuanced, in which a single, vast horror – the persecution and attempted extermination of the Jews in Europe – coexisted with evidence of guilt and innocence of varying degrees among combatants on both sides, including those, like Johnston himself, who wished to brand themselves as neutrals. The promise of facticity held out by the 'sound pictures' of front-line radio reporting proved insufficient to the task of accurately representing a conflict with so many versions of meaningful, actionable reality. In the end, Johnston returned to the written word, not as some vehicle for a monolithic truth, but as a medium capable of sustaining the plurality, the contradictions and the revisions necessary for the capture of one man's experience of the war.

Notes

1. Johnston's *The Brazen Horn* (1976: 2–3) also relates this anecdote, with slight differences and some omissions.

2. Johnston's journal-keeping was extensive; his output included pocket notebooks, daily diaries, scrapbooks and 'Omnibus' journals, the latter of which fill in missing details and add a retrospective gloss to the more immediate impressions of the daily entries. For an overview of the assemblage of life writing that constitutes what Johnston called his 'Record', see Adams (2002: x–xii). References to 'journals' and 'diaries' throughout this chapter, unless otherwise stated, refer to the 'War Field Books'.
3. *Nine Rivers from Jordan* foregrounds its own temporal and factual slipperiness: at one point, Johnston quotes from a letter, ostensibly written by a friend pseudonymised as Yourman, which claims that Johnston's published memoirs are not wholly reliable: 'In his statements of fact he is substantially accurate, except that events and conversations did not necessarily occur in the manner in which he describes them. He constantly condenses three or four interviews into one, and even three or four characters into one, alleging that the literal truth usually conveys a lie, and that the only way to paint an honest picture in the round, is to "produce" it by filling in the background, and maybe by adding things that have occurred on other occasions' (Johnston 1953: 294). The clearest statements of Johnston's revisions, however, appear in the memoir's first version, *Dionysia*, and in his 'Correction' to the War Field Books. In the latter, he states plainly that he conflated certain events for reasons of narrative efficiency (Johnston [n.d.], MS 3751).
4. While occasional references will be made to divergences between *Dionysia* and *Nine Rivers from Jordan*, the emphasis in this chapter will be on the Verschoyle edition of *Nine Rivers*. An American edition, published by Little, Brown in 1955, lacks the final chapters of the British edition, an omission that Johnston resisted and subsequent scholars have found deprives the conclusion of much of its force and complexity (Barnett 1978: 120–1; Adams 2002: 311).
5. For an account of Johnston's contributions to the Northern Ireland Region of the BBC, see Cathcart (1984: 81–4, 115–22).
6. As with the Regional services, it was feared that the particular and localisable signal of the television mast at Alexandra Palace could provide a useful point of orientation for approaching German bombers, a technique called 'meaconing' (Adams 2002: 195–6; Briggs 1970: 72).
7. Johnston's cross-appointment, which saw him moving frequently between Belfast, Dublin, Manchester and occasionally London, caused no small amount of confusion among his superiors and colleagues, who were uncertain as to whom he ultimately answered (L1/225/1).
8. Clair Wills (2007: 180–219) gives a comprehensive overview of radio (neutral, Axis and Allied) over wartime Ireland. For Johnston's specific role in sounding Irish attitudes to BBC broadcasts, see especially pp. 195–8.
9. For an overview of changes to the news-gathering operations of the BBC, see Nicholas (1996: 196–221) and Hawkins ([1946] 2014: 22–6).
10. Some of Johnston's dispatches are preserved at the British Library's National Sound Archive and at the Imperial War Museum (IWM), including his Churchill interview.
11. These efforts to secure recordings in the field were not always matched, or believed, by their Axis competitors. In *Nine Rivers from Jordan*, Johnston

recalls meeting a former Italian propagandist in Rome in 1944, who presumed the BBC's actuality recordings had been faked in a studio and who remarked that 'sometimes he had felt that the BBC timed their effects very badly' (1953: 252–3).
12. There is some indication in *Nine Rivers from Jordan* that Johnston found the Riverside Portable difficult to use, but it is unclear whether he continued to use the Type C or ultimately adopted the Riverside (1953: 302).
13. As fruitful as Bolter and Grusin's conceptual framework is, it is worth noting, as they themselves do (2001: 14), that virtually all of their media examples – Renaissance painting, photography, film, television and computer graphics – are visual. Even their frequent replacement of 'immediacy' with the term 'transparency' betrays the visual bias of their work.
14. On the reluctance of BBC News and propaganda services to engage in 'deliberate perversions of the truth', see Briggs (1970: 6–7) and Robert Calder (2004: 43–4, 206).
15. On 'Lili Marleen' (the spelling of which varies), see Baade (2012: 162–3). Johnston makes an appearance in a 1944 GPO propaganda film called *The True Story of Lilli Marlene*.
16. Piette (1995: 29–38) and Rawlinson (2000: 119–38) offer insightful analyses of this moment of recognition during the war in North Africa, as Allied writers including Keith Douglas and Dan Davin encountered the corpses, possessions and other material traces of their Axis adversaries.
17. 'Convention Relative to the Treatment of Prisoners of War' (Geneva, 1929), Part VII, Art. 1–3, 81; 'Convention (IV) Respecting the Laws and Customs of War on Land' (The Hague, 1907), 'Annex', Art 1–3.
18. In addition to its general connotations of moral compromise, Johnston's use of the pseudonym 'Faustus' may be intended to resonate with *Doktor Faustus*, the 1947 novel by German author (and broadcaster) Thomas Mann, who was exiled by the Nazis for the duration of the war. But another reason suggests itself: at this stage of *Nine Rivers from Jordan*, Johnston has just visited the concentration camp at Buchenwald, for which the Nazis had cleared a beech forest (the literal translation of 'Buchenwald') once frequented by Johann Wilhelm von Goethe and his close companion Charlotte von Stein. At the centre of the camp, the Nazis left standing a single oak tree, under which (according to legend) Goethe had written the 'Walpurgisnacht' section of his own *Faust* (1808). Now reduced to a stump, this tree is still known as the 'Goethe Oak', and has appeared in Alain Resnais's *Night and Fog* ([1955] 2003) and in a BBC 3 radio feature by Christopher Cook entitled *Goethe's Oak* (2011). Though he does not make this chain of signification explicit, Johnston's embrace of the morally compromised Faustus as his avatar in the wake of a visit to Buchenwald indicates that he saw himself as enmeshed in similarly fraught ethical exchanges.
19. Both of these exclamations translate as appeals for Johnston's longevity; *hoch* is an abbreviated form of the German *hoch lebe* ('long life'), while *viva* means 'live' in Italian (*OED*).
20. Indeed, in a sign that he was listening to the war with the ears of a broadcaster, Johnston remarks throughout *Nine Rivers from Jordan* as much on the persistence of sonic memories as on visual ones. Popular songs and

soldiers' slang pepper the text; Johnston becomes attuned to the sounds of mortar fire, shelling and small arms; philosophical exchanges are presented as dialogues rather than excursus. Most fundamental to the text, we can hear in the liturgical framework of *Nine Rivers* an attention to how sound can structure ceremony. For example, in the 'Canon of an unknown Mass' that comes near the end of the book, Johnston describes a scene in which, 'in the silence of final things, all the overtones of the past can be heard without distraction'; in this setting, the Antiphon sings out prominent sonic memories from Johnston's journey through Jordan, Italy and Ireland: 'The voice of a Muezzin in Azrak, / The High, clear note of a lark at Assisi, / The bell of a church in Dungannon' (1953: 446).

21. Winston Burdett was a CBS journalist (and secret communist) who worked alongside Edward R. Murrow. When Majdanek camp, near Lublin, Poland, was liberated by the Soviets in July 1944, vast piles of shoes taken from several hundred thousand dead prisoners provided British readers with their first images of what would become an iconic means of quantifying the seemingly incomprehensible loss of life of the Holocaust (Kushner 1994b: 138).
22. There is a similar gap in Johnston's dispatches in the available records at the IWM, the Johnston papers at Trinity College Dublin and correspondence at the BBC WAC.
23. Tony Kushner (1994a and 1994b), David Cesarani (1996), Walter Laqueur (1980) and Jean Seaton (1987), among others, have contributed important insights into this seeming paradox. McLaine (1979) provides valuable documentation of the perspective on Jewish persecution in Europe, and anti-Semitism in Britain, from within the wartime MoI.
24. Captain C. A. G. Burney, a prisoner at Buchenwald, interviewed by Robert Reid, April 1945, qtd in Hawkins ([1946] 2014: 447).
25. In one example of the overt recognition of Jewish suffering on the air, a Home News Bulletin dated 27 April 1945 about the report of a Parliamentary Delegation to Buchenwald notes that Jews were the victims of 'scientific experiments' in the camp, and describes artefacts made of human skin (Films 5/6).
26. While the 'Canon' is obviously a fantastic scene, Johnston maintains in a later work, *The Brazen Horn*, that he discarded his Luger in the Alps in a symbolic renunciation of violence, although he later went back and collected the weapon (1976: 207, 212). The anecdote that opens the present chapter presumably refers to this discarded and recovered weapon.
27. This 'Correction' appears between his final wartime entry of 21 May 1945 and the circa-1956 anecdote about the return of his pistol in the Belfast BBC studio; in the 'Correction', he mentions already having completed *Dionysia*, which would mean it dates from 1947 or later.

Chapter 5

Calling the West Indies:
Una Marson's Wireless Black Atlantic

If questions of propaganda, politics and national identity proved troubling to writers who broadcast to domestic and American audiences, they were even more vexing for those writers of colonial extraction who were tasked with representing Britain and its objectives to the imperial periphery. As an agency charged with projecting a positive image of Britain to its colonies and allies abroad, the Overseas Service had little time for dissenting views of the Empire. And yet, as with the Home Service, administrators and producers at the Overseas Service recognised that in the context of total war and significant civilian sacrifice, programming would need to reflect the communities it was intended to reach. As it grew in size and importance over the course of the war, the Overseas Service therefore engaged its international audience in a complex and contradictory act of cultural *rapprochement.* It engaged broadcasters of colonial origin who understood first-hand the experience of listening in to the metropole from its periphery. As nationalists of varying degrees of commitment, these writers had to contend with the fact that the BBC was, first and foremost, an agent of imperial diffusion. The story of their participation in Second World War broadcasting, however, indicates that the need of the state to propagandise to its subjects could yield consequences unintended by official institutions of communication and persuasion. In handing the microphone to late imperial writers, the BBC opened the airwaves to coded articulations of political and cultural autonomy.

Though these writers participated with reservations, many recognised that the war offered opportunities for shaping political and cultural debate both at the point of reception and at the point of transmission. Focusing on *Calling the West Indies* (1941–5), a programme hosted by Jamaican activist and poet Una Marson, this chapter examines the ways in which the imperial networks of the BBC offered colonial writers a means of voicing previously unrepresented identities that ranged from the regional to the transnational. Marson offers a productive case study because of the dedication with which she approached the task of representing West Indian and diasporic black experiences at the BBC.[1] Through her promotion of black poetry, music, journalism and activism from multiple continents, Marson helped to forge a wireless black Atlantic that connected West Indian listeners to a global network of cultural production and activism. Like the diasporic writers on whom Paul Gilroy focuses in *The Black Atlantic*, Marson and her fellow broadcasters found in *Calling the West Indies* a means of 'crossing borders in modern machines that were themselves micro-systems of linguistic and political hybridity' (1993: 12). The chronotope of the ship to which Gilroy's quotation refers – a central emblem, in *The Black Atlantic*, of the transatlantic flow of bodies, goods, texts and ideas – finds its midcentury echo in the shortwave radio beam. Like the ship, shortwave radio served as a vehicle of both domination and resistance.[2] In harnessing this ambivalent technology, Marson and the intellectuals she gathered together shaped wartime and postwar discussions about poetry, politics and transnational solidarity.

Gilroy's reorientation of black history and poetics away from strict national boundaries and towards more dynamic processes of oceanic migration offers important insights into the work of Marson and her collaborators. As late imperial subjects, West Indians did not have recourse to a single stable national identity; rather, their identities were elaborated between their Caribbean origins and the diffuse and abstract Empire to which they were expected to show fealty. The legacy of slavery, however, grants a different inheritance – a diasporic one rooted in the historical violence of the slave trade and sustained by subsequent migrations of black populations to and from major centres in the Americas, Europe and Africa. As a West Indian intellectual living in London and connected to cultural and political circles on all of those continents, Marson was well positioned to use the wireless as a means of articulating a new identity for the West Indies, one that did not operate on a bilateral axis of metropole and colony, but instead opened up to include aspects of racialised experience drawn from North American and African culture and history.

For all of her achievements at the wartime BBC, Marson has been marginalised in studies of West Indian transmissions in favour of a focus on postwar broadcasters. In separate accounts, John Figueroa (1966–70: vol. 1, xiv), George Lamming ([1960] 1984: 65–6) and Edward Kamau Brathwaite (1984: 87) have all cited the importance of hearing West Indian poetry over the airwaves from the 1940s into the 1950s. Perhaps most influentially, Brathwaite emphasises the role of the BBC's West

Indian programming in the international promotion of what he calls the 'nation languages' of Caribbean poetry, the varieties of non-'standard' English developed following colonisation (1984: 5–6, 87). However, Brathwaite – like Figueroa and Lamming – focuses on *Caribbean Voices* (1945–58), the successor programme to *Calling the West Indies*, and on the efforts of long-time producer Henry Swanzy. Under the Anglo-Irish Swanzy's direction, *Caribbean Voices* introduced listeners to such talents as Sam Selvon, George Lamming, V. S. Naipaul and Brathwaite himself. The programme was so influential that Figueroa borrowed its name for the title of the first major anthology of Caribbean verse. More recently, scholars including Peter Kalliney, Laurence Breiner and Glyne Griffith have contributed valuable analyses of *Caribbean Voices* and its role in the formation of a Caribbean literary community and even a particular Caribbean aesthetic. In Kalliney's words, 'Metropolitan cultural institutions designed to consolidate imperialism . . . became modes of anti-imperialist cultural production through the incorporation of late colonial intellectuals partial to modernist aesthetics but also resentful of metropolitan political dominance' (2013: 5; see also 116–45). Programmes like *Caribbean Voices* therefore served, during the final years of the British Empire, as sources of both institutional validation and cultural incubation.

This postwar focus, however, has had the unfortunate effect of minimising Marson's wartime role in building networks of communication between geographically dispersed black populations. The relative lack of attention to *Calling the West Indies* may reflect anxieties about Marson; her poetic works are difficult to assimilate into postwar constructions of the radical Caribbean literary tradition. Furthermore, Marson's tenure at the BBC was clouded by conflicts with performers and staff. Some of these conflicts were of her own making, but at least some of them were caused by resentment that a black West Indian woman might achieve Marson's position of power and influence. These conflicts took their toll: after repeated stress leaves, Marson was institutionalised for mental illness in January 1946. Upon her release in October that year, she returned to Jamaica. She did not broadcast for the BBC again.

Beyond such questions of marginalisation, the postwar emphasis of Caribbean radio scholarship also obscures the global conflict that catalysed the growth of broadcasting services for West Indian men and women both in Britain and in the Americas. The context of total war demanded that the British government secure the cooperation of all subjects, both at home and abroad. Though unwilling to grant political concessions at the time, the British government came to realise the importance of representing West Indian subjects on the radio in order to shore up support for the war effort. Under wartime censorship and propaganda directives, Caribbean broadcasting could not be entirely revolutionary; indeed, many of Marson's contributors genuflect to Britain, a gesture that fits awkwardly with the established postwar canon of anti- or postcolonial literature from the region. As *Calling the West Indies* developed, however, it enabled the projection of colonial identities distinct from Anglocentric versions of British identity; combined with the intimate and polysemic aural registers of radio, this projection fostered new forms of cultural expression for West Indian artists. Marson's programme forged connections among anti-racist and anti-imperial intellectuals from the West Indies, America and Britain; it encouraged the establishment of a West Indian literary tradition by praising poets past and present; and it began, slowly, to recognise and celebrate the particular linguistic heritage of the West Indies by broadcasting 'nation language' literature in the form of folk tales and poems. By representing aspects of identity beyond the binary of mother country and colony, *Calling the West Indies* contributed to the formation of post-imperial communities of belonging at regional, national and transnational levels.

Projecting the Empire to the West Indies

Over the course of the 1930s, major European nations had matched their increasing belligerence with an expansion of international broadcast networks designed to further their political and ideological interests. Yet despite reports of increasingly effective German and Italian broadcasts to British territories, the British government was slow to expand the overseas role of the BBC. An Empire Service had been provisionally operational since 1932, but it had only limited funding and no guarantee of long-term operation. Finally, the Ullswater Committee – established in 1935 to consider the renewal of the BBC charter in 1936 – recommended that the Empire Service be officially enshrined in a new charter, with a commensurate rise in operational funds. As the war of words continued to build over the course of the late 1930s, much of the attention and funding for international broadcasting was directed towards propaganda broadcasts in languages other than English, in order to compete with similar initiatives by Italy and Germany (Briggs 1965: 395; Briggs 1970: 18). The Empire Service was folded into the Overseas Service, which initially included broadcasts to the Continent as well, shortly after war broke out in 1939 (Potter 2012: 117–18). Within this increasingly polyglot environment, English-language broadcasts to

West Africa, the Caribbean, India and the Dominions still went out with the intention of reaffirming imperial ties.

Many late-colonial writers were reluctant to broadcast on behalf of the BBC because of the complicated signals such cooperation sent to listeners overseas. Writers were wary of a process of ideological slippage in which an anti-fascist position could be read as implicitly pro-Empire. In another branch of the Overseas Service, Indian nationalist and novelist Mulk Raj Anand resisted invitations for almost a year from both George Orwell and Sir Malcolm Darling, head of the India Section, to deliver broadcasts to the Subcontinent. In a letter to Darling in March 1941, Anand argued that broadcasting on behalf of the government that had imprisoned members of the Indian Congress party would enforce on him 'a kind of vague neutrality, the strain of which can be very harrowing for the more timid individual, who is torn between conflicting loyalties' (qtd in W. J. West 1985: 15). While English anti-imperialists like Orwell and E. M. Forster understood the injustice of the British Empire as a problem of moral hypocrisy, Anand foregrounded the disciplinary violence of imperialism and shied away from defending it. It was only when he realised the global ambitions of Germany and Japan that Anand felt he had no choice but to contribute to the British Empire's propaganda war. Anand's compromise captures the ambivalent power wartime broadcasting offered to British colonial subjects; forced to choose between principled non-involvement in the radio war and a vexed form of agency, many chose the latter.

The subtle process of give-and-take through which writers collaborated in order to participate in an anti-fascist war complicates narratives which present imperial broadcasting in binary terms, as a tool of either subjugation or revolution. Many accounts of mid-twentieth-century broadcasting figure networks like the BBC Overseas Service as invasive tentacles of Empire deliberately working against the political aspirations of colonised populations. Frantz Fanon, in 'This Is the Voice of Algeria' (from *A Dying Colonialism*, 1959), offers a characteristic assessment when he argues that before the emergence of pro-independence stations in the mid-1950s, Arab Algerians saw the radio set itself as 'a symbol of French presence'; so long as it was identified with French-operated Radio-Alger, the radio could only ever be 'a material representation of the colonial configuration' (1976: 73). This is not, as Fanon explains, a predetermined effect of the medium: under the right circumstances, radio can as easily become an agent of radical transformation as of colonial subjugation. Most often, radio manifests its transformative potential through illicit broadcasts operating outside the control of colonial powers, as in the revolutionary *Voice of Free Algeria* broadcasts that began emanating from Egypt in late 1956 (Fanon 1976: 82). With the advent of this new channel of radio resistance, listening in became a political act, 'not the adoption of a modern technique for getting news, but the obtaining of access to the only means of entering into communication with the Revolution, of living with it' (Fanon 1976: 83). Radio became a dissident channel through which revolutionary discourse could circulate and thereby link dispersed listeners.

In describing illicit listening as 'entering into communication with the Revolution', Fanon indicates the power of the radio public to instil a sense of communally generated meaning.[3] As Ian Baucom has argued, radio listening in such circumstances is not simply a passive acceptance of one group identity (free Algerian) over another (colonised subject). Rather, tuning in combines individual agency and group solidarity by giving each audience member a role in the constitution of a new public entity mediated through the wireless: though oriented around the radio as a common source of discourse, listening and interpretation remain individual actions that enable a collective politics (2001: 25). In an echo of Michael Warner's theory of the affiliative 'public', Baucom argues that Fanon's prototypical radio listeners 'assemble themselves as Algerians through their common, but discrete, consumption of a narrative of Algerianness, which, on consuming, they differentially reproduce' (2001: 27). More specifically, this mediated and communal self-recognition as 'Algerian' against a backdrop of colonial French occupation represents what Warner calls a 'counterpublic': a subordinate grouping whose formation and operation represent a challenge to the dominant discursive field (2002: 119). The illicit radio broadcast becomes a venue through which dissident listeners constitute themselves as distinct from the official publics imagined by colonial Algerian broadcasters.

Baucom and Fanon provide useful models for thinking about dissident listening practices, but their theories require some adaptation in the case of wartime broadcasts to the West Indies, where the interplay between official and alternative cultural formations was more nuanced. For one thing, the relationship between mother country and colony was very different to that in operation between France and Algeria; the West Indian territories, especially their politically and culturally engaged middle classes, had always considered themselves culturally aligned with the 'mother' country (Rush 2011: 1–8 and *passim*). This affective connection was partly due to the foreshortening of history by colonialism; the erasure of indigenous populations on the islands meant there was effectively no unitary pre-colonial tradition that could be drawn upon in order to build a narrative of nation-formation. As diverse islands brought together under the aegis of colonialism, the geographically far-flung and socio-culturally distinct West Indies did not have a particularly stable collective identity separate from the Empire itself (Rush 2011: 178). Furthermore, as each colony had its own administrative link to the mother country, political relations tended to operate directly between Britain and each individual territory, rather than multilaterally among the colonies themselves. The idea of an independent 'West Indies' was therefore a notion grounded in imperial history and articulated through imperial means.

For many years, the strong affective and administrative bonds linking individual colonies to the imperial metropole dampened the political will necessary for regional independence. Unlike Fanon's account of Algeria in the 1950s, there was no organised insurrection in the British West Indies in the lead-up to the Second World War. For much of the 1930s, however, the Caribbean colonies endured significant labour and class unrest connected to the larger global depression and to a pattern of social and economic neglect by Britain. The waves of rioting and protest, which reached a peak in 1937–8, were sufficiently disruptive to occasion a West Indian Royal Commission led by Lord Moyne (Walter Edward Guinness), which was tasked with proposing solutions to the economic and social troubles of the islands.[4] Such overtures could not undo the strains that had begun to appear in the fabric of British–West Indian relations. The breakdown of order in the Caribbean in the late 1930s was enough to disabuse many West Indian intellectuals and leaders of their residual faith in the ability of Britain to provide for its colonies (Schwarz 2003: 6). Because the geographical dispersal of the islands made coordination of an independence movement difficult, however, much of the work of building political alliances and networks took place among West Indian intellectuals who had moved to Britain, including George Padmore and C. L. R. James (Schwarz 2003: 7).

Woefully underdeveloped broadcasting resources in the Caribbean exacerbated the problem of inter-island communication and served as a metonym for British neglect of the West Indian colonies (Jarrett-Macaulay 1998: 146; E1/1294/1). There was little in the way of local, island-based radio, which meant that most transmissions received on the islands in the 1920s and 1930s came via shortwave from the United States or Britain. Even in London, where a growing number of intellectuals were based, broadcasting opportunities were limited; despite interest within the Corporation in providing the West Indies with programming that would reinforce ties to Britain, BBC broadcasts to the colonies had evolved haphazardly, largely due to underfunding. Initially, the West Indies had received broadcasts through the Empire Service, a generalised daily programme begun in 1932 and designed for transmission to the colonies and Dominions of Britain at staggered intervals throughout the day (Briggs 1965: 370–5). Though not entirely neglected, the Caribbean region was far from a high priority. The main targets of the Empire Service were the settler populations of the British colonies; little attention was paid to indigenous populations or (in the West Indies) those of African, South Asian or East Asian descent (Potter 2012: 111–12; Rush 2011: 154–5). Consequently, the BBC offered what might be characterised as an oblique listening experience in the Caribbean: listeners heard programming directed primarily at much larger audiences in Canada, while the vagaries of shortwave transmission through variable atmospheric conditions meant that West Indian listeners could also occasionally pick up broadcasts directed towards India (Briggs 1965: 375, 381, 387). Given the tensions caused by decades of socio-economic neglect, this lack of representation over the wireless made it difficult for many West Indians to imagine a meaningful role for themselves in the British Empire. The BBC, like the British government, seemed uninterested in acknowledging the concerns and culture of a region with a specific history of colonisation and creolisation.

The build-up to war precipitated growth and change in the Overseas Service. As the propaganda war with Germany accelerated in the late 1930s, international broadcasting hours increased from 16 hours a day in 1936 to 20.5 hours a day in 1943 (Briggs 1965: 392; Briggs 1970: 492). If the extension of overseas broadcasting succeeded in linking Britain and its colonies, it also brought the war into the homes of colonial subjects who might have otherwise tried to ignore it. Despite the fact that over 10,000 West Indians enlisted in the armed services (mainly in the RAF), and many thousands more volunteered for other forms of war work, the war seemed to be unfolding half a world away (Deer 2009: 109). But radio took a war that had seemed 'over there' and brought its realities to bear on daily life in the colonies, especially once combat flared up in spring 1940.

What people did with news of the conflict was another question. Jamaican poet and historian Philip Sherlock's 'Dinner Party 1940' (1943) offers one illustration of the negotiation of distance and empathy that could take place when radio accounts of the war intruded on the lives of the middle classes of the West Indies. As the guests at a dinner party sit down to eat, their host turns on the wireless to hear the latest news from Britain:

> The well-bred voice from Daventry
> Mingled with sounds from the pantry

And slowly through the ether spilled
Its syllables . . .
[. . .]
. . . 'and at Narvik
   Where for five days a storm has raged
   a few were killed . . .' (Sherlock [1943] 2005: 156)

Depending on the date of the depicted scene, news of the engagement at Narvik might be slightly positive or devastating: between April and June 1940, a series of battles took place in which German forces eventually succeeded at occupying the northern Norwegian port, despite an initial maritime defeat at the hands of the British Navy. The dinner party – one hesitates to call them an audience – appears unperturbed by news of the struggle: '"More mutton, Alice?" "Yes, it's delicious, dear, / Yesterday at bridge I held three aces, three . . ."' (156). The poem is largely an exercise in ironic contrast; by juxtaposing the two worlds of dinner party and mediated battle, the speaker indicates the difficulties inherent in communicating the urgency of the conflict across the sea, and implies frustration at those insensible to that urgency.

Despite the diners' apparent unconcern, news of Narvik and of 'a number of dead' in the Baltic weaves in and out of the conversation, suturing colonial commonplaces together with global conflict (156). After wavering on the bifurcated soundscape of colonial dinner party and European carnage, the poem moves to claim that the news from the failed British campaign at Narvik cannot affect the lives of British subjects thousands of miles from the war: the news 'did not really silence the sounds from the pantry / Or the show of wit which never fails / Thanks to 7.30 cock-tails' (156). And yet the closing lines of the poem indicate that the trauma of war has entered the lexicon of the speaker: 'Cold mutton is delicious with guava-jelly / And does not seriously incommode / Like cold lead in the belly' (156). This contrast between meat on the table and meat on the battlefield amplifies the ironic ambivalence of an earlier claim about the news 'not silencing' but rather 'augmenting' the sparkling conversation of the diners (156). Even thousands of miles away, the 'well-bred voice' of the BBC brings the conflict to listeners who might prefer to ignore it; one detects in Sherlock's diners not apathy but a defensive performance of genteel inanity. In their mission to secure colonial support for Britain, Overseas Service broadcasts to the West Indies would have to overcome this self-protective 'tuning out' as the debacle at Narvik yielded to the invasions of Belgium, the Netherlands and France, events which ended the period of the 'Phoney War' and brought new threats to the British home front.

While such poems dramatise the psychological split between colonial home and European conflict, BBC officials were troubled by the more fundamental question of just how many people were listening. Estimates for the number of wireless sets spread across the islands are hard to verify. In 1933, the *BBC Yearbook* estimated that the total listening audience in Jamaica, Trinidad, British Guiana and Barbados was between 38,000 and 40,000 (Rush 2011: 155). By the war, the number of listeners had increased, but not exponentially as it had in Britain. On 23 December 1941, an unidentified official wrote to John Grenfell-Williams, who served as Assistant Controller for the Overseas Service for much of the war, and who became the first head of the postwar BBC Colonial Service; the official cited estimates from the Trinidadian government that the total potential radio audience in Trinidad numbered between 20,000 and 30,000.[5] In a later memo, Grenfell-Williams quotes a report by the Empire Parliamentary Association, just back from a tour of the West Indies. The report describes the state of broadcasting infrastructure in the Caribbean as

> nothing short of a scandal ... [I]n Jamaica, there is nothing except an amateur equipment which was taken over on the outbreak of war ... There are estimated to be only 12,000 sets in an Island with a population of over a million. (Grenfell-Williams 1944)

Furthermore, officials could not determine how many tuned in to *Calling the West Indies*; the Department of Listener Research, while very useful on the home front, allocated few resources to surveying overseas audiences. There was some secondary evidence of public interest; internal correspondence indicates that Marson's presence, especially in the early months of the programme, received considerable attention in the West Indies, and that the contents of broadcasts were summarised in newspapers, thereby extending the reach of the programme through print (R46/92). 'While we have proof of a great deal of publicity in the West Indian press,' wrote Grenfell-Williams in November 1941, 'and while we get a fairly large number of letters, most of them favourable in their criticism, we are badly in need of information and comment of a constructive kind' (Grenfell-Williams 1941). The impressionistic and anecdotal responses the BBC received did not help them to describe or quantify precisely the tastes and expectations of their listening audience.

Despite this lack of firm information, officials knew that they could neglect the West Indies only at the risk of further alienating a restive population. Starting in 1940, the BBC implemented regular programming designed specifically for the West Indies as part of a broader attempt to reach out to audiences throughout the colonies – as opposed to the better-served Dominions (Potter 2012: 117). The increase in specialised programming was designed to reinforce ties between the metropole and its colonial sources of material and human resources. Reinforcing those ties involved more than simply talking *about* colonial contributions to the war; listeners in the Caribbean and elsewhere had to feel as though they were part of the national community being imaginatively constructed over the radio.

But for many colonial listeners, identification with the sound of British radio had meant relinquishing an embodied social identity. As with domestic broadcasts, the Overseas Service had presented a uniform acoustic profile of radio citizenship analogous to Warner's universalised liberal subject at the centre of public discourse: speakers had usually been marked as male, metropolitan, middle- or upper middle-class and educated at an elite level.[6] Overseas listeners, if they wished to enter into the imagined community of British cultural life via their participation as radio listeners, had to abandon their particularity as colonial subjects, whether that difference manifested itself in rurality, accent, pigment or class. While changes to this pattern would be gradual and piecemeal, the global conflict helped to spur movement towards a less limited representation of the varieties of Britishness.[7]

Una Marson: poetry, activism and cultural independence

As the war ramped up, BBC Overseas producers strove to depict, acoustically, an Empire that was inclusive, tolerant and representative of its listeners. For the West Indies, this resulted, after a few sporadic broadcasts, in a series of 'parties' which aired every few weeks beginning in December 1940. The broadcasts were a combination of propaganda and entertainment in which messages from soldiers and other war workers stationed in Britain alternated with performances from musical groups, including Rudolph Dunbar and his Negro Choir.[8] Cecil Madden, head of the Empire Entertainment Unit (later the Overseas Entertainment Unit), was so pleased with the atmosphere of a West Indian 'party' broadcast on Boxing Day 1940 that he scheduled another for early 1941 and, soon thereafter, arranged for the establishment of a regular series of West Indian broadcasts (Madden 1940; Madden 1941).

In arranging for more regular West Indian programming, Cecil Madden specifically praised Una Marson for her success in arranging and hosting the Boxing Day broadcast. Marson was not altogether unfamiliar to the BBC, or to Madden. She had periodically contributed scripts and suggestions to the Empire Service in the late 1930s and into 1940, but her BBC debut had come not through radio but through television. The BBC had launched a short-lived television service – the first of its kind – in November 1936 (Briggs 1965: 594–622). Marson visited the experimental television headquarters at Alexandra Palace in summer 1939 while showing a visiting Miss Jamaica around London. She caught Cecil Madden's attention while at the studios, and he offered her freelance work securing interviewees for the television programme *Picture Page*, which he was then producing (Jarrett-Macaulay 1998: 144). The war forced the cancellation of all experimental television broadcasts, but when *Calling the West Indies* began to take shape for the wireless Overseas Service, Madden sought Marson out. She joined *Calling the West Indies* as a full-time staff member in March 1941, shortly after its launch. In doing so, she became the first woman of colour to host a BBC programme. Indeed, her unprecedented appointment caused consternation at high levels within the BBC. Marson's staff file records an exchange among administrators regarding whether the Ministry of Information (MoI) or the Colonial Office was opposed to the hiring of persons of colour for such a position (S. G. Williams 1941). Director of Empire Services R. A. Rendall checked with the Colonial Office and assured the hiring committee that 'they were very anxious that we should make this experiment though they suggested that we should take the probationary two months rather seriously in this case' (Rendall 1941a). Though willing to break new ground in hiring Marson, Rendall and other officials at the BBC seemed unsure of her abilities – or her allegiances.

This wariness on the part of BBC officials stemmed from the fact that, in hiring Marson, they were securing the services of a well-connected and prolific representative of interwar black progressivism. Remarkable though her appointment at the BBC was, it was only one of a series of firsts for Marson. Born in 1905 into a middle-class household in the countryside of Jamaica, she became that country's first female editor–publisher when she launched a magazine called *The Cosmopolitan* in 1928. Marson's intentions for the magazine were socially progressive and feminist, as she made clear in one of her editorials from spring 1928: 'This is the age of woman. What man has done, women may do' (qtd in Jarrett-Macaulay 1998: 30). Her 1932 play *At What a Price* was the first all-black production in Kingston; it went on to be the first all-colonial play staged in London's West End (Jarrett-Macaulay 1998: 43, 53–4). Marson also contributed actively to a number of political and social causes: in the late 1930s she helped establish the Jamaican chapter of the Save the Children foundation and edited *The Keys*, the journal of the League of Coloured Peoples. Through her commitment to feminist and anti-racist causes, she became an important figure among the West Indian intelligentsia not only in Jamaica but also in London, where she lived from 1932 to 1936 and from 1938 to 1946.

Marson's political development was shaped in part by two sustained encounters with prominent African leaders. In summer 1934, Marson welcomed Sir Nana Ofori Atta to London on behalf of the League of Coloured Peoples. Ofori Atta was the flamboyant ruler of the Gold Coast kingdom of Akyem Abuakwa and a relatively forward-thinking leader who welcomed the advancement of women and promoted education among his subjects (Jarrett-Macaulay 1998: 68). The pair became close over the course of that summer, and their frequent conversations sharpened Marson's critique of colonial policy. She began to make connections with African students and intellectuals in London, to read extensively about African issues and literature, and to speak out about the failures of British rule over Jamaica and other colonies (Jarrett-Macaulay 1998: 71–3).

Events of the following summer crystallised her Africanist sympathies: having been offered a temporary post at the League of Nations in Geneva, Marson watched as tensions escalated over Italy's plan to invade Abyssinia. As her position in Geneva came to a close, Marson approached the Abyssinian government and was offered an administrative position with their legation in London. Her employment began just as Italy invaded; over the next few months, Marson watched in despair as the League of Nations proved ineffectual at protecting the African nation (Jarrett-Macaulay 1998: 98–103). The failure of the League (and of Britain in particular) to defend its more vulnerable members convinced Marson – along with many other interwar intellectuals – of the severity of the fascist threat and of the need for a more vigorous defence of progressive principles. Unlike some British intellectuals, however, Marson grounded these new convictions in an anti-colonial Africanism that challenged the notion of Britain as a virtuous imperial force. The reluctance of Britain to defend the League's purported ideals of national self-determination in the case of Abyssinia, together with the larger fact of the British Empire itself, reinforced the hollowness of its claims to benevolent leadership in international affairs.

Marson's critiques of imperial racism emerge, if somewhat sporadically, in her poetry of the late 1930s. Over the course of her career, she produced four volumes of verse and published her work in such venues as *The Keys* and *Poetry of the Negro*, a 1949 anthology compiled by Langston Hughes. Alison Donnell and Delia Jarrett-Macauley have done much to recover Marson's artistic legacy following years of neglect.[9] As both scholars point out, Marson is in some ways a difficult subject for rehabilitation in the post-independence era of Caribbean literary canonisation because she does not adhere to a consistent political tone of national liberation. Much of her verse is, as Jarrett-Macauley phrases it, 'pure Romantic derivation' which draws heavily on the conventions of English nature poetry (Jarrett-Macaulay 1998: 41). Furthermore, her first two collections, *Tropic Reveries* (1930) and *Heights and Depths* (1931), tend to portray a female speaker eager for male affection and attention. Such imitative and seemingly anti-feminist poetics run counter not only to Marson's work as an activist and publisher but also to the emphasis placed on nationalist or regionalist poetry since the consolidation of a corpus of Caribbean literature in the 1970s (Donnell 2006: 42).

Despite the limitations of some of her works, Marson includes in her later collections *The Moth and the Star* (1937) and *Towards the Stars* (1945) several poems that remain remarkable documents of her position as a black female West Indian intellectual. In 'Cinema Eyes' (1937), for example, she warns a younger acquaintance against the racialised standards of beauty that dominate the film-going experience: 'I used to go to the Cinema / To see beautiful white faces . . . / My ideal man would be a Cinema type – / No kinky haired man for me, / No black face, no black children for me' (Marson 2011: 139). Many of her most effective poems refer specifically to her experience of racial ostracism in London, a city that had yet to experience substantial immigration from the Caribbean such as would arrive with the postwar *Windrush* generation. Her poem 'Little Brown Girl' (1937) expresses the urban alienation faced by new arrivals:

> Little brown girl
> Why do you wander alone
> About the streets
> Of the great city
> Of London?
> Why do you start and wince
> When white folk stare at you?
> Don't you think they wonder
> Why a little brown girl
> Should roam about their city
> Their white, white city?
> [. . .]
> You speak good English
> Little brown girl,
> How is it you speak
> English as though it belonged
> To you? (2011: 92–4)

Through poems such as 'Little Brown Girl', 'Kinky Hair Blues' and 'Cinema Eyes', Marson sought to intervene in debates about what it meant to be both black and British, and what it meant to be a subject, but not a citizen, of the British Empire. Though raised on Wordsworth's *Lyrical Ballads* and Palgrave's *Golden Treasury*, Marson quickly realised that the world described by her poetic influences accommodated neither her racial difference nor her desire for greater political rights for the West Indies (Jarrett-Macaulay 1998: 19).

Yet Marson believed that things could change. Her father had been a minister, and she never deviated from the faith in which she was raised. She saw in Christianity a moral weapon in the struggle for political freedom and the alleviation of want. 'He Called Us Brethren!' (1937) apostrophises the mother country with a plea that Christian universalism might overwhelm imperial complacency:

> England, England, heart of an Empire
> That reaches to remotest parts of earth [. . .]
> How slow thou art to comprehend the truth,
> The universal truth that all must learn –
> And thou the foremost for thou hast set
> Great claim upon the holy words of God.
> [. . .] [S]tronger than the bonds
> That bind the peoples of one Race
> Is the same blood that flows –
> That flows alike through black and white
> Making us one in Christ. (2011: 94–5)

While Marson advocated a cross-race unity under God, she also came to believe that, in order to be recognised as equal, any cultural group had to realise its potential through intellectual and artistic achievement. Her faith-based conviction of the fundamental equality of all peoples had been modified by her exposure, in her late twenties, to the cultural nationalism espoused by Indian intellectuals including Rabindranath Tagore, Pandit Nehru and Gandhi, as well as the African–American writer James Weldon Johnson. As Jarrett-Macaulay has pointed out, Marson became convinced that the path to political independence lay through cultural independence: many of her articles published in the Jamaican journal *Public Opinion* in the late 1930s echo Johnson's assertion that no 'people that has produced great literature and art has ever been looked upon by the world as distinctly inferior' (qtd in Jarrett-Macaulay 1998: 118). Marson thus set out on her radio career with a deeply religious sense of the moral injustice of racial prejudice, and a commitment to manifesting cultural pride through artistic excellence. In mobilising both a Christian doctrine of equality under God and an Anglophone literary tradition of liberal humanism and freedom of expression, Marson effectively turned the discourses of colonialism back on themselves. Her apparently moderate politics, as compared to postwar anticolonial poets, belie the agency provided by her religious and aesthetic outlook. For the rest of her life, these convictions would guide Marson's efforts at promoting West Indian independence and prosperity through work as a broadcaster and activist.

Wireless Black Atlantic, part one: transnational solidarity

Marson's extensive résumé and her connections within West Indian and African literary and political circles proved indispensable to her work as producer and host of *Calling the West Indies*. Although intended to strengthen ties between the West Indies and Britain, and thereby reinforce a sense of loyal 'Britishness' among West Indians, the programme allowed Marson to champion other vectors of identity and cultural affinity that were at times Africanist, anti-colonialist and regionalist. Her broadcasts explored the shared experience of racialisation common to many people of African or Asian descent, the disjuncture between ideals of liberal democracy and the realities of colonialism, and the linguistic particularities that distinguish the West Indies as a region. Little changed about the medium involved in this renegotiation of identity; the shortwave beam still moved information in a single direction, from Britain to the Caribbean colonies. But Marson repurposed this imperial channel by virtue of the voices she invited to the airwaves. She contributed to a refiguring of the dynamic between Britain and the West Indies by changing the input at the source point in order to foreground racial, ideological and linguistic markers. In a pattern typical of black internationalism, the exchanges that Marson broadcast depended on the social and cultural resources of the very imperial metropolis of which they were a critique (Edwards 2003: 5).

The aural community that Marson forged at the BBC exists in a complicated relationship to the question of Caribbean nationalism. The 'West Indies' were in some senses a construction, a community imagined by an imperial master. And yet this imperial imagining had palpable consequences, both historically and in everyday life: the Caribbean colonies were bound by a common language and a shared experience of slavery, colonisation and British education. Tasked with addressing the linked but heterogeneous islands of the West Indies, Marson had to balance representation from across the islands while emphasising their unity in diversity. It was a fundamentally diasporic approach, one which, by drawing on the internationals gathered in wartime London, enabled a consideration of both the commonality and plurality of black experience (Gilroy 1993: 80). Inflected by contributions from other corners of the black Atlantic, *Calling the West Indies* enabled the elaboration of a provisional and quasi-nationalist West Indian consciousness, rooted in imperial history but informed by the experiences of others of African descent and colonial extraction. This consciousness was 'quasi-nationalist' in the sense that it was not articulated as an outright independence movement over the wireless, much less as one rooted in ethnic absolutism; rather, the image of the West Indies Marson promoted through her broadcasts was an intermediate construction, somewhere between the dependence of the colonies and the full independence they secured in the 1960s. In its measured approach to the question of West Indian political and cultural identity, it both projected a cultural community that had yet to find full political expression, and reflected the mingled affinity and heteronomy many West Indians felt under British rule.

Marson's vision of cultural independence dovetailed with the wish of the BBC to include more colonial voices in its projections of the Empire, even if the Corporation would have balked at outright calls for political self-rule. When *London Calling*, the BBC magazine for overseas listeners, announced the expansion of broadcasts to the West Indies in March 1941, it stressed the efforts that the Corporation was making to secure colonial participation: 'As far as is possible West Indians and people with West Indian interests over here will be brought to the microphone in talks, special West Indian News, interviews and variety' ('Extended Service' 1941). Early episodes of *Calling the West Indies* were modest in ambition; their scope was limited to musical performances and messages from soldiers to relations back home. Over time, however, Marson began to change the format of the programme. On 6 May 1941, she invited Dr Harold Moody, President of the League of Coloured Peoples, to deliver a 'message home' to the West Indies. Unlike most contributors, who spoke only briefly, Moody spoke for four minutes and was paid for his contributions (Gilbert 1941). Speeches like Moody's opened the door for longer interviews with West Indians who could provide a glimpse of their life in Britain; these interviews began to appear in late May 1941, with broadcasts including 'In a Munitions Factory' and 'A Minister in the Blitz'. Such broadcasts did double duty: they instilled pride in the West Indian contributions to the conflict while reinforcing the sense of duty that imperial subjects owed to the mother country.

Over the next four years, Marson brought dozens of speakers to the microphone. The list of intellectuals, artists and activists featured on

Calling the West Indies includes not only Harold Moody but also his brother Ronald, a prominent modernist sculptor; Elizabeth McDougald of the Red Cross; Maida Springer, an American labour organiser of West Indian descent; and Randolph Dixon, correspondent for the *Pittsburgh Courier*, the most widely circulated African–American newspaper during the war. With each of these guests, Marson explored how issues of race intersected with their larger artistic and political projects. Maida Springer, for example, stresses the multiracial character of the American labour movement in her interview of 30 March 1945, and represents unions as vehicles for the advancement of racial equality as much as labour rights (Marson and Spring 1945). Other figures captured the complex dynamics of moving in predominantly white cultural circles as non-white artists and intellectuals. In discussing his sculpture, Ronald Moody makes casual reference to the racialised lens through which critics perceive art by non-white artists. He notes that critics have often said that his work 'has remained faithful to my racial origin, and my early environment', although Moody claims no conscious attempt on his own part to sculpt in a 'Primitive' style. He goes on to express hope for an art form beyond racial essentialism:

> [I]n the West Indies we lack the rich heritage of an indigenous art. I feel that we'll produce a culture that is neither African nor English, but will be something which, for want of a better name, we shall call West Indian. (Marson and Moody 1943)

This sampling indicates that, beyond her literary concerns, Marson wanted to build a transatlantic community of thinkers and cultural producers in the service of progressive causes of all kinds. Overt revolutionary content was impossible; there were limits to what could be broadcast to the colonies. In a memo from 17 November 1941, John Grenfell-Williams addressed the constraints of broadcasting to the Caribbean. In particular, he noted the impossibility of fully addressing the kinds of political unrest documented in the Report of the West Indian Royal Commission, completed the previous year:

> As far as the real problems of the West Indies are concerned, for obvious reasons we have had to strike a middle course between demonstrating our interest in and sympathy with the difficulties of the people of the West Indies and giving vent to grievances, which would be of assistance to the enemy ... We could not, for example, handle fully the Report of the West Indies Commission, publication of which was withheld. (Grenfell-Williams 1941)

Given that administrators like Grenfell-Williams were obliged to avoid any topic that might undermine official British policy in the West Indies, political discourse on programmes like *Calling the West Indies* had to remain unprovocative. Censorship protocol ensured that any taboo topics raised during the initial scripting of an interview would be cut in transmission.[10] For example, in an interview with Roi Ottley, the first African–American war correspondent for a major US newspaper, the censors struck out Ottley's mention of a US organisation 'carrying on a programme to persuade the United States government to support a West Indian Federation' (Marson and Ottley 1944). The censor also deleted Ottley's praise of Marson as the only woman of colour in the UK or US to host a radio programme; a note in the margins claims that this would be acceptable to US audiences but not for 'W.I.' (West Indian) audiences. Despite such censorship, Ottley and Marson engage in a long conversation about the changes in race relations brought about by the war, and offer predictions about black economic opportunities in the postwar period, which Ottley expects will worsen in the short term. While direct discussions of decolonisation and nationalism may have been forbidden on the imperial networks of the BBC, Ottley's comment that '[t]he condition of the negro in the world is the barometer of Democracy' would have struck a chord with progressive listeners oriented towards independence.[11]

A more pointed example of the intervention of the censor occurs in an interview between Marson and George Orwell that aired on *Calling the West Indies* on 7 May 1942.[12] This interview is the first collaboration between the two for which any script remains; they would go on to record two episodes of the poetry programme *Voice* for the India Section, alongside other writers including T. S. Eliot and Mulk Raj Anand.[13] The interview details Orwell's experiences in Burma and in the Spanish Civil War, his commitment to socialism and his thoughts about the future of English-language literature. The interview was cleared for broadcast with the exception of a short passage, which reads as follows:

MARSON: When did you consciously become left-wing?
BLAIR: About 1927 or so, while I was in Burma.
MARSON: Did the poverty there strike you?
BLAIR: Properly speaking, there is no poverty in Burma. It is a very rich country, but all the same, imperialism is not defensible really, even when it does not happen to oppress that particular area. (Marson and Orwell 1942)

Orwell's remark about imperialism comes across as offhand, as if the indefensibility of imperialism were a *fait accompli*, as indeed it would have seemed to many West Indian listeners. It is perhaps the casualness of this remark that earned the intervention of the censor, because later on Orwell makes a more mitigated comment about the future of British imperialism, which remains uncensored:

> BLAIR: I think the basic fact about countries like India or the African colonies, or the West Indies, etc., is that we can't any longer govern them on the old terms. On the other hand, they can't defend themselves, and they can't be entirely self-supporting, so one must make some sort of loose partnership on comparatively generous terms before it is too late. Because if we don't, they might be lost to some new imperial power like Japan, and they will simply be worse off than before. (Marson and Orwell 1942)

This comment aligns with Orwell's self-justifications for contributing to the wartime BBC as a broadcaster in the India Section: for all its injustice, the British Empire was preferable to a Nazi or Japanese empire, and until the Axis was defeated, Britain and its colonies had to work together. Despite the fact that censors muted the more strident anti-imperial content of Orwell's interview, the very mention of an alternative governance structure – a 'loose partnership' rather than a paternalistic imperial relationship – represents a significant achievement.

Beyond his statements about imperialism itself, Orwell would, for many listeners, have represented a degree of literary respectability that affected the reception of *Calling the West Indies* as a whole. He was one of several established British writers and intellectuals whom Marson and her team invited to participate in the programme. Marson unsuccessfully sought contributions from Louis MacNeice (Jarrett-Macaulay 1998: 160), but she succeeded in bringing Scottish critic, writer and broadcaster L. A. G. Strong to the microphone to offer his assessments of the growing body of West Indian poetry and prose being aired. Strong's participation presages contributions to the postwar series *Caribbean Voices* by critics including MacNeice and Stephen Spender. Most of these authors would have considered themselves anti-imperialists. As Peter Kalliney argues, the involvement of metropolitan writers like Orwell, Strong, Spender and MacNeice in Caribbean broadcasting is important for reasons beyond their support for, or disavowal of, colonial independence. Regardless of such brass-tacks political considerations, interactions between the London literary establishment and the nascent Caribbean literary scene effected complex relations of institutional validation and assimilation (Kalliney 2013: 120–2). Affiliation with colonial intellectuals contributed to the progressive credentials of white British writers and actualised the role many had hoped radio would play in bringing together cultures from around the world. For West Indian intellectuals, the involvement of British writers lent *Calling the West Indies* even greater cultural capital. Especially in later years, as *Calling the West Indies* became *Caribbean Voices* and played host to an ever more vibrant Caribbean literary boom, this process of exchange became a means of pursuing ideals of aesthetic autonomy that benefited intellectuals on both sides of the Atlantic (Kalliney 2013). Transatlantic solidarity thus validated and reinforced the aspirations to autonomy – both political and artistic – embedded in the cultural production of the West Indies.

Wireless Black Atlantic, part two: Caribbean poetry and nation language

Beyond these international connections, *Calling the West Indies* served to strengthen proto-national sentiment among West Indian listeners and participants. Marson was keen to demonstrate a radio-generated *rapprochement* between islands that often seemed as far apart from one another as they were far from Britain. Speaking of West Indian soldiers in Britain on 3 September 1942, Marson noted that

> what I think is proving most valuable is their growing consciousness of belonging not to Jamaica, or Trinidad or Antigua – but to the West Indies ... The thing that has interested me most is the growth of real friendships between lads from different islands who only met over here for the first time. (Marson 1942c)

Calling the West Indies was not simply facilitating the expression of a previously existing and stable regional identity; rather, the wartime expatriate experience enabled what Laurence Breiner describes as a 'West Indianification', as a group of people who had, up to that point, been dispersed both geographically and intellectually endured a common isolation in the imperial metropolis (2003: 96). For one thing, their respective home islands appeared more alike from the vantage point of London, forging a kind of inter-island solidarity; moreover, West Indians who considered themselves 'British' were often shocked to discover upon arrival in London that native Britons did not see them as such, and often labelled all West Indians as 'Jamaicans' (Rush 2011: 170–2). Encouraging connections between West Indians became, for Marson, a way of recovering a positive collective identity from the exclusionary operations of normative Britishness.

For Marson, the key to cementing this nascent identity was the development of a shared language and a shared literature. As the programme evolved, Marson increasingly used *Calling the West Indies* as a vehicle for the promotion of West Indian poetry.[14] Much of the poetry broadcast on *Calling the West Indies* was formally and politically conservative. Nonetheless, these poems were a means of building up a sense of literary tradition in the West Indies, and could thereby serve as exercises in nation-formation. In an explicit celebration of the racial and cultural hybridity of the islands, one transmission broadcast in November 1942 focused on the poetry of the various ethnic groups in the West Indies. Although Marson announces that listeners will hear from the four 'major races', the script contains poetry celebrating only the Indian, Chinese and African heritage of the islands, indicating that the fourth example (presumably European) had been cut (Marson 1942d).[15]

Marson and her contributors were eager to demonstrate the burgeoning artistic and intellectual culture of the islands. In a broadcast that aired on 14 June 1942, the programme featured works written and read by Grenada-born poet Calvin Lambert, which were set to music. Though stylistically unadventurous, Lambert's poetry succeeds in answering its own call for the development of a regional literature: 'Let us awake and give the world our share / Of literature to mould the destiny / Of the tempestuous age in which we live' (Lambert 1942a). At the same time, however, Lambert directs this call for a new regional literature towards the aims of Britain as a global power: 'This world-catastrophe is spread / To native man, in native lands. / What will remain to speak of Europe's Art? / Who will survive to write the page of time?' (Lambert 1942b). While Lambert was and remains a relative unknown, Marson also praised the contributions of more established Caribbean poets, including Tom Redcam, J. E. Clare MacFarlane and Vivian Virtue. On the occasion of the death of Constance Hollar, an early pioneer of Jamaican poetry, Marson dedicated an entire episode of the new programme *Caribbean Voices* to Hollar's memory, and featured poems written in her honour by Lena Kent, A. C. Hutton and Alan Wiles (Marson 1945b).

For writers like Lambert, MacFarlane and Hollar, mother country and colony were bound fast by both sentiment and poetic form; gestures at regional consciousness had to proceed through pre-modernist models of English-language literature and with an understanding that the West Indies existed within the Empire. As the programme evolved, *Calling the West Indies* would move beyond these Euro-centric poetic forms, to include idioms more specific to the West Indies. On 12 November 1942, Marson and her team presented a folk story collected by Dorothy Clarke and published in the *Daily Gleaner*, Jamaica's largest newspaper. Titled 'Brer Nancy and de Woss-woss', the story participates in the anancy (or 'nancy') tradition, which was one of the most prominent narrative forms to survive the journey from West Africa to the West Indies. Anancy narratives usually feature as their central character a trickster figure in the form, or with some attributes, of a spider; indeed, the form derives its title from the word *ananse,* which means 'spider' in the Akan language of Ghana ('Anancy'). Originally an oral storytelling form, these narratives tend to be written in dialect when transcribed in order to represent their spoken origins more closely. The opening of 'Brer Nancy' gives a sense of the narrative voice:

> One day, Brer Blackbud siddung pan one tree-limb ab tek sun, an him see tree butcher come wid a cow, and him mek no nize, him watch dem when dem kill de cow. When it down, him see dem cut up de meat so carry it to one lock-up place. When dem ketch ah do', dem say 'One, two, tree, me no touch libber' an de do' open, mek them carry in de meat. Bamby dem come out again an gone.' (Clarke 1942)

As in most anancy stories, 'Brer Nancy and de Woss-woss' celebrates the protagonists' clever subversion of established order. In this case, having learned the secret of entering and exiting the storeroom, Brer Blackbud tips Brer Nancy off about the stash of meat. Although Brer Blackbud informs Brer Nancy that escape from the storeroom requires that one not leave with a cut of liver ('One, two, tree, me no touch libber'), Brer Nancy ignores this advice, and becomes trapped in the storeroom while Brer Blackbud escapes. Once they discover Brer Nancy, the butchers tie him to a tree and prepare to brand him as punishment. Only through Brer Blackbud's intervention (with the assistance of a small army of 'woss-woss', or wasps) does Brer Nancy succeed in escaping from the butchers, before sharing the spoils of victory with Brer Blackbud and the wasps.

This synopsis indicates some of the political valences of the story, not least of which is the triumph of trickster figures coded as black (the West African anancy figure and the blackbird) over the butchers. The apparent slippage of characters between animal and human forms – a spider able to walk away with a great quantity of meat, and large enough to be tied to a tree – indexes a parallel generic slippage from fable to historical representation. The branding with which Brer Nancy is threatened, for example, is at once an element of the fable-world and a representation of the bodily trauma inflicted on those, like slaves and dispossessed agricultural workers, caught on the wrong side of the islands' often violent and inequitable system of discipline. At a level beyond the overt diegesis, the very act of sharing anancy stories is culturally freighted. The history of anancy storytelling is rooted in Afro-Caribbean folk culture and based on the assumption that fictional subversions of authority can in some way model real-world resistance, or at the very least compensate for the difficulties of achieving that resistance. As a coded form of subversion and a vestige of African culture in the West Indies, the telling of anancy stories was prohibited in colonial educational institutions; furthermore, well into the middle of the twentieth century, anancy stories were frowned upon by a growing black cultural establishment that sought to foster literary respectability along European lines rather than encourage ties to the slavery-era past (Arnold, Rodriguez-Luis and Dash 2001: 56–7). It was not until the late 1960s that folk poets such as Louise Bennett would achieve recognition *as poets* for their work in demotic traditions and dialects (Brathwaite 1984: 26–8).

Although examples of folk literature like 'Brer Nancy' occurred far less often on *Calling the West Indies* than literature that emulated European models, their frequency grew as the war went on. Late in the war, the programme began to include dialect poems by Marson, Claude MacKay and others, which collectively depict aspects of lived experience in a language closer to that spoken by many residents of the islands. In the blind medium of radio, shadings of vocal difference became an important vehicle for the communication of 'West Indianness' as distinct from 'Britishness'. Robert Warren's poem 'Poor We Country Folk', which aired on 27 May 1945, offers an example of a poem spoken from the perspective of an agricultural labourer selling his produce at a Kingston market:

> Inna market people poke
> Ya tings an' tink a joke
> Wen ye tell dem nuh fe dweet.
> 'n laugh like sinting ketch dem sweet.
>
> Kingston people? Dem aal right.
> Sink we ride jackass aal night
> Fe seel dem peas an' corn fe nuttin!
> Dem kyan nyam dem ham an' muttin! (Warren 1945)

From today's perspective, this kind of poem can sound uncomfortably close to a kind of auto-minstrelsy, in which a racial identity is performed for an outside audience. And yet questionable appropriations seem not to obtain in this situation; the poem was written by a Jamaican, chosen by the editors of the *Yearbook of the Jamaican Poetry League 1940* and then by the producers of *Calling the West Indies*, and broadcast back to a West Indian audience. The possibility that this poem represents an act of class ventriloquism is harder to adjudicate, but Warren's adoption of an agricultural produce-seller's voice is in any case sympathetic. The speaker complains about the inequalities between city and country, and silently reproves urbanites who presume they can take advantage of him and his labours. Like 'Brer Nancy', 'Poor We Country Folk' stages resistance to figures of authority through the use of local dialect and literary forms.

The inclusion of folk literature on *Calling the West Indies* directed listeners' attention to a tradition at once synchronous with and distinct from British poetry of the twentieth century. Transmission of non-standard accents and regional dialects encouraged a sense of West Indian cultural autonomy by foregrounding the differences between the linguistic and poetic traditions of the colonies and Britain. In this sense, broadcasting poetry from the West Indies back to the West Indies contributed to the formation of what Brathwaite has called nation language, a more celebratory term than 'dialect' and one that entails liberation from certain metrical constraints of English-language poetry (Brathwaite 1984: 5–17). Nation language, for Brathwaite, emerges from a pluralistic linguistic condition; the term encompasses all of the varieties of spoken and written English from the Caribbean that exhibit a tension resulting from the suppression, and eventual re-emergence, of the rhythms and inflections of the African and indigenous languages that circulated among early slave populations (1984: 5–7). West Indian nation language is a product of the linguistic contact zone between a dominant idiom and other, subordinate idioms, whether residual (African) or emergent (demotic Afro-Caribbean). While nation language has the potential to challenge the linguistic hegemony of English as a colonial language, it does not replace standard English with a unified, positivist version of Caribbean English; rather, as Matthew Hart has argued (adapting the work of Simon Gikandi), the condition of the emergence of nation language is one of reaction and relation, not pure linguistic identity (Hart 2010: 123).

The extra-verbal variations of speech audible via shortwave – inflections, cadence, vowel tones – produce meaning beyond the lexical inheritance of English. In doing so, they echo Brathwaite's claims about Caribbean orality in *History of the Voice*:

> The poetry, the culture itself, exists not in a dictionary but in the tradition of the spoken word. It is based as much on sound as it is on song. That is to say, the noise that it makes is part of the meaning, and if you ignore the noise (or what you would *think* of as noise, shall I say) then you lose part of the meaning. (1984: 17)

The celebration of Caribbean nation language on the air shifted the particularities of accent and dialect from the realm of noise – unwanted sound or distortion – to a productive dimension of poetic meaning.

Laurence Breiner argues that this emphasis on the heard sound of language had a profound effect on the development of Caribbean poetry, beyond simply validating nation language. It trained West Indian audiences to listen for differences in accents, dialects and delivery, and laid the groundwork for the privileging of oral and performance poetry in the later twentieth century (Breiner 2003: 98–9).

Indeed, one can trace a lineage from the first wireless articulations of nation language to Paul Gilroy's shift, in *The Black Atlantic*, away from the poststructuralist obsession with textuality in favour of a music-derived rhetoric of gesture, inflection and kinesis (Gilroy 1993: 77–8). Though Gilroy focuses on the transatlantic history of black musical forms, his argument that textuality deprives scholars of a language by which to analyse 'performances in which identity is fleetingly experienced in the most intensive ways' holds true for broadcast poetry as well (1993: 78). Both the spoken word and performed music are embodied forms, experienced ephemerally when broadcast. Both assert the material origin of the artwork, whether voice or bodily movement. In doing so, they bear traces of the bodily particularity of the artist. In the case of broadcast poetry, the effect of nation language inheres, partly, in the inflections, cadences, tones and stresses of the voice, which connect speaker and listener. In asserting a regional identity, nation language asserts a measure of bodily particularity on the part of the speaker by indicating island of origin, socio-economic class and commitment to one register of speech or another. While radio cannot reliably represent the most contested aspect of West Indian identity – race – it can nonetheless approximate the aural trace of disenfranchisement and material dispossession by representing non-metropolitan and working-class accents. In representing this disenfranchisement and dispossession in the context of the West Indies, it offers a reminder of Stuart Hall's claim that race is the modality in which class is lived; that in a racially binarised society, poverty disproportionately affects the subjugated half of the binary (Hall 1980: 341). In introducing a spectrum of West Indian voices to the wireless, *Calling the West Indies* claimed for the radio public a measure of embodied history, a colonial otherness which had previously been excluded from the airwaves emanating from the metropole.

The representation of atypical accents and dialects in West Indian broadcasts met with resistance from listeners at the time. Some listeners found it difficult to escape internalised prejudices about accents; John Figueroa has noted that 'many people in the Caribbean felt that poetry on the BBC, even Caribbean poetry, should be read by English voices' (qtd in Griffith 2003: 204), although this may have as much to do with preconceptions about appropriate 'literary voices' as about 'radio voices'. The Colonial Office, whose cultural politics were often more responsive to those of the colonial plantocracy than those of non-white West Indians, was critical of the show and its host, summing up its response as '[t]oo much Jamaica, too much Una Marson' (Rendall 1943). At times, the question of accent proved divisive even among listeners supportive of regional variety; an undated and anonymous internal report from late 1941 or early 1942 notes that

> We are accused, too, on occasions, of using too many speakers from some particular island. But we do recognise the friendly rivalry which exists between the islands, and we try very hard to find men from all parts of the West Indies to take part in our programmes. ('Notes on Broadcasting to the West Indies' [n.d.])

On 19 May 1941, the West Indian programmes division received a telegram from Port of Spain, Trinidad, which claimed that public interest in *Calling the West Indies* was virtually non-existent in Trinidad owing to a perceived focus on Jamaican speakers and issues (R46/92). Such regional frictions preoccupied the producers of *Calling the West Indies* throughout the war, but despite such complaints, the producers largely succeeded at their task of providing a representative sample of voices from across the West Indies while drawing from a limited pool of students, soldiers, intellectuals and war workers.

While *Calling the West Indies* struggled to represent the racial diversity of the Caribbean vocally, it came nonetheless to play a mediating role between West Indians and white Britons. In a broadcast of 3 September 1942, Marson notes that war had brought citizens of the British Isles into contact with colonial citizens whose existence had, up to that point, been all too easy to ignore: 'If we want understanding and sympathy among peoples of different races and colours, we must first have knowledge of each other – and at least the war is compelling us to meet one another over here' (Marson 1942b). In reality, things were more difficult than Marson's on-air assessment might indicate. She clashed frequently with the Colonial Office and the West Indian Commission, both of which favoured increased representation of white guests on *Calling the West Indies*.[16] In a long, undated report from early in 1942, Marson responded to allegations that she allowed non-white West Indians to broadcast at the expense of white West Indians: 'We usually have a good mixture – white, brown, black – and the number of white lads [broadcasting messages home] keeps up and is a good percentage when we realise only 3% are white in the West Indies' (Marson 1942a: 2). For its part, the upper administration tended to side with Marson. In addition to Grenfell-Williams's regular support for Marson's efforts, R. A.

Rendall (then the Assistant Controller for Overseas Services) noted in a memorandum to upper administrators that Marson had 'special difficulties' to deal with, including 'the proper holding of the balance between white and black and the criticism of the West India committee on this point' (Rendall 1942).

Addressing the mother country: *West Indies Calling*

Despite the importance of *Calling the West Indies* in introducing vocal diversity to the imperial airwaves, few recordings remain of Marson's voice. The episodes of *Calling West Africa* or George Orwell's programme *Voice* in which Marson participated have not survived. The National Sound Archive of the British Library possesses three acetate discs (out of four recorded) from an episode of *Calling the West Indies* featuring L. A. G. Strong; on this recording, Marson's voice introduces Strong and closes the programme, which is to say that her presence is minimal. There is, however, one other recording of Marson's voice, preserved in a 1943 propaganda film entitled *West Indies Calling*. Produced by the MoI, this was part of a larger effort to highlight West Indian contributions in Britain, and would have been shown between or before feature films at British cinemas. This film uses the format of the radio message programme that Marson hosted, but reverses the direction of transmission in order to introduce Britons to the various war jobs West Indians were performing. In the film, a large and ethnically heterogeneous group of West Indians gather at Broadcasting House in an informal party setting, during which Marson approaches the microphone and introduces a number of speakers, all of whom are men of colour. Beginning with the first guest – Learie Constantine, a well-known Trinidadian cricketer employed during the war by the Ministry of Labour – the audience is introduced to a variety of war jobs being performed by Caribbean Britons, which the speakers continue to narrate in voice-over. Marson's voice, though seemingly altered by many years in London, nonetheless retains hints of a distinctly non-British cadence and inflection in certain moments. The other speakers possess a range of accents.

By pairing the brown bodies of its presenters with their varied West Indian accents, the film presents a visual correlative to the insistence in radio on the bodily particularity of its announcers. Viewers not only watch and hear them speak while learning about West Indian contributions to the war; the film actually ends with the image of white and black West Indians dancing together, a rare if not unprecedented depiction of wartime interracial intimacy. The moment of intimacy is gestured at rather than boldly asserted: most of the dancing couples are not interracial, but one interracial couple features in close-up, while two others feature in the background. However fleeting, the staged romance of the dance is especially remarkable, given the ample evidence collected by scholars like Sonya Rose about the extent of racial prejudice in the UK during the war (Rose 2004: 245–86). While British authorities in the Colonial Office and elsewhere promoted interracial cooperation, officials often stressed that acceptable interactions did not include romantic fraternisation (Rose 2004: 246–9). This visual defiance of Colonial Office policy may simply be a case of one hand not knowing what the other is doing. The MoI, whose mandate of maintaining public morale and order would have included the smoothing over of racial tensions, may not have been fully attuned to the Colonial Office's mandate to bear in mind colonial attitudes to race while West Indians were in Britain.

The closing scene of black, brown and white West Indians dancing together can, of course, also be read in less liberatory terms, as a bracketing off of the creolised world represented by the Caribbean colonies. Given the long history of cultural and racial intermixing in the West Indies – to which the film alludes in its introduction – the film can be seen as representing a particularly 'West Indian' situation. The framing device of the roomful of West Indians broadcasting to Britain becomes a means of safely containing the perceived threat of miscegenation and treating it as a peculiarly 'colonial' situation. That some Britons resisted the return and continued presence of West Indians in the 1950s – even of former soldiers in areas where they had been stationed during the war – indicates that Britain may not have been ready for the return of the imperially repressed. Nonetheless, the decision to represent this kind of fraternisation was a bold one because it gives visual form to the social barriers that came under pressure during the war. Once presented with the image of a multiracial community, no matter how it may be framed or contained, the audience must at least entertain as a possibility the notion of a creolised British Empire.

The ambiguity of this final scene, its presentation of bodily difference within a particular, limited frame, encapsulates the constraints inherent in broadcasting a new version of Britain that included a plethora of racial, regional and class identities. Marson, Anand, Orwell and others accepted such constraints as the price of reaching a large audience and participating actively in wartime discussions of national and imperial belonging, social organisation and postwar planning. But there was constant tension between official and unofficial uses of radio, between maintaining the vast imperial war effort and daring to challenge its shape and objectives. To a certain extent, even such mitigated forms of dissent could be folded back into the larger propaganda aims of the British government: the more dissent and diversity could be aired through the BBC, the more the government could claim to be a tolerant, democratic and pluralist imperial nation. The imperial networks of the BBC were thus precisely hegemonic, in the sense that they provided an elastic form of containment for the class and colonial unrest that might otherwise have destabilised Britain and its Empire (Raymond Williams 1977: 113–14; Hall 1977: 334). Nevertheless, Britain left the Second World War a transformed polity, with a Labour government in power and possessed of a mandate for substantial social reform, with the independence of India essentially a matter of when, not if; even Jamaica, whose independence from Britain would not arrive until 1958, was granted a new Constitution with full suffrage in 1945. The success of Caribbean decolonisation movements in the late 1950s and 1960s indicates that wartime articulations of national consciousness formed part of a larger, and ultimately productive, movement for regional autonomy.

In the context of war, Marson's deployment of regionally specific poetry was thus always doubly voiced. The demands of propaganda ensured a message of colonial cooperation with Britain at a time of crisis, and prevented overtly pro-independence messages from reaching Caribbean listeners. At the same time, by making late-colonial voices audible from the centre of the British Empire, *Calling the West Indies* challenged simple models of exchange between centre and periphery, and accentuated the mutual implication of white and black British subjects in the mediated projects of modernity. The semantic effect of hearing West Indian poetry read in West Indian voices extended far beyond the literal content of words; it expanded the horizon of national possibility in a manner analogous to the belated inclusion of Northern and working-class English accents on the BBC in the late 1930s and 1940s, and prompts consideration of the relationship between audibility, representation and citizenship in late modernist texts generally. By seizing the modern mechanisms of control and using them for their own patterns of circulation, these writers offered a reminder that, in accounts of late imperialism and culture, sound matters. The articulation of alternate cultural formations depends on the audible as much as on the legible, and emerges in practices that work through technologies and institutions of mediation.

Notes

1. The term 'British West Indies' (usually shortened to 'West Indies') refers to the political formation of British colonies that dotted the Caribbean Sea

– namely, the Bahamas, Jamaica, the Leeward Antilles, the Lesser Antilles (including Barbados and Trinidad and Tobago) and other smaller dependencies – and technically excludes mainland territories near the Caribbean, including British Guiana (Guyana) and British Honduras (Belize). However, when used at the wartime BBC, 'West Indies' tended to include these outlying colonies. Some critics (including Alison Donnell and Sarah Lawson Welsh) avoid the term 'West Indies' in order to free the literature from 'the (re-)centering tendencies of a colonial and Commonwealth framework' (Donnell and Welsh 1996: 6). This chapter uses both 'Caribbean' (as a spatial descriptor) and 'West Indian' (as a political and cultural descriptor) in order to recognise the layered historical and geographical identities of the region and its inhabitants; during the war, residents participated simultaneously in multiple communities at the local, island, regional and imperial levels. This layering of regional and political identities aligns with the metropolitan perspective of the BBC North American Service, for whose broadcasting purposes the Caribbean was coterminous with the Anglophone West Indian (and Central/South American) colonies. See Rush (2011: 14–15) for further discussion of this nomenclature.
2. Peter Kalliney discusses the combined imperial and anti-imperial tendencies of programmes including *Calling the West Indies* in *Commonwealth of Letters* (2013: 4–7, 116–45).
3. On Michael Warner's notion of 'publics' as communities shaped by the circulation of discourse, and how those communities relate to radio listening, see the Introduction to this volume. On publics and counterpublics more generally, see Warner (2002: 65–124).
4. Though the Commission would complete its report in 1940, the British government blocked publication of it for fear that its frank discussion of poor social and economic conditions in the West Indies, and its recommendation of regional self-government, would stoke further unrest and provide fodder for Axis propaganda (Morley 2007).
5. Memo from official with initials 'WMM' and the occupational acronym 'A/EID', to John Grenfell-Williams, 23 December 1941 (R46/92). BBC Staff Lists are incomplete for this date, making it difficult to identify 'WMM'.
6. Entry into the public sphere often requires the erasure of any class, ethnic, racial or sexual identity that is seen as 'particular' because not middle-class, white, male and heterosexual, as Warner notes (2002: 39–44, 51). This erasure of individuality applies to both the wielders and the audience of a discourse.
7. For more on these changes at the wartime BBC, see Chapter 1.
8. An accomplished bandleader and composer born in British Guiana, Dunbar would go on to become the first black conductor to lead the London Symphony Orchestra at the Royal Albert Hall. This 1942 concert included pieces by Mendelssohn and Dvořák, as well as William Grant Still's 'Afro-American Symphony' (1931) ('Rudolph Dunbar's Albert Hall Triumph' 1942: 5).
9. Donnell has produced an edition of Marson's *Selected Poems* (Marson 2011) and features Marson prominently in her literary–historical survey *Twentieth-Century Caribbean Literature* (Donnell 2006) and her co-edited *Reader in Caribbean Literature* (Donnell and Lawson Welsh 1996).

Jarrett-Macauley's contributions include *The Life of Una Marson, 1905–1965* (1998) and a short overview of Marson's wartime contributions to radio entitled 'Putting the Black Woman in the Frame: Una Marson and the West Indian Challenge to British National Identity' (1996).

10. BBC censorship policy demanded that all broadcasts be scripted beforehand, including interviews, which then had to be read out verbatim. A switch censor present in the studio would cut the microphone of any presenter who strayed from his or her script.
11. Ottley documented his stay in the UK, including his experience broadcasting with Marson and his meetings with intellectuals including George Padmore and unnamed writers from the British colonies, in his diaries and letters. On first observing a BBC broadcast, Ottley noted, 'Nothing of the fierceness that characterizes American productions was apparent here. Everything was conducted on a casual level' (Ottley 2011: 72). Of his own broadcast, Ottley remarked, 'It went well – I was in good voice' (2011: 82).
12. Currently housed in the *Calling the West Indies* files of the WAC, this interview does not feature in the *Complete Works of George Orwell* (ed. Davison 1998), nor does it appear in W. J. West (1985; [1985] 1987). While Marson refers to him as 'George Orwell' in her remarks, the script itself calls him by his real surname, Blair.
13. Marson and Orwell first worked together in August 1941, just before he officially joined the BBC. Orwell had a small role, playing a colonial slave owner alongside Marson, in a radio play written by Orwell's future India Section colleague Venu Chitale (Bowker 2003: 284; Davison 1998: vol. 12, 544).
14. Glyne Griffith links this transformation to Marson's participation in George Orwell's Eastern Service radio poetry programme *Voice* in late 1942 (Griffith 2003: 9). However, while *Voice* undoubtedly spurred Marson to emulate its audio 'magazine' format, she had already broadcast several poetry-themed programmes to the West Indies by the end of 1942.
15. This may not have been intentional; Marson was known to prepare too much material for her broadcasts, often cutting poems and paragraphs as she assembled her scripts (R46/92). Still, the lack of any white West Indian poetry in the script indicates that, by the time the show went on air, only three cultural groups were to be represented.
16. This aligns with the resistance to anti-racist propaganda and the abolition of the colour bar by agencies like the Bermuda Information Office, as noted by Rose (2004: 271).

Coda: Coronation

Let us pray then that *all* the media survive. (Louis MacNeice, 'A Plea for Sound' [1953: 135])

In autumn 1953, Louis MacNeice – no longer the rising talent of the BBC Features Department but one of its aging statesmen – published a *cri de cœur* in which he lamented the passing of a sceptre the previous spring. On 2 June, Elizabeth Windsor had been crowned Queen of the United Kingdom and the Commonwealth realms. It was not with the monarch, however, but with the televisual medium of her accession that MacNeice was concerned. 'It was prophesied by some that sound broadcasting would die on Coronation Day,' MacNeice observes in 'A Plea for Sound', but he cannot help but feel that television had let its public down: 'to my mind and that of many others the coronation procession became a bore on the television screen and, paradoxically, regained both sweep and colour when one went over to the sound broadcast' (1953: 129). MacNeice concedes that the ceremony itself, within Westminster Abbey, was well served by television, but the procession outside had 'clutter[ed] up the poor little screen in [an] unsignificant way' (129–32). Worse in MacNeice's view is the possibility that television, more so than sound broadcasting, may 'shackle' the imaginations of its audience (134).

The title of MacNeice's article communicates both his continued interest in the medium of radio and his awareness that, whatever he might wish to be true, television was in the ascendant. Indeed, in conventional accounts of British media history, the installation of Queen Elizabeth II serves as a double coronation in which Britain appointed a successor not only to their wartime monarch but also to the medium of their national self-representation. Television had been around for years; while its early, experimental phase at the interwar BBC had been suspended with the outbreak of hostilities, by 1946 the Corporation was once again in the business of vision. Before 1953, however, uptake of the new medium had been slow. It took a ceremony of national importance and visual splendour to prompt a public still emerging from years of austerity to spend £45 for an entry-level television set.[1] Coronation afforded that opportunity. For the first time, television cameras were to be allowed within the walls of Westminster Abbey on Coronation Day, having been restricted to the procession outside for the 1937 coronation of George VI and similarly excluded for the wedding of Elizabeth in 1947. Access begat interest: the 1953 coronation marked the first time that more people watched a major national ceremony on television than listened to it on the radio (Hajkowski 2010: 97, 100).

But if television emerged from the coronation as the dominant medium, radio did not go gently into the good night of technological obsolescence. Beginning in 1952 but gathering steam by April 1953, the BBC Home Service, Light Programme and Third Programme – the postwar trifecta of hierarchised cultural output – produced a flood of radio broadcasts in anticipation of the ceremony. Coronation-themed episodes aired on established programmes from *The Children's Hour* (which aired a six-part series on the queens regnant in Britain's past) to *Mrs. Dale's Diary* (in which the eponymous doctor's wife welcomes a Pakistani family in London to witness the coronation), while special programmes aired about municipal planning for the event (*London Prepared*), details on coronation customs (*The Holy Oil*, on the ritual anointing of the monarch) and more demotic cultural traditions (such as the brewing of triple-strength Coronation Ales).[2] MacNeice produced a feature for the Home Service named after Elizabeth I's declaration upon her coronation, *Time Has Brought Me Hither*, and described as a 'historical panorama showing the continuity in diversity of the British tradition with glimpses of various coronations through the last four hundred years' ('Time' 1953: 12; Hajkowski 2010: 101). That these radio broadcasts were remediated through periodicals including *The Listener*, *Radio Times* and *London Calling* reminds us that while the coronation may have marked a decisive moment in television's rise, that rise took place in a media system that was, and remains, a contested field of communication and representation. Like radio before it, television would be able to assert its particular function only in relation to the representations offered by print, cinema, phonography and other media.

Ultimately, however, the more enduring media of the double coronation might be the material instantiations that mark the ritual transfer of sovereign power. On screen and on the wireless, British and Commonwealth audiences encountered a ceremony resonant with, and through, the tangible past: orb, sceptre, robes, carriage and crown.

The Abbey itself – described in *The Stones Cry Out* as 'a great stone ship becalmed in the night' – was and is a vehicle for the articulation of national identity, its constitutive role in the fabulation of Britishness reimagined and remediated at regular intervals over centuries (MacNeice 1941c: 4). Churches, as MacNeice well knew, are intermedial spaces. They offer a multisensory experience antecedent to technologies of mass communication: an immersive language of stone that is at once sculpture, gallery and resonant chamber for voice and music. If MacNeice's wartime broadcast honouring the Abbey and its inhabitants had marked one means of bringing that deep history into the present by suturing scripture and stone to the sounds of bombardment, the televised coronation in 1953 marked only the newest way of realising national identity through the circulation of meaningful forms.

While the death of George VI, whose rule encompassed the war, may have seemed to mark the end of one chapter in the life of the nation, it is equally true that Elizabeth had endured the Blitz along with the rest of Britain. If wartime propaganda, both at home and abroad, had stressed the contributions of average Britons to the war effort, the royal family's determination to stay in London throughout the conflict had lent credibility to their claims to represent the beleaguered nation, and the Empire, as a whole.[3] It is precisely this legacy of shared wartime vulnerability that Elizabeth Bowen draws on in 'Coronation', a talk prepared weeks in advance of the event and aired 31 May 1953 on the Third Programme. For Bowen, Elizabeth's coronation marks a larger celebration of the victories earned through struggles so severe that their scars persist:

> This is a nation great in its endurances. We commemorate the wounds which have been survived, the losses outfaced, the sorrows which ran their course. The Queen's Coronation is taking place in a London of spaces of cleared ruins. The dead who should still be living, the dead of two wars, are among the concourse: the Queen is victorious in their name – she is to reign, also, over a living race of slow but undeterrable rebuilders. (2010: 104–5)

Bowen's rhetoric of endurance, renewal and rebuilding reflects the emphasis the BBC as a whole put on the coronation event. Like the Festival of Britain that had taken place in summer 1951, the celebration surrounding Elizabeth's investiture was to mark the continued progress of the nation out of the depths of the war and into a brighter future (Hilmes 2012: 208). The coronation was therefore framed not as a feudal remainder in a modern constitutional monarchy, but as a well-deserved moment of joyous unity in a welfare state and a larger Commonwealth. Programmes in the lead-up included *The Queen's People*, featuring portraits of sailors, soldiers and farmers who 'fought and worked to preserve the heritage of Britain', as well as repeated references to the Commonwealth as a united family and a source of pride; the coronation was, as Charles Max-Mueller of BBC Outside Broadcasts noted, 'a Commonwealth affair' (qtd in Hajkowski 2010: 101–2). If radio – as the medium that had tracked the social and political changes thrust upon Britain by the war – was no longer dominant, the reformed structures whose arrival it had chronicled nonetheless conditioned the coverage of this new media event.

Television might traffic in representations of the same decolonising welfare state that radio had augured, but subtle differences in the embodied experience of each medium provided Britons with a shifting and multiform perspective on this collective turning point. Bowen, ever attuned to the different ways in which media spoke to Britons of themselves, saw the coronation as an instance of multiple mediation for both the figure of the monarch and the nation itself:

> The actuality of her movements is being photographed, not only on the consciousness of the bystanders – it is recorded on films as history – and cast from moment to moment, fugitive as real life, on to television screens. Listeners more closely watch with the mind's eye: voice after voice takes up every golden turning flash of her coach-wheels, each inclination of her head. These hours – day here, night elsewhere, focus the world. The size, the intensity, the silence of the global attention can be felt – or, can it? Does the Queen feel it? Is it too vast to feel? (2010: 103–4)

Photography, film, television, radio: each affords an impression, a way of participating in the event by perceiving it, which together add up to a monumental interpellation into a new, postwar nation. By projecting herself into the moment of the mass-mediated coronation that had yet to happen, Bowen entertains the idea that the Queen might *just* register the immensity of the popular enthusiasm for the event: '[D]o they, do the Royal, record vibrations?', she wonders (2010: 106).

Writers who broadcast over the wireless during the war did not entirely turn their backs on television, but it might be said that the transition suited few of them. Following his wartime stint as a correspondent, Denis Johnston had returned to BBC Television as Director of Programmes in 1946, although he found the work less creative in an austerity Britain where radio still reigned; he resigned in 1947 to pursue freelance television work in New York, but found his BBC reputation did not carry him very far there, and eventually moved into academia (Adams 2002: 284–302). In April 1953, BBC Director of Television (and former Third Programme Controller) George Barnes reached out to Johnston about returning to the now-vigorous television department, but Johnston was busy with his academic career and in the thick of preparations for the publication of *Nine Rivers from Jordan* later that year, and so demurred (Adams 2002: 386).

In an echo of the initial mistrust that some felt towards radio, many other writers found it even more difficult than Johnston did to embrace television with any fervour. Though he was enthusiastic about radio, T. S. Eliot resisted the new audio-visual medium because he thought it further distanced the public from what he considered appropriately elevating and challenging forms of art (Coyle 2009: 192). W. H. Auden was outright dismissive; in a 1972 interview with the *Paris Review*, he declaimed, 'I don't see how any civilised person can watch TV, far less own a set' (qtd in Carey 1992: 214). For some writers, television simply represented another imperfect medium that, while it had its drawbacks, offered certain advantages. MacNeice may have grudgingly acknowledged that television captured the spectacle of the coronation ceremony, but he worried that, as television and other media continued to grow in popularity, the audience might forget the ability of radio to offer an imaginative experience free of visual determinants:

> Let us pray then that *all* the media survive. Radio and the films have not yet killed books and there are many words including many poems which it is best to read on the page. Above all do not let us, with 3D and such impinging on us, think that a multiple technique is necessarily 'better' than a simple technique. Many music lovers prefer to hear music with their eyes shut and who wants to live all the time in the world of Mr. Disney's *Fantasia*? (1953: 135)

MacNeice never tried his hand at 3-D filmmaking. He would go on to direct two August Strindberg plays for television in 1958, but he never felt at home in the medium (Stallworthy 1995: 429). Although theoretically open to the possibilities of television, it may simply have been too late in his career for him to take the same kinds of risk with television as he had with radio less than twenty years earlier.

Writing in 1957, Priestley gave voice to a similarly resigned acceptance of new media. He could not hide his disappointment that the public enthusiasm that had animated British writers' success in radio broadcasting in earlier decades was passing. No matter how resistant he may have been to the seductions of the postwar consumer society he dubbed 'Admass' (Priestley and Hawkes 1955: 50), Priestley saw adaptation to new media as the only choice open to the midcentury intellectual, who must 'go after his audience wherever that audience may be':

> You may wish, as I have often wished, that the media of mass communications had never been invented; but they have been invented, they are with us

... Therefore, if we think of ourselves not simply as exponents of the printed word, but as creators, as makers, as inventors; as belonging to one of those eternal types I mentioned earlier, we should go for the audience wherever it may be found and try to learn those new techniques demanded by the new media ... I feel very strongly that, certainly in this country, we would have had better films, we would have had better radio and we would be having better television if more writers had thought it their duty to learn how to use these media and so found new audiences; in the hope, of course, of bringing those audiences to the older arts of the printed word and the theatre. (Priestley 1957: 27–8)

Priestley's shift in tense when referring to the media of mass communication, from the film and radio the public 'would have had' to the television they 'would be having', is telling. In consigning film and radio, rather prematurely, to the dustbin of media past, he indicates a belief that their eclipse by television is all but complete. Reports of the death of cinema and of radio remain greatly exaggerated. Priestley's nostalgic tone nonetheless reflects a sense that the moment of primacy for both media, as well as for himself, had passed.

The loss of this historically contingent confluence of mass-mediated public cultural authority, directed towards progressive goals, was perhaps especially crushing for Priestley because it had once seemed so full of potential. Following the war, the spirit of participatory democracy and common endeavour that had animated the early years of the People's War seemed to fade in favour of a government run by faceless technocrats: 'One day in the late summer of '45,' Priestley wrote in 1958, 'Revolutionary Young England was invited to 10 Downing Street, to be thanked for its election services, and was shot as it went upstairs. Who pulled the trigger, I don't know' (1958: 15). Against the sense of possibility that his 'Postscripts' had at once captured and engendered, an exhausted resignation to officialdom seemed to set in amongst the public. Instead of inheriting a culture of creation and community, the nation had been taken over by something he dubbed 'Topside', a new form of Establishment England (and he was back to calling it 'England') that blended tradition, bureaucracy and the love of power. *'Topside'*, Priestley states, is *'the reaction against a revolution that never happened'* (1958: 14; emphasis in original).

With public attention fixated on the future of the nation during the war, radio had opened up a vast field of engagement for writers interested in framing the character of British cultural and political life, a field characterised by feedback and iteration, and by a process of constant negotiation between dictating and reflecting public expectations and tastes. But the same forces of public opinion that had forced the BBC to appeal more directly to listeners' tastes from the late 1930s onwards effected a postwar diffusion of the power held by the Home Service on the domestic front and the Overseas Service on the international front. While the launch of the Third Programme in 1946 would ensure a forum for highbrow content for decades to come, the tripartite division of broadcasting services served to institutionalise cultural hierarchies while splitting the attention of the national radio public. The resumption of BBC television broadcasting in 1946 only added to a media landscape already populated by radio, cinema and print.

The pre-eminence of radio as a site for discourses of politics, culture and identity did not last long. As a medium for propagating stories of national and transnational belonging, radio reached its apogee during the Second World War and would sustain it for some years afterwards before beginning a slow fade-out that continues to this day. But, for that brief historical period, the sound of an individual's voice and the weight of that individual's words could affect the shape of debate on a national scale. The same crisis that cemented writers' resolve to participate in the public sphere brought that public sphere to new life, as listeners tuned in to hear representations of the events and ideas that shaped both the immediate and the more distant future. Writing the radio war demanded an attention to the tenor of public discussion and a willingness to step in and influence that same discussion. In bringing a diversity of opinions, accents and aesthetics to the radio, British writers moved beyond entertainment and information to open up new possibilities for belonging to Britain and to the nations of the Commonwealth to come.

Notes

1. In terms of commodity purchasing power, £45 in 1953 was equivalent to approximately £1,100 in 2016. As a comparison, the brand-new Olivetti Lettera 22 typewriter was advertised at £28.15s in the 11 June 1953 issue of *The Listener* ('Olivetti' 1953: 936). A 1951 Pye P43 table-top Superhet radio receiver retailed for £12.5s.2d when first introduced ('Pye P43' 1952).
2. On these and other programmes, see the *Radio Times* schedules for the months of April, May and June 1953. *The Listener* reprinted portions of Douglas Willis's report on Coronation Ales on 5 March 1953 ('Did You Hear That?' 1953: 377) and C. H. Williams's 'The Legend of the Holy Oil' on 28 May 1953 (C. H. Williams 1953: 875).
3. On the relation of the royal family to broadcasting during the war, see Hajkowski, *The BBC and National Identity* (2010: 93–7).

Bibliography

Archival sources
British Broadcasting Corporation Written Archives Centre (BBC WAC), Caversham

Calling the West Indies script files, Boxes 21–23.

Caribbean Voices script files (microfilm).

Day Lewis, Cecil. *Ariel in Wartime*. Original transmission 8 March 1941 on BBC Home Service.

E1/1294/1: Countries: West Indies/Broadcasting in W. Indies/File 1a/Sept 1940–1942.

E1/1294/2: Countries: West Indies/Broadcasting in W. Indies/File 1b/1943–1944.

E1/1301: Countries: West Indies/General/1936–1950.

E2/584: Foreign General/West Indies.

Films 5/6, Home News Bulletins, War 1943–4 A–Z.

Hanley, James, 'Atlantic Convoy', *Freedom Ferry* (ep. 1) script files: D. G. Bridson, Manchester. Overseas Service transmission 14 May 1941.

Hanley, James, 'Pilots', *Freedom Ferry* (ep. 11) script files: John Glyn-Jones. Overseas Service transmission 23 July 1941.

Hanley, James, 'Men in Darkness', *Freedom Ferry* (ep. 13) script files: D. G. Bridson. Overseas Service transmission 6 August 1941.

Hanley, James, 'Open Boat', *Freedom Ferry* (ep. 18) script files: D. G. Bridson. Overseas Service transmission 10 September 1941.

Home News Bulletin Index.

L1/225/1: Left Staff/Johnston, William Denis. 1936–1948.

L1/285/1: Left Staff/MacNeice, Frederick Louis. 1941–1961.

L1/290/1: Left Staff/Marson, Una Mavis Victoria. 1941–1946.

LR/151: Listener Research Report: 'Listeners' Comments on Mr. Duff Cooper, Mr. J.B. Priestley, and Sir Hugh Elles'. 2 August 1940. File R9/9/4.

LR/231: Listener Research Report: 'Mr. J.B. Priestley's Postscripts'. 2 March 1941. File R9/9/5: Audience Research: Special Reports 5: Sound and General, 1941.

LR/493: Listener Research Report: 'Alexander Nevsky'. 23 December 1941. File R9/64/4.

LR/882: Listener Research Report: 'Alexander Nevsky'. 14 May 1942. File R9/64/4.
LR/1175: Listener Research Report: 'USSR: Public Opinion on the Function of British Broadcasting in Interpreting the USSR to British Listeners'. 11 September 1942. File R9/9/6.
LR/1264: Listener Research Report: 'Christopher Columbus'. 29 October 1942. File R9/64/4.
MacNeice, Louis (1941), *Alexander Nevsky*, Dallas Bower (prod.), BBC Home Service. Original transmission 9 December 1941.
MacNeice, Louis (1941), 'Dr. Johnson Takes It (17 Gough Square)', *The Stones Cry Out*, E. A. F. Harding (prod.), BBC Eastern Service. Original transmission 5 May 1941.
MacNeice, Louis (1941), 'The House of Commons', *The Stones Cry Out* (ep. 10), John Glyn-Jones (prod.), BBC Eastern Service. Original transmission 7 July 1941.
MacNeice, Louis (1941), 'St. Paul's', *The Stones Cry Out* (ep. 8) (prod. unknown), BBC Eastern Service. Original transmission 23 June 1941.
MacNeice, Louis (1941), 'The Temple', *The Stones Cry Out* (ep. 18), John Glyn-Jones (prod.), BBC Eastern Service. Original transmission 1 September 1941.
MacNeice, Louis (1941), 'Westminster Abbey', *The Stones Cry Out* (ep. 8), Malcolm Baker-Smith (prod.), BBC Eastern Service. Original transmission 26 May 1941.
R19/174: 'Entertainment: Christopher Columbus: 1941–1949'.
R19/352/3: Entertainment: Features Head Office Memos: July–Dec 1940.
R19/1222/1: Entertainment: 'The Stones Cry Out': File 1: May–Aug 1941.
R28/280/1: 'FOREIGN NEWS COMMITTEE: Report to Controller (News) on Radio War Correspondence and News Service from the Fighting Fronts'. 8 December 1942.
R45/78: Recorded Programmes: 'The Stones Cry Out: 1941'.
R46/92: Recorded Programmes: 'Calling the West Indies: 1940–1950'.
RCont1/Hanley.
RCont1/Talks/J.B. Priestley/File 1/1927–39.
RCont1/Talks/J.B. Priestley/File 2/1940.
RCont1/Talks/J.B. Priestley/File 3/1941.

British Library (BL), London

Christopher Columbus. Prod. Dallas Bower. 12 October 1942. Shelf Number T573–574W S1–4. National Sound Archives.
'Not too bad, really/Bower'. 27 January 1992, BBC Radio 3. Shelf Mark B9031/1. National Sound Archives.

Harry Ransom Humanities Research Center, Austin

Ms. (Priestley, J.B.) Recip.

Imperial War Museum (IWM), London

Johnston, Denis. BBC Field Recording (1945–02–21). Shelf mark 1973.
Johnston, Denis. BBC Field Recording (1945–04–18). Shelf mark 2048.
Johnston, Denis. BBC Field Recording (1942–11–08). Shelf mark 1243.

Trinity College Dublin Manuscripts and Archives Research Library (TCD), Dublin

MS 10066/188: 'Denis Johnston War Field Book I (Middle East), 30 April 1942 – 31 Oct 1942'.
MS 10033/190: 'Denis Johnston War Field Book III (Italian Campaign, 8 Sept 1943 – 15 Feb 1944'.
MS 10066/362/125: 'Denis Johnston: World War II Correspondence, 1944'.
MS 10066/362/315: 22 April 1945.
MS 10066/Misc. Photocopies 103 Denis Johnston, diary 8 Nov 1944 – 17 March 1945.
MS 10066/Misc. Photocopies 104 Denis Johnston, diary 22 March – 21 May 1945 + 1961 Postscript.
MS 3208: Dionysia I (Book I).
MS 3213: Dionysia III (Book VI).
MS 3751: Misc. Box XI.

University of Bradford Special Collections Library (UB), Bradford

PRI 13/22: Priestley Papers: Correspondence: Letters to Gene [Saxton] and Cass Canfield, 1940–1942.
PRI 19/4: Biography: 'Radio Lives: J.B. Priestley' (audiocassette). 13 June 1991, BBC Radio Four.

University College, London (UCL)

George Orwell Papers (GB 0103 Orwell [H]): Letters to Orwell.

University of Oxford, Bodleian Library Special Collections (Bodleian), Oxford

Bodleian Manuscripts Collection: MS. Eng. Lett. C.465: Louis MacNeice Papers: Uncatalogued Papers, Box 9.

Printed sources

Adams, Bernard (2002), *Denis Johnston: A Life*, Dublin: Lilliput Press.
Addyman, David (2014), 'J. B. Priestley: By Radio to a New Britain', in Matthew Feldman, Erik Tonning and Henry Mead (eds), *Broadcasting in the Modernist Era*, New York: Bloomsbury, pp. 155–68.

'Anancy', *OED Online*, Oxford University Press, December 2016, <http://www.oed.com> (last accessed 10 March 2017).
Anderson, Benedict ([1983] 2006), *Imagined Communities*, New York: Verso.
Arnheim, Rudolf ([1936] 1986), *Radio*, Salem: Ayer.
Arnold, A. James, Julio Rodriguez-Luis and J. Michael Dash (2001), *A History of Literature in the Caribbean: English- and Dutch-speaking Regions*, Philadelphia: J. Benjamins.
Avery, Todd (2006), *Radio Modernism: Literature, Ethics, and the BBC, 1922–1938*, Burlington, VT: Ashgate.
Baade, Christina (2012), *Victory through Harmony: The BBC and Popular Music in World War II*, New York: Oxford University Press.
Baker-Smith, Malcolm (1941), letter to Laurence Gilliam, 8 December 1941. RCont1/Hanley, James/Scriptwriter/1a, BBC Written Archives Centre, Caversham.
— (1942), 'Report on James Hanley', letter to Laurence Gilliam, 11 November 1942. RCont1/Hanley, James/Scriptwriter/1a, BBC Written Archives Centre, Caversham.
Barnett, Gene (1978), *Denis Johnston*, Boston: Twayne.
Barrett, Gerard (2007), 'James Hanley and the Colours of War', in Marina MacKay and Lyndsey Stonebridge (eds), *British Fiction After Modernism: The Novel at Mid-Century*, London: Palgrave.
Baucom, Ian (2001), 'Frantz Fanon's Radio: Solidarity, Diaspora, and the Tactics of Listening', *Contemporary Literature* 42.1 (Spring 2001), pp. 15–49.
Baxendale, John (2007), *Priestley's England: J. B. Priestley and English Culture*, New York: Manchester University Press.
BBC (British Broadcasting Corporation) (1942), *Engineering Division Training Manuals*, London: British Broadcasting Corporation.
BBC Features (1941), unsigned memo (possibly by Laurence Gilliam) to Sir John Forsdyke, 9 July 1941. R45/78, Recorded Programmes, 'The Stones Cry Out', 1941, BBC Written Archives Centre, Caversham.
BBC Foreign News Committee (1942), 'Report to Controller (News) on Radio War Correspondence and News Services from the Fighting Fronts', 8 December 1942. R28/280/1, BBC Written Archives Centre, Caversham.
Bloom, Emily (2017), *The Wireless Past: Anglo-Irish Writers and the BBC, 1931–1968*, Oxford: Oxford University Press.
Bluemel, Kristin (2004), *George Orwell and the Radical Eccentrics: Intermodernism in Literary London*, London: Palgrave MacMillan.
Bolter, David Jay and Richard Grusin (2001), *Remediation: Understanding New Media*, Cambridge, MA: MIT Press.
Boswell, Ronald (1940), letter to J. B. Priestley, 28 May 1940. RCont1/Talks/J.B. Priestley/2/1940, BBC Written Archives Centre, Caversham.
Bourdieu, Pierre ([1979] 1984), *Distinction: A Social Critique of the Judgement of Taste*, trans. Richard Nice, Cambridge, MA: Harvard University Press.
— (1993), *The Field of Cultural Production: Essays on Art and Literature*, ed. Randal Johnson, New York: Columbia University Press.
Bowen, Elizabeth ([1969] 1986), 'The People's War by Angus Calder', in *The Mulberry Tree: Writings of Elizabeth Bowen*, ed. Hermione Lee, New York: Harcourt Brace Jovanovich.

— (1986), *The Mulberry Tree: Writings of Elizabeth Bowen*, ed. Hermione Lee, New York: Harcourt Brace Jovanovich.
— (2010), *Listening In*, ed. Allan Hepburn, Edinburgh: Edinburgh University Press.
Bower, Dallas (1942a), letter to Sir Adrian Boult, 2 October 1942. R19/174: 'Entertainment: Christopher Columbus: 1941–1949', BBC Written Archives Centre, Caversham.
— (1942b), 'Christopher Columbus', draft copy of promotional material, 14 September 1942. R19/174: 'Entertainment: Christopher Columbus: 1941–1949', BBC Written Archives Centre, Caversham.
— (1942c), letter to William Walton, 14 October 1942. R19/174: 'Entertainment: Christopher Columbus: 1941–1949', BBC Written Archives Centre, Caversham.
— (1942d), letter to Sir Adrian Boult, 14 October 1942. R19/174: 'Entertainment: Christopher Columbus: 1941–1949', BBC Written Archives Centre, Caversham.
Bowker, Gordon (2003), *George Orwell*, London: Little, Brown and Co.
Brathwaite, Edward Kamau (1984), *History of the Voice: The Development of Nation Language in Anglophone Caribbean Poetry*, London: New Beacon Books.
Breiner, Laurence (2003), 'Caribbean Voices on the Air: Radio, Poetry, and Nationalism in the Anglophone Caribbean', in Susan Merrill Squier (ed.), *Communities of the Air: Radio Century, Radio Culture*, Durham, NC: Duke University Press, pp. 93–108.
Brewer, Susan A. (1997), *To Win the Peace: British Propaganda to the United States during World War II*, Edinburgh: Edinburgh University Press.
Bridson, D. G. (1971), *Prospero and Ariel: The Rise and Fall of Radio*, London: Gollancz.
Briggs, Asa (1961), *The History of Broadcasting in the United Kingdom, Vol. 1: The Birth of Broadcasting*, London: Oxford University Press.
— (1965), *The History of Broadcasting in the United Kingdom, Vol. 2: The Golden Age of Wireless*, London: Oxford University Press.
— (1970), *The History of Broadcasting in the United Kingdom, Vol. 3: The War of Words*, London: Oxford University Press.
'Britain Speaks' (1940), J. B. Priestley Contract, 30 May 1940. RCont 1/Talks/J.B. Priestley 2 (1940), BBC Written Archives Centre, Caversham.
Brooks, Tim (2007), *British Propaganda to France, 1940–1944: Machinery, Method and Message*, Edinburgh: Edinburgh University Press.
Brown, Erica and Mary Grover (eds) (2012), *Middlebrow Literary Cultures: The Battle of the Brows, 1920–1960*, London: Palgrave MacMillan.
Buitenhuis, Peter (2000), 'J. B. Priestley: The BBC's Star Propagandist in World War II', *English Studies in Canada* 26.4 (2000), pp. 445–72.
Burnham, Barbara (1938), Memo to John Pudney, 11 August 1938. RCont1/Hanley, James/Scriptwriter/1a, BBC Written Archives Centre, Caversham.
Calder, Angus (1969), *The People's War: Britain 1939–1945*, London: Cape.
— (1993), *The Myth of the Blitz*, London: Pimlico.
Calder, Robert (2004), *Beware the British Serpent: The Role of Writers in British Propaganda in the United States 1939–1945*, Montreal: McGill-Queen's University Press.

Cardiff, David and Paddy Scannell ([1987] 2009), 'Radio in World War II', in Andrew Crisell (ed.), *Radio*, vol. 2, New York: Routledge.
Carey, John (1992), *The Intellectuals and the Masses*, London: Faber.
Casanova, Pascale (2004), *The World Republic of Letters*, trans. M. B. DeBevoise, Cambridge, MA: Harvard University Press.
Cathcart, Rex (1984), *A Most Contrary Region: The BBC in Northern Ireland*, Belfast: Blackstaff Press.
Cesarani, David (1996), 'Great Britain', in David S. Wyman (ed.), *The World Reacts to the Holocaust*, Baltimore: Johns Hopkins University Press.
Chamberlain, Neville (1939), 'Declaration of War with Germany', Rec. 3 September 1939. *Greatest Speeches of All Time*, Master Classics Records/The Orchard. Audio MP3.
Chapman, James (1998), *The British at War: Cinema, State and Propaganda*, London: I. B. Tauris.
Chignell, Hugh (2009a), 'Co-presence', *Key Concepts in Radio Studies*, London: SAGE UK, <http://www.credoreference.com/entry/sageukrs/co_presence> (last accessed 27 March 2013).
— (2009b), 'Imagined Community', *Key Concepts in Radio Studies*, London: SAGE UK, <http://www.credoreference.com/entry/sageukrs/co_presence> (last accessed 27 March 2013).
Christopher Columbus (1942). Written Louis MacNeice. Prod. Dallas Bower. BBC Home Service, 12 October 1942. Shelf Number T573–574W S1–4, National Sound Archives, British Library, London.
Churchill, Winston (1951), *The Grand Alliance*, Boston: Houghton Mifflin.
Clarke, Dorothy (ed.) (1942), 'Brer Nancy and de Woss-woss', 12 November 1942. CWI Box 21 Folder 1941–43, BBC Written Archives Centre, Caversham.
Cohen, Debra Rae (2009), 'Annexing the Oracular Voice: Form, Ideology, and the BBC', in Debra Rae Cohen, Michael Coyle and Jane Lewty (eds), *Broadcasting Modernism*, Gainesville: University Press of Florida.
— (2010), 'Modernism on Radio', in Peter Brooker, Andrzej Gąsiorek, Deborah Longworth and Andrew Thacker (eds), *The Oxford Handbook of Modernisms*, Oxford: Oxford University Press.
— (2012), 'Intermediality and the Problem of *The Listener*', *Modernism/modernity* 19.3 (September 2012), pp. 569–92.
— (2015), '"Strange Collisions": Keywords Toward an Intermedial Periodical Studies', *English Studies in Canada* 41.1 (March 2015), pp. 93–104.
Cole, Robert (2006), *Propaganda, Censorship and Irish Neutrality in the Second World War*, Edinburgh: Edinburgh University Press.
Colley, Linda (1992), *Britons: Forging the Nation, 1707–1837*, New Haven, CT: Yale University Press.
'Convention (IV) Respecting the Laws and Customs of War on Land', 1907, <https://ihl-databases.icrc.org/ihl/INTRO/195> (last accessed 7 June 2016).
'Convention Relative to the Treatment of Prisoners of War', 27 July 1929, Geneva Convention, <https://ihl-databases.icrc.org/ihl/INTRO/305?OpenDocument> (last accessed 7 June 2016).
Cook, Christopher (2011), *Goethe's Oak*, radio broadcast on BBC 3, Weimar, Germany: Mark Burman, 2011.

Cook, Judith (1998), *Priestley*, London: Bloomsbury.
Cottrell, Leonard (1942), memos to Louis MacNeice and Dallas Bower, 13 October 1942. R19/174: 'Entertainment: Christopher Columbus: 1941–1949', BBC Written Archives Centre, Caversham.
Coulton, Barbara (1980), *Louis MacNeice at the BBC*, Boston: Faber.
Coyle, Michael (2009), 'We Speak to India: T. S. Eliot's Wartime Broadcasts and the Frontiers of Culture', in Debra Rae Cohen, Michael Coyle and Jane Lewty (eds), *Broadcasting Modernism*, Gainesville: University Press of Florida.
Craxton, Anthony (1942), memo to Dallas Bower, 13 October 1942. R19/174: 'Entertainment: Christopher Columbus: 1941–1949', BBC Written Archives Centre, Caversham.
Crisell, Andrew ([1986] 1994), *Understanding Radio*, 2nd edn, London: Routledge.
Cull, Nicholas (1995), *Selling War: The British Propaganda against American 'Neutrality' in World War II*, Oxford: Oxford University Press.
Davison, Peter (ed.) (1998), *The Complete Works of George Orwell*, 20 vols, London: Secker and Warburg.
Day Lewis, Cecil (1941), *Ariel in Wartime*, BBC Home Service, 8 March 1941. Microfilm. BBC Written Archives Centre, Caversham.
— ([1943] 1992), 'Where Are the War Poets?', *Complete Poems*, Stanford: Stanford University Press, p. 335.
Deer, Patrick (2009), *Culture in Camouflage: War, Empire, and Modern British Literature*, New York: Oxford University Press.
Dentith, Simon (2003), 'James Hanley's *The Furys*: The Modernist Subject Goes on Strike', *Literature & History* 12.1 (2003), pp. 41–56.
'Did You Hear That?' (1953), *The Listener* 1253 (5 March 1953), p. 377.
Dillon, Francis (1942), letter to Laurence Gilliam, 13 October 1942. RCont1/Hanley, James/Scriptwriter/1b, BBC Written Archives Centre, Caversham.
Dinsman, Melissa (2015), *Modernism at the Microphone: Radio, Propaganda, and Literary Aesthetics During World War II*, London: Bloomsbury.
Doherty, Martin (2000), *Nazi Wireless Propaganda: Lord Haw-Haw and British Public Opinion in the Second World War*, Edinburgh: Edinburgh University Press.
Donnell, Alison (2006), *Twentieth-Century Caribbean Literature: Critical Moments in Anglophone Literary History*, New York: Routledge.
Donnell, Alison and Sarah Lawson Welsh (eds) (1996), *The Routledge Reader in Caribbean Literature*, New York: Routledge.
Douglas, Susan (1999), *Listening In: Radio and the American Imagination*, Minneapolis: University of Minnesota Press.
Drakakis, John (ed. and 'Introduction') (1981), *British Radio Drama*, Cambridge: Cambridge University Press.
E1/1294/1: Countries: West Indies/Broadcasting in W. Indies/File 1a/Sept 1940–1942, BBC Written Archives Centre, Caversham.
'Eclipse of the Highbrow' (1941), *Times* [London], 25 March 1941, p. 5.
Edwards, Brent Hayes (2003), *The Practice of Diaspora: Literature, Translation, and the Rise of Black Internationalism*, Cambridge, MA: Harvard University Press.

Ellul, Jacques (1962), *Propaganda: The Formation of Men's Attitudes*, trans. Konrad Kellen and Jean Lerner, New York: Knopf.
'Extended Service to West Indies' (1941), *London Calling* 81 (27 March 1941), p. 81.
Fanon, Frantz (1976), *A Dying Colonialism*, trans. Haakon Chevalier, New York: Grove.
Fielden, Lionel (1929), memo to Hilda Matheson and Roger Eckersley, 21 November 1929. RCont 1/Talks/J.B. Priestley 1 (1927–1939), BBC Written Archives Centre, Caversham.
Fifield, Peter (2014), '"I Often Wish You Could Answer Me Back: And So Perhaps Do You!" E. M. Forster and Radio Broadcasting', in Matthew Feldman, Erik Tonning and Henry Mead (eds), *Broadcasting in the Modernist Era*, New York: Bloomsbury, pp. 57–78.
Figueroa, John (ed.) (1966–1970), *Caribbean Voices: An Anthology of West Indian Poetry*, 2 vols, London: Evans Brothers.
Films 5/6, Home News Bulletins, War 1943/1944 A-Z. Microfilm. BBC Written Archives Centre, Caversham.
Fleay, C. and M. L. Sanders (1989), 'Looking into the Abyss: George Orwell at the BBC', *Journal of Contemporary History* 24.3 (July 1989), pp. 503–18.
Fordham, John (2002), *James Hanley: Modernism and the Working Class*, Cardiff: University of Wales Press.
'Foreword' (1941), *Picture Post* 10.1 (4 January 1941), p. 4.
Friedman, Susan Stanford (2015), *Planetary Modernism: Provocations on Modernity Across Time*, New York: Columbia.
Gilbert, Joan (1941), memo to Mr. Boswell, 15 May 1941. R46/92, BBC Written Archives Centre, Caversham.
Gilliam, Laurence (1941a), memo to D. G. Bridson, Jack Dillon and John Glyn-Jones, 15 July 1941. R45/78, Recorded Programmes, 'The Stones Cry Out' 1941, BBC Written Archives Centre, Caversham.
— (1941b), letter to James Hanley, 31 July 1941. RCont1/Hanley, James/Scriptwriter/1a, BBC Written Archives Centre, Caversham.
— (1941c), letter to D. G. Bridson, 31 July 1941. RCont1/Hanley, James/Scriptwriter/1a, BBC Written Archives Centre, Caversham.
— (1941d), memo to D. G. Bridson, Jack Dillon and John Glyn-Jones, 17 August 1941. R45/78, Recorded Programmes, 'The Stones Cry Out' 1941, BBC Written Archives Centre, Caversham.
— (1941e), memo to Peter Watts, 9 September 1941. R45/78, Recorded Programmes, 'The Stones Cry Out' 1941, BBC Written Archives Centre, Caversham.
— (1941f), memo to Controller (Programmes), 30 September 1941. R45/78, Recorded Programmes, 'The Stones Cry Out' 1941, BBC Written Archives Centre, Caversham.
— (1941g), letter to Francis Dillon, 29 December 1941. RCont1/Hanley, James/Scriptwriter/1a, BBC Written Archives Centre, Caversham.
— (1950), *B.B.C. Features*, London: Evans Brothers.
Gilroy, Paul (1993), *The Black Atlantic: Modernity and Double Consciousness*, Cambridge, MA: Harvard University Press.
Goble, Mark (2010), *Beautiful Circuits: Modernism and the Mediated Life*, New York: Columbia University Press.

Goldie, Grace Wyndham (1941a), 'The Critic on the Hearth: Broadcast Drama: War, MacNeice and Such', *The Listener* XXVI.662 (18 September 1941), p. 416.
— (1941b), 'The Critic on the Hearth: Broadcast Drama: The Rise of the Feature', *The Listener* XXVI.675 (18 December 1941), p. 832.
Greene, Graham (1940), 'A Lost Leader', *Spectator* (13 December 1940), p. 646.
Grenfell-Williams, John (1941), memo to unknown recipient ('Programmes to the West Indies'), 17 November 1941. E1/1294/1, BBC Written Archives Centre, Caversham.
— (1944), memo to Acting Controller (Overseas Service) R. A. Rendall, 30 May 1944. E1/1301, BBC Written Archives Centre, Caversham.
Griffith, Glyne (2003), '"This is London Calling the West Indies": The BBC's *Caribbean Voices*', in Bill Schwarz (ed.), *West Indian Intellectuals in Britain*, New York: Manchester University Press, pp. 196–207.
Hajkowski, Thomas (2010), *The BBC and National Identity in Britain, 1922–53*, New York: Manchester University Press.
Haley, W. H. (1944), memo to Assistant Controller (News) re: 'Proposed Live Broadcast on an Allied Bomber over Berlin', 6 April 1944. R28/280/1, BBC Written Archives Centre, Caversham.
Hall, Stuart (1977), 'Culture, the Media, and the Ideological Effect', in James Curran, Michael Gurevitch and Janet Woollacott (eds), *Mass Communication and Society*, London: Edward Arnold.
— (1980), 'Race, Articulation and Societies Structured in Dominance', *Sociological Theories: Race and Colonialism*, Paris: UNESCO, pp. 305–45.
Hammill, Faye (2007), *Women, Celebrity, and Literary Culture between the Wars*, Austin: University of Texas Press.
Hanley, James (1941a), 'Atlantic Convoy', *Freedom Ferry* (ep. 1), prod. D. G. Bridson. Overseas Service, 14 May 1941. Microfilm. BBC Written Archives Centre, Caversham.
— (1941b), 'Pilots', *Freedom Ferry* (ep. 11), prod. John Glyn-Jones. Overseas Service, 23 July 1941. Microfilm. BBC Written Archives Centre, Caversham.
— (1941c), 'Men in Darkness', *Freedom Ferry* (ep. 13), prod. D. G. Bridson. Overseas Service, 6 August 1941. Microfilm. BBC Written Archives Centre, Caversham.
— (1941d), 'Open Boat', *Freedom Ferry* (ep. 18), prod. D. G. Bridson. Overseas Service, 10 September 1941. Microfilm. BBC Written Archives Centre, Caversham.
— (1941e), letter to Laurence Gilliam, 28 October 1941. RCont1/Hanley, James/Scriptwriter/1a, BBC Written Archives Centre, Caversham.
— ([1941] 1999), *The Ocean*, London: Harvill Press.
— (1942a), letter to Laurence Gilliam, n.d. (between April and August 1942). RCont1/Hanley, James/Scriptwriter/1b, BBC Written Archives Centre, Caversham.
— (1942b), letter to Val Gielgud, 6 November 1942. RCont1/Hanley, James/Scriptwriter/1b, BBC Written Archives Centre, Caversham.
— (1943), *Sailor's Song*, London: Nicholson & Watson.
Hanley, James and Malcolm Baker-Smith (1942), *Return to Danger*, BBC

Home Service, 15 January 1942. Microfilm. BBC Written Archives Centre, Caversham.
Hanley, James and Brigid Maas (1942), *Shadows Before Sunrise*, prod. Leonard Cottrell. BBC Home Service, 6 December 1942. Microfilm. BBC Written Archives Centre, Caversham.
Hannon, Brian (2008), 'Creating the Correspondent: How the BBC Reached the Frontline in the Second World War', *Historical Journal of Film, Radio and Television* 28.2 (June 2008), pp. 175–94.
Hart, Matthew (2010), *Nations of Nothing but Poetry: Modernism, Transnationalism, and Synthetic Vernacular Writing*, New York: Oxford University Press.
Hawkes, Nicholas (2008), *The Story of J. B. Priestley's Postscripts*, Bradford: J. B. Priestley Society.
Hawkins, Desmond (ed.) ([1946] 2014), *War Report*, London: BBC Books.
Hendy, David (2000), *Radio in the Global Age*, Malden, MA: Blackwell.
— (2013), 'Painting with Sound: The Kaleidoscopic World of Lance Sieveking, a British Radio Modernist', *Twentieth Century British History* 24.2 (2013), pp. 169–200.
Hepburn, Allan (ed. and Introduction) (2010), *Listening In: Broadcasts, Speeches, and Interviews by Elizabeth Bowen*, Edinburgh: Edinburgh University Press.
Hewison, Robert (1977), *Under Siege: Literary Life in London, 1939–45*, New York: Oxford University Press.
Hiller, Eric (1942), letter to Francis Dillon, 6 October 1942. RCont1/Hanley, James/Scriptwriter/1b, BBC Written Archives Centre, Caversham.
Hilmes, Michele (1997), *Radio Voices: American Broadcasting, 1922–1952*, Minneapolis: University of Minnesota Press.
— (2012), *Network Nations: A Transnational History of British and American Broadcasting*, New York: Routledge.
'Hoch lebe', *OED Online*, Oxford University Press, June 2016, <http://www.oed.com> (last accessed 27 August 2016).
Holmes, Christopher (1981), 'The Radio Drama of Louis MacNeice', in John Drakakis (ed.), *British Radio Drama*, Cambridge: Cambridge University Press.
Home News Bulletin Index (n.d.), 'Johnston, Denis', BBC Written Archives Centre, Caversham.
Humble, Nicola (2001), *The Feminine Middlebrow Novel, 1920s to 1950s: Class, Domesticity, and Bohemianism*, New York: Oxford University Press.
Jarrett-Macauley, Delia (1996), 'Putting the Black Woman in the Frame: Una Marson and the West Indian Challenge to British National identity', in Christine Gledhill and Gillian Johnson (eds), *Nationalising Femininity: Culture, Sexuality, and British Cinema in the Second World War*, New York: Manchester University Press, pp. 119–26.
— (1998), *The Life of Una Marson, 1905–65*, New York: Manchester University Press.
Johnston, Denis (n.d.), 'Correction' (undated, post-1947) in MS 3751: Misc. Box XI: War Field Books 2–21st May 1945. Denis Johnston Papers, Trinity College Manuscripts and Archives Research Library, Dublin.
— ([1931] 1960), *The Moon in the Yellow River*, in Denis Johnston, *'The Old*

Lady Says "No"' and Other Plays, ed. Joseph Ronsley, Boston: Little, Brown and Co.
— (1942a), MS 10066/188: 'Denis Johnston War Field Book I (Middle East), 30 April 1942 – 31 Oct 1942.' Denis Johnston Papers, Trinity College Manuscripts and Archives Research Library, Dublin.
— (1942b), BBC Field Recording (1942–11–08). Shelf mark 1243, Imperial War Museum, London.
— (1943–4), MS 10033/190: 'Denis Johnston War Field Book III (Italian Campaign), 8 Sept 1943 – 15 Feb 1944.' Denis Johnston Papers, Trinity College Manuscripts and Archives Research Library, Dublin.
— (1944), MS 10066/362/125: 'Denis Johnston: World War II Correspondence, 1944.' Denis Johnston Papers, Trinity College Manuscripts and Archives Research Library, Dublin.
— (1944–5), MS 10066/Misc. Photocopies 103 Denis Johnston, diary 8 November 1944 – 17 March 1945. Denis Johnston Papers, Trinity College Manuscripts and Archives Research Library, Dublin.
— (1945a), MS 10066/362/315: 22 April 1945. Denis Johnston Papers, Trinity College Manuscripts and Archives Research Library, Dublin.
— (1945b), BBC Field Recording (1945–02–21). Shelf mark 1973, Imperial War Museum, London.
— (1945c), BBC Field Recording (1945–04–18). Shelf mark 2048, Imperial War Museum, London.
— (1945d), MS 3751: Misc. Box XI: War Field Books 2–21st May 1945. Denis Johnston Papers, Trinity College Manuscripts and Archives Research Library, Dublin.
— (1945–61), MS 10066/Misc. Photocopies 104 Denis Johnston, diary 22 March – 21 May 1945 + 1961 Postscript. Denis Johnston Papers, Trinity College Manuscripts and Archives Research Library, Dublin.
— (1947a), MS 3208: Dionysia I (Book I). Denis Johnston Papers, Trinity College Manuscripts and Archives Research Library, Dublin.
— (1947b), MS 3213: Dionysia III (Book VI). Denis Johnston Papers, Trinity College Manuscripts and Archives Research Library, Dublin.
— (1953), *Nine Rivers from Jordan*, London: Derek Verschoyle.
— (1976), *The Brazen Horn*, Dublin: Dolmen Editions.
Kalliney, Peter (2013), *Commonwealth of Letters: British Literary Culture and the Emergence of Postcolonial Aesthetics*, New York: Oxford University Press.
Keane, Damien (2014), *Ireland and the Problem of Information: Irish Writing, Radio, Late Modernist Communication*, University Park: Pennsylvania State University Press.
Kerr, Douglas (2002), 'Orwell's BBC Broadcasts: Colonial Discourse and the Rhetoric of Propaganda', *Textual Practice* 16.3 (2002), pp. 473–490.
— (2004), 'In the Picture: Orwell, India and the BBC', *Literature and History* 13.1 (2004), pp. 43–57.
Kushner, Tony (1994a), 'Different Worlds: British Perceptions of the Final Solution in the Second World War', in D. Cesarani (ed.), *The Final Solution*, London: Routledge, pp. 244–67.
— (1994b), *The Holocaust and the Liberal Imagination*, Cambridge, MA: Blackwell.

LaCapra, Dominick (1998), *History and Memory after Auschwitz*, Ithaca: Cornell University Press.
Lacey, Kate (2013), *Listening Publics: The Politics and Experience of Listening in the Media Age*, Malden, MA: Polity Press.
Lago, Mary (1990), 'E. M. Forster and the BBC', *Yearbook of English Studies* 20 (1990), pp. 131–55.
Lago, Mary, Linda K. Hughes and Elizabeth MacLeod Walls (eds and 'Introduction') (2008), *The BBC Talks of E. M. Forster*, Columbia: University of Missouri Press.
Lambert, Calvin (1942a), 'A Request to the West', on 'Calling the West Indies: Poems by Calvin Lambert', 14 June 1942. CWI Box 21/File 1941–43, BBC Written Archives Centre, Caversham.
— (1942b), 'War Planes', on 'Calling the West Indies: Poems by Calvin Lambert', 14 June 1942. CWI Box 21/File 1941–43, BBC Written Archives Centre, Caversham.
Lamming, George ([1960] 1984), *The Pleasures of Exile*, London: Allison and Busby.
Laqueur, Walter (1980), *The Terrible Secret: Suppression of the Truth about Hitler's Final Solution*, Boston: Little, Brown and Co.
Lawrence-Curran, Zelda (1999), '"All the things that might have been": *Christopher Columbus*', in Stewart R. Craggs (ed.), *William Walton: Music and Literature*, Brookfield, VT: Ashgate.
LeMahieu, D. L. (1988), *A Culture for Democracy: Mass Communication and the Cultivated Mind in Britain Between the Wars*, Oxford: Clarendon Press.
Levine, Caroline (2015), *Forms: Whole, Rhythm, Hierarchy, Network*, Princeton: Princeton University Press.
L1/225/1: Left Staff/Johnston, William Denis. 1936–1948. BBC Written Archives Centre, Caversham.
Longley, Edna (1988), *Louis MacNeice: A Study*, London: Faber.
Loviglio, Jason (2005), *Radio's Intimate Public: Network Broadcasting and Mass-Mediated Democracy*, Minneapolis: University of Minnesota Press.
LR/151 (1940), Listener Research Report: 'Listeners' Comments on Mr. Duff Cooper, Mr. J. B. Priestley, and Sir Hugh Elles', 2 August 1940. File R9/9/4, BBC Written Archives Centre, Caversham.
LR/231 (1941), Listener Research Report: 'Mr. J. B. Priestley's Postscripts', 2 March 1941. File R9/9/5: Audience Research: Special Reports 5: Sound and General, 1941. BBC Written Archives Centre, Caversham.
LR/493 (1941), Listener Research Report: 'Alexander Nevsky', 23 December 1941. File R9/64/4, BBC Written Archives Centre, Caversham.
LR/882 (1942), Listener Research Report: 'Alexander Nevsky', 14 May 1942. File R9/64/4, BBC Written Archives Centre, Caversham.
LR/1175 (1942), Listener Research Report: 'USSR: Public Opinion on the Function of British Broadcasting in Interpreting the USSR to British Listeners', 11 September 1942. File R9/9/6, BBC Written Archives Centre, Caversham.
LR/1264 (1942), Listener Research Report: 'Christopher Columbus', 29 October 1942. File R9/64/4, BBC Written Archives Centre, Caversham.
McDonald, Peter (1991), *Louis MacNeice: The Poet in his Contexts*, New York: Oxford University Press.

— (2002), *Serious Poetry: Form and Authority from Yeats to Hill*, New York: Oxford University Press.
Mackarness, R. S. P. (1942), 'My Name Is Atkins' (memo to James Hanley), 8 October 1942. RCont1/Hanley, James/Scriptwriter/1b, BBC Written Archives Centre, Caversham.
MacKay, Marina (2007), *Modernism and World War II*, Cambridge: Cambridge University Press.
Mackay, Robert (2006), 'An Abominable Precedent: The BBC Ban on Pacifists in the Second World War', *Contemporary British History* 20.4 (2006), pp. 491–510.
McLaine, Ian (1979), *The Ministry of Morale: Home Front Morale and the Ministry of Information in World War II*, Boston: Allen and Unwin.
MacNeice, Louis ([1938] 1968), *Modern Poetry*, 2nd edn, Oxford: Clarendon.
— ([1939] 2007), 'Autumn Journal', in Peter McDonald (ed.), *Collected Poems*, London: Faber.
— (1941a), letter to Elizabeth Dodds, 27 April 1941. MacNeice papers, MS. Eng. Lett. C.465, Bodleian Library, Oxford.
— (1941b), 'Dr. Johnson Takes It (17 Gough Square)', *The Stones Cry Out*, E. A. F. Harding (prod.), BBC Eastern Service, 5 May 1941. BBC Written Archives Centre, Caversham.
— (1941c), 'Westminster Abbey', *The Stones Cry Out* (ep. 8), Malcolm Baker-Smith (prod.), BBC Eastern Service, 26 May 1941. BBC Written Archives Centre, Caversham.
— (1941d), 'St. Paul's', *The Stones Cry Out* (ep. 8) (prod. unknown), BBC Eastern Service, 23 June 1941. BBC Written Archives Centre, Caversham.
— (1941e), 'The House of Commons', *The Stones Cry Out* (ep. 10), John Glyn-Jones (prod.), BBC Eastern Service, 7 July 1941. BBC Written Archives Centre, Caversham.
— (1941f), 'The Temple', *The Stones Cry Out* (ep. 18), John Glyn-Jones (prod.), BBC Eastern Service, 1 September 1941. BBC Written Archives Centre, Caversham.
— (1941g), *Alexander Nevsky*, Dallas Bower (prod.), BBC Home Service, 9 December 1941. BBC Written Archives Centre, Caversham.
— (1942), synopsis for *Christopher Columbus* (in memo from Dallas Bower to Adrian Boult), 28 January 1942. R19/174: 'Entertainment: Christopher Columbus: 1941–1949', BBC Written Archives Centre, Caversham.
— ([1944] 1993), *Christopher Columbus*, in Louis MacNeice, *Selected Plays of Louis MacNeice*, ed. Alan Heuser and Peter McDonald, Oxford: Oxford University Press, pp. 1–67.
— ([1944] 1993), 'Some Comments on Radio Drama', in Louis MacNeice, *Selected Plays of Louis MacNeice*, ed. Alan Heuser and Peter McDonald, Oxford: Oxford University Press, pp. 393–402.
— ([1946] 1993), 'Introduction to *The Dark Tower and Other Radio Scripts*', *Selected Plays*, ed. Alan Heuser and Peter McDonald, Oxford: Oxford University Press, pp. 403–8.
— (1953), 'A Plea for Sound', *BBC Quarterly* 8.3 (Autumn 1953), pp. 129–35.
— ([1954] 2007), 'Autumn Sequel', in Peter McDonald (ed.), *Collected Poems*, London: Faber.
— ([1965] 2007), *The Strings Are False*, London: Faber.

— (1969), *Persons from Porlock and Other Plays for Radio*, London: BBC.
— (1987), *Selected Literary Criticism of Louis MacNeice*, ed. Alan Heuser, Oxford: Oxford University Press.
— (1990), *Selected Prose of Louis MacNeice*, ed. Alan Heuser, Oxford: Oxford University Press.
— (1993), *Selected Plays of Louis MacNeice*, ed. Alan Heuser and Peter McDonald, Oxford: Oxford University Press.
— (2010), *The Letters of Louis MacNeice*, ed. Jonathan Allison, London: Faber.
Madden, Cecil (1940). Memorandum to unknown recipient ('West Indian Party'), 28 December 1940. R46/92, BBC Written Archives Centre, Caversham.
— (1941). Memorandum to Mrs. Fitzgerald ('West Indian Party [W. Indian Programmes]'), 3 January 1941. R46/92, BBC Written Archives Centre, Caversham.
Marshall, Howard (1944), 'Circular Instruction: All Correspondents' (telegram), circa May 1944. MS 10066/362/125/Denis Johnston: World War II Correspondence, 1944, Denis Johnston Papers, Trinity College Manuscripts and Archives Research Library, Dublin.
Marson, Una (1937), *The Moth and the Star*, Kingston, Jamaica: self-published.
— (1942a), 'West Indian Message Programmes'. E2/584, BBC Written Archives Centre, Caversham.
— (1942b), 'Calling the West Indies', 3 September 1942. *CWI* Box 21/File 1941–1943, BBC Written Archives Centre, Caversham.
— (1942c), 'Calling the West Indies: Talk by Una Marson', 3 September 1942. *CWI* Box 21/File 1941–1943, BBC Written Archives Centre, Caversham.
— (1942d), 'Calling the West Indies: At the Barbecue', 26 November 1942. *CWI* Box 21/File 1941–43, BBC Written Archives Centre, Caversham.
— (1945a), *Towards the Stars: Poems*, Bickley, Kent: University of London Press.
— (1945b), 'Caribbean Voices: Tribute to Constance Hollar', 25 March 1945. *Caribbean Voices* microfilm scripts, BBC Written Archives Centre, Caversham.
— (2011), *Selected Poems*, ed. Alison Donnell, Leeds: Peepal Tree.
Marson, Una and Ronald Moody (1943), 'Calling the West Indies: Close-Up: Ronald Moody', 31 January 1943. *CWI* Box 21/File 1941–1943, BBC Written Archives Centre, Caversham.
Marson, Una and George Orwell (1942), 'Calling the West Indies: Close-Up: George Orwell Interviewed by Una Marson', 7 May 1942. *CWI* Box 21/File 1941–1943, BBC Written Archives Centre.
Marson, Una and Roi Ottley (1944), 'Calling the West Indies: Mr. Roi Ottley Interviewed by Una Marson', 17 September 1944. *CWI* Box 22/File 1944, BBC Written Archives Centre, Caversham.
Marson, Una and Maida Springer (1945), 'Calling the West Indies: Interview with Mrs. Springer', 30 March 1945. *CWI* Box 22/File 1945, BBC Written Archives Centre, Caversham.
Matheson, Hilda (1929), memo to Roger Eckersley, 18 November 1929.

RCont 1/Talks/J.B. Priestley 1 (1927–1939), BBC Written Archives Centre, Caversham.

Mellor, Leo (2011), *Reading the Ruins: Modernism, Bombsites and British Culture*, Cambridge: Cambridge University Press.

'The Men who Speak for Britain: 1. J. B. Priestley' (1940), *London Calling* 43 (4 July 1940), p. 2.

Merritt, Russell (1994), 'Recharging "Alexander Nevsky": Tracking the Eisenstein–Prokofiev War Horse', *Film Quarterly* 48.2 (Winter 1994–5), pp. 34–47.

'Middlebrow', *OED Online*, Oxford University Press, June 2016, <http://www.oed.com> (last accessed 9 September 2012).

Midkiff, Sheri P. (1998), 'James Hanley', in George M. Johnson (ed.), *Dictionary of Literary Biography Volume 191: British Novelists Between the Wars*, Detroit: Gale Research.

Morley, Jason (2007), 'Caribbean, British Colonies in the', in David Dabydeen, John Gilmore and Cecily Jones (eds), *The Oxford Companion to Black British History*, New York: Oxford University Press, pp. 83–6.

Morse, Daniel Ryan (2011), 'Only Connecting?: E. M. Forster, Empire Broadcasting and the Ethics of Distance', *Journal of Modern Literature* 34.3 (2011), pp. 87–106.

— (2015), '"An Impatient Modernist": Mulk Raj Anand at the BBC', *Modernist Cultures* 10.1 (2015), pp. 83–98.

Murphet, Julian (2009), *Multimedia Modernism: Literature and the Anglo-American Avant-Garde*, Cambridge: Cambridge University Press.

Murphy, Kate (2016), *Behind the Wireless: A History of Early Women at the BBC*, London: Palgrave MacMillan.

Nicholas, Siân (1995), '"Sly Demagogues" and Wartime Radio: J. B. Priestley and the BBC', *Twentieth Century British History* 6.3 (1995), pp. 247–66.

— (1996), *The Echo of War: Home Front Propaganda and the Wartime BBC, 1939–45*, Manchester: Manchester University Press.

'Notes on Broadcasting to the West Indies' (n.d.). E2/584. BBC Written Archives Centre, Caversham.

'Not too bad, really/Bower' (1992), Carol Rosen interviews Dallas Bower, BBC Radio 3, 27 January 1992. Shelf Mark B9031/1. National Sound Archives, British Library, London.

'Olivetti Lettera 22' (1953), *The Listener* XLIX.1267 (11 June 1953), p. 936.

'On! Sail On!' (1942), *The Listener* XXVIII.717 (8 October 1942), p. 456.

Orwell, George ([1968] 1970), *Collected Essays, Journalism, and Letters*, 4 vols, ed. Sonia Orwell and Ian Angus, Markham, ON: Penguin.

— (1998), *Complete Works*, 20 vols, ed. Peter Davison, London: Secker and Warburg.

Ottley, Roi (2011), *Roi Ottley's World War II: The Lost Diary of an African American Journalist*, ed. Mark A. Huddle, Lawrence: University Press of Kansas.

Owen, Wilfred ([1919] 1996), 'Strange Meeting', in Jon Silkin (ed.), *The Penguin Book of First World War Poetry*, New York: Penguin, pp. 206–8.

Piette, Adam (1995), *Imagination at War: British Fiction and Poetry, 1939–1945*, London: Papermac.

Plain, Gill (2013), *Literature of the 1940s: War, Postwar and 'Peace'*, Edinburgh: Edinburgh University Press.
Pollentier, Caroline (2011), 'Everybody's Essayist: On Middles and Middlebrows', in Kate Macdonald (ed.), *The Masculine Middlebrow 1880–1950: What Mr. Miniver Read*, London: Palgrave MacMillan, pp. 119–34.
— (2012), 'Configuring Middleness: Bourdieu, *l'Art Moyen* and the Broadbrow', in Erica Brown and Mary Grover (eds), *Middlebrow Literary Cultures: The Battle of the Brows, 1920–1960*, New York: Palgrave MacMillan, pp. 37–51.
Poovey, Mary (1998), *A History of the Modern Fact: Problems of Knowledge in the Sciences of Wealth and Society*, Chicago: University of Chicago Press.
Potter, Simon (2012), *Broadcasting Empire*, New York: Oxford University Press.
Priestley, J. B. (1927a), *The English Novel*, London: Ernst Benn.
— (1927b), *Open House*, London: Heinemann.
— (1930), letter to Hilda Matheson, 11 July 1930. RCont 1/Talks/J.B. Priestley 1 (1927–1939). BBC Written Archives Centre, Caversham.
— (1931), letter in reply to correspondence signed PT/LF, 21 January 1931. RCont 1/Talks/J.B. Priestley 1 (1927–1939), BBC Written Archives Centre, Caversham.
— (1932a), 'Tell Us More about these Authors', *Evening Standard* (13 October 1932), p. 11.
— (1932b), 'To a High-Brow', BBC Home Service, 17 October 1932. Microfilm. BBC Written Archives Centre, Caversham.
— (1934), *English Journey*, London: Heinemann.
— (1939), *Let the People Sing*, London: Heinemann.
— (1939–40), *[Untitled Novel] Book One: Birmanpool*. Typescript, c. 1939–1940. Priestley Misc. Works. Harry Ransom Humanities Research Center, University of Texas at Austin.
— (1940a), *Britain Speaks*, New York: Harper.
— (1940b), 'A New English Journey', BBC Home Service, 24 April 1940. Microfilm. BBC Written Archives Centre, Caversham.
— (1940c), *Postscripts*, London: William Heinemann.
— (1941a), letter to Cass Canfield, 29 April 1941. PRI 13/22 (Correspondence: Letters to Gene [Saxton] and Cass Canfield, 1940–1942). J. B. Priestley Papers, University of Bradford Special Collections.
— (1941b), *Out of the People*, New York: Harper.
— (1942), *Britain at War*, New York: Harper.
— (1943a), *British Women Go to War*, London: Collins.
— (1943b), *Daylight on Saturday*, New York: Harper.
— (1957), 'The Author and the Public', in the International Congress of P.E.N. Clubs, *The Author and the Public*, London: Hutchinson, pp. 27–8.
— (1958), *Topside, or The Future of England*, London: Heinemann.
— (1962), *Margin Released*, London: Heinemann.
— (1970), *The Edwardians*, London: Heinemann.
— (1973), *The English*, London: Heinemann.
Priestley, J. B. and Jacquetta Hawkes (1955), *Journey Down a Rainbow*, London: Heinemann.

'Pye P43' (1952), service sheet supplement to *Wireless and Electrical Trader* (1 March 1952), n.p.

R46/92: Recorded Programmes: 'Calling the West Indies: 1940–1950', BBC Written Archives Centre, Caversham.

'Radio Lives: J.B. Priestley' (1991), audiocassette of radio broadcast, original transmission 13 June 1991, BBC Radio Four. PRI 19/4 (Biography), J. B. Priestley Papers, University of Bradford Special Collections.

Rajewsky, Irina (2005), 'Intermediality, Intertextuality, and Remediation: A Literary Perspective on Intermediality', *Intermédialités* 6 (Autumn 2005), pp. 43–64.

Ranasinha, Ruvani (2007), *South Asian Writers in Twentieth-Century Britain: Culture in Translation*, Oxford: Clarendon Press.

— (2008), 'Talking to India: The Literary Production and Consumption of South Asian Anglophone Writers in Britain and the USA', *Books Without Borders* 2 (2008), pp. 170–80.

— (2010), 'South Asian Broadcasters in Britain and the BBC: Talking to India (1941–1943)', *South Asian Diaspora* 2.1 (2010), pp. 57–71.

Rawlinson, Mark (2000), *British Writing of the Second World War*, Oxford: Clarendon.

Reith, Sir John (1949), *Into the Wind*, London: Hodder and Stoughton.

Rendall, R. A. (1941a), memo to S. G. Williams, 28 January 1941. L1/290/1, BBC Written Archives Centre, Caversham.

— (1941b), memo to J. C. S. Macgregor, 18 December 1941. R19/1222/2, BBC Written Archives Centre, Caversham.

— (1942), memo to C (N.C.), 7 January 1942. E2/584, BBC Written Archives Centre, Caversham.

— (1943), memo to John Grenfell-Williams, 2 January 1943. E1/1294/2, BBC Written Archives Centre, Caversham.

Resnais, Alain ([1955] 2003), *Night and Fog*, Criterion Collection.

Rice, Anne (2002), '"A Peculiar Power about Rottenness": Annihilating Desire in James Hanley's "The German Prisoner"', *Modernism/modernity* 9.1 (2002), pp. 75–89.

Rodger, Ian (1982), *Radio Drama*, London: MacMillan.

Rolo, Charles (1942), *Radio Goes to War: The 'Fourth Front'*, New York: G. P. Putnam's Sons.

Rose, Sonya (2004), *Which People's War? National Identity and Citizenship in Britain 1939–1945*, Oxford: Oxford University Press.

'Rudolph Dunbar's Albert Hall Triumph' (1942), *London Calling* 140 (14 May 1942), p. 5.

Rush, Anne Spry (2011), *Bonds of Empire: West Indians and Britishness from Victoria to Decolonization*, New York: Oxford University Press.

Ryan, A. P. (1940), memo to Frederick Ogilvie, 7 October 1940. RCont1/Talks/J.B. Priestley/2, BBC Written Archives Centre, Caversham.

Sassoon, Siegfried ([1918] 1996), 'Glory of Women', in Jon Silkin (ed.), *The Penguin Book of First World War Poetry*, New York: Penguin, p. 132.

Scannell, Paddy and David Cardiff (1987), 'Broadcasting and National Unity', in James Curran, Anthony Smith and Pauline Wingate (eds), *Impacts and Influences: Essay on Media and Power in the Twentieth Century*, New York: Routledge, pp. 157–74.

— (1991), *A Social History of British Broadcasting*, Cambridge, MA: Blackwell.
Schwarz, Bill (2003), 'Introduction: Crossing the Seas', in Bill Schwarz (ed.), *West Indian Intellectuals in Britain*, New York: Manchester University Press, pp. 1–30.
Seaton, Jean (1987), 'Reporting Atrocities: The BBC and the Holocaust', in Jean Seaton and Ben Pimlott (eds), *The Media in British Politics*, Aldershot: Avebury, pp. 154–82.
Sherlock, Philip ([1943] 2005), 'Dinner Party 1940', in Paula Burnett (ed.), *The Penguin Book of Caribbean Verse in English*, London: Penguin, p. 156.
Sieveking, Lance (1934), *The Stuff of Radio*, London: Cassell and Co.
Silvey, R. J. (1940), memo to Laurence Gilliam, 28 August 1940. R19/352/3, BBC Written Archives Centre, Caversham.
Stallworthy, Jon (1995), *Louis MacNeice*, New York: Norton.
Sterne, Jonathan (2003), *The Audible Past: Cultural Origins of Sound Reproduction*, Durham, NC: Duke University Press.
Talks Booking Form (1940), 17 May 1940. Talks/JBP2/1940, BBC Written Archives Centre, Caversham.
'Time Has Brought Me Hither' (1953), *Radio Times* 1542 (29 May 1953), p. 12.
Trotter, David (2013), *Literature in the First Media Age: Britain Between the Wars*, Cambridge, MA: Harvard University Press.
Verma, Neil (2012), *Theater of the Mind: Imagination, Aesthetics, and American Radio Drama*, Chicago: University of Chicago Press.
'Viva', *OED Online*, Oxford University Press, June 2016, <http://www.oed.com> (last accessed 27 August 2016).
Warner, Michael (2002), *Publics and Counterpublics*, New York: Zone Books.
Warren, Robert (1945), 'Poor We Country Folk', *Caribbean Voices*, 27 May 1945. *Caribbean Voices* microfilm scripts, BBC Written Archives Centre, Caversham.
West, Rebecca (1947), *The Meaning of Treason*, New York: Viking.
West, W. J. (ed. and 'Introduction') (1985), *Orwell: The War Broadcasts*, London: Duckworth/BBC.
— (ed. and 'Introduction') ([1985] 1987), *Orwell: The War Commentaries*, Toronto: Penguin.
White, Antonia (1941), 'A Great Stone Ship', *London Calling* 107 (25 September 1941), pp. 16–17.
Whittington, Ian (2014), 'Radio Studies and 20th-Century Literature: Ethics, Aesthetics, and Remediation', *Literature Compass* 11.9 (2014), pp. 634–48.
— (2015), 'Archaeologies of Sound: Reconstructing Louis MacNeice's Wartime Radio Publics', *Modernist Cultures* 10.1 (2015), pp. 44–61.
Williams, C. H. (1953), 'The Legend of the Holy Oil', *The Listener* 1263 (28 May 1953), p. 875.
Williams, Keith (1996), *British Writers and the Media, 1930–45*, Basingstoke: Macmillan Press; New York: St Martin's Press.
Williams, Raymond (1977), *Marxism and Literature*, New York: Oxford University Press.

Williams, S. G. (1941), Memorandum to Mr. Chesterton, 21 January 1941. L1/290/1, BBC Written Archives Centre, Caversham.

Williams, W. E. (1940), 'The Critic on the Hearth: The Spoken Word: Priestley Steals the Show', *The Listener* 590 (2 May 1940), p. 903.

Wills, Clair (2007), *That Neutral Island: A Cultural History of Ireland During the Second World War*, Cambridge, MA: Harvard University Press.

Wollaeger, Mark (2006), *Modernism, Media, and Propaganda*, Princeton: Princeton University Press.

Wollaeger, Mark and Matthew Eatough (eds) (2012), *The Oxford Handbook of Global Modernisms*, Oxford: Oxford University Press.

Woolf, Virginia ([1932] 1942), 'Middlebrow', *The Death of the Moth and Other Essays*, London: Hogarth.

Index

1941 Committee, 59–60
4'33", 90

Abyssinia *see* Ethiopia
accents, 23, 40–3
 and national identity, 5, 23, 62n2, 63n7
 Northern English, 42, 47, 68, 182
 Priestley, 5, 24, 30, 32, 40–3, 45, 47–9
 West Indian, 163, 173–80, 182
Adams, Bernard, 118, 150n2
Agee, James, 114
air raids *see* Blitz
Alexander Nevsky, 19, 24, 85, 96–104, 114n1, 115n10
 as intermedial text, 14–15, 98–101
Algeria, 157–8
Allied bombings, 125, 132–4, 141
anancy tradition, 174–6
Anand, Mulk Raj, 29n27, 157, 171, 181
Anderson, Benedict, 9, 27n11
anti-fascism, 4, 5–6, 15–18, 85, 95, 157, 165
appeasement, 1, 15
Ariel in Wartime, 15–16
Arlott, John, 47, 63n10
Arnell, Skipper, 123, 125
Arnheim, Rudolf, 7
Arnold, Matthew, 6, 32–3
At What a Price (Marson), 164
Auden, W. H., 85, 86, 189
audiences, 8–12, 115n8, 158, 183n6
 audioposition in *Christopher Columbus*, 104–7
 boredom of, 44, 87
 for *Calling the West Indies*, 153, 162–3, 171
 for features, 69, 71, 77, 88, 112–14, 114n2
 for frontline reporting, 120, 124–5, 129, 149
 for 'middlebrow' content, 40–1, 44
 for *Postscripts*, 30, 32, 47, 51–2, 55
 surrogates in *Alexander Nevsky*, 100–2
 television vs. radio, 185–6, 189–90
 see also Listener Research Department; publics
audile technique, 72, 102, 105
audioposition, 96, 104–7
autonomy
 aesthetic, 13–15, 17, 19–20, 22–3, 153, 173
 colonial, 25, 173, 177, 182
 of facts, 20, 128, 135, 145–8
 propaganda value of, 18, 45–6
Autumn Journal (MacNeice), 84
Autumn Sequel (MacNeice), 84
Avery, Todd, 10, 27n9, 28n19

Baker-Smith, Malcolm, 76–7
Barnes, George, 45, 188–9
Baucom, Ian, 158
Baxendale, John, 2, 62n1
Beckett, Samuel, 66
Bennett, Louise, 176
Berridge, Elizabeth, 80, 82n12
Beveridge Report, 60, 111, 116n19
Bible, 91–3, 114n5
'Birmanpool' (Priestley), 38–9, 63n6
black Atlantic, 4, 25, 153–6, 168–82
blindness, 100–1, 103, 114, 176

Blitz, 3, 8, 21, 24, 187
  audile technique in, 102
  evacuation of Features Department, 69
  in *No Directions*, 79–80
  Postscripts featuring, 50, 54, 55, 61
  in *The Stones Cry Out*, 87–96, 97, 114n2, 114n7
  see also Allied bombings
Bloom, Emily, 27n8, 28n19, 115n9
Bolter, David Jay, 126–7, 151n13
Bourdieu, Pierre, 13, 34, 37, 62n5
Bowen, Elizabeth, 2, 26n4, 29n27, 122, 187–8
  'Coronation', 187–8
  Demon Lover, The, 102
Bower, Dallas, 14, 104, 106, 107–8
Boy (Hanley), 70
Brathwaite, Edward Kamau, 25, 63n10, 154–5, 176–8
Brazen Horn, The (Johnston), 149, 149n1, 152n26
Breiner, Laurence, 155, 173, 178
'Brer Nancy and de Woss-woss', 174–6, 177
Bridson, D. G., 42, 68, 76, 77, 81n6, 114n7
Briggs, Asa, 41, 47
Britain
  England vs., 10, 53–4, 64n14
  national identity of, 5, 8–12, 52–8
  radio history of, 4, 6–8
  regional identities within, 9–10, 27n13
  see also British Empire; England; Northern Ireland; Scotland; Wales
Britain Speaks (Priestley), 10, 21, 23–4, 45–6, 51, 54, 56, 57
Britain to America, 67
British Broadcasting Corporation (BBC)
  British Empire and, 4, 7, 153–63, 168–82
  and coronation of Queen Elizabeth II, 25–6, 185–91
  democratisation of, 32, 40–7
  development of, 6–8, 27n9
  Forces Programme, 9, 12, 44, 62n4
  Holocaust reporting, 138–45
  Home Service, 8–10, 20, 30, 44, 62n4, 69, 89, 93, 186
  Light Programme, 12, 44, 62n4, 186
  middlebrow role of, 30–6, 43
  Munich Crisis response, 18–19
  and national identity, 2–3, 5–6, 8–11, 18, 27n13, 52–8
  National Programme, 8, 42
  North Region, 8, 42, 68, 69
  Radiophonic Workshop, 27n8
  Regional Programme, 8, 10, 42, 43, 121
  response to outbreak of war, 1–2, 7–8, 43–4, 69, 160–3
  Talks Department, 40–1, 42, 45
  television, 14, 25, 98, 121, 150n6, 164, 185–91
  Third Programme, 24, 45, 66, 67, 80, 186, 187, 191
  UK government relation to, 17–19, 29n24, 57, 61, 62n1, 97, 110, 119, 123
  War Liaison Office, 78, 79
  see also accents; *Calling the West Indies*; censorship; Features Department; Listener Research Department; Ministry of Information; News Division; Overseas Service; propaganda
British Empire
  and British identity, 3, 4, 16, 17, 181, 187
  Commonwealth, 25, 185, 186, 187–8
  and imperial identity, 5, 17, 154, 158–9, 174, 181
  postwar changes to, 3, 4, 25, 26n3, 60, 156, 187–8
  and radio, 4, 7, 153–63, 168–82
  resistance to, 4, 15, 16, 153–5, 157, 163–9, 171
  see also India; Jamaica; Marson, Una; Trinidad; West Indies
British Museum, 114n4
broadbrow, 31, 35–9, 45, 49, 58–9, 62n3
  middlebrow vs., 36–7
Buchenwald, 117, 134–9, 145–6, 151n18, 152nn24–5
Burdett, Winston, 136, 152n21
Burnham, Barbara, 71

Cage, John, 90
Calling the West Indies, 4, 25, 153–84
  and accent, 163, 177–80, 182
  and black Atlantic, 25, 153–6, 168–82
  and Caribbean poetry, 154–5, 173–80

and nation language, 25, 154–5, 174–80
Canfield, Cass, 46, 63n6
Cardiff, David, 19, 27nn9–10, 27n12, 80n1, 81n6
Caribbean *see* West Indies
Caribbean Voices, 155, 172–3, 174
censorship, 3, 17, 19, 88, 184n10
 of James Hanley, 70, 79
 of Denis Johnston, 19, 119, 125, 129–31, 138, 148
 of Una Marson, 19, 156, 170–2
 of J. B. Priestley, 19, 57–8, 61
Cesarani, David, 142, 152n23
Chamberlain, Neville, 1, 16, 49
Chitale, Venu, 184n13
Christopher Columbus (MacNeice), 17, 24, 87, 104–14, 114n1, 115nn12–15, 116nn16–17
Churchill, Winston
 conduct of war, 59, 131, 134
 and official war culture, 17, 30, 52, 55
 popularity, 45, 49
 radio appearances, 103, 124, 132, 150n10
 voice, 5, 30
cinema *see* film
'Cinema Eyes' (Marson), 166
Clark, R. T., 20, 128
Cleverdon, Douglas, 66, 71, 80
Cohen, Debra Rae, 11–12, 27n15, 28n19
collaboration
 aesthetic, 16–17, 23, 85–7
 political compromise as, 15–19, 153, 157–9, 169, 181–2
 see also hegemony
Colonial Office, 164, 179, 181
Comedy of Danger, A (Hughes), 101
Common Sense (periodical), 45, 111
Commonwealth, British *see* British Empire
Conrad, Joseph, 73
Conservative Party, 60, 61
 response to Priestley, 30, 56–8, 62n1, 110
Constantine, Learie, 180
Cook, Christopher, 151n18
Cooper, Duff, 57
'Coronation' (Bowen), 187–8
Cosmopolitan, The, 164
'Critique of the Gotha Programme' (Marx), 57

Dark Tower, The (MacNeice), 101
Darling, Sir Malcolm, 157
Day Lewis, Cecil, 26n4, 85
 Ariel in Wartime, 15–16
 'Where are the War Poets?', 15–16
Daylight on Saturday (Priestley), 38, 59
Deer, Patrick, 17, 26n1, 79, 80, 81n3; *see also* Second World War: official war culture
Demon Lover, The (Bowen), 102
Dillon, Francis ('Jack'), 68, 71, 79, 80, 114n7
Dimbleby, Richard, 123, 129, 144
'Dinner Party 1940' (Sherlock), 160–1
Dinsman, Melissa, 28n19, 27n29, 115n14, 116n17
Dionysia (Johnston), 118–19, 124, 131, 150nn3–4, 152n27
Disney, Walt, 14, 189
Dixon, Randolph, 170
Dodds, E. R., 83, 85, 91
Dodds, Elizabeth, 83
Donnell, Alison, 165–6, 182n1, 183n9
dramatic control panel, 67, 81n5
Dunbar, Rudolph, 163, 183n8
Dunkirk, 49–50

Eckersley, Roger, 40–1
'Eclipse of the Highbrow', 31, 61
Eisenstein, Sergei, 14, 98–9
Eliot, T. S. (Thomas Stearns), 86, 171, 189
Elizabeth II (queen), 25–6, 185–91
Ellul, Jacques, 21–2
Emergency Powers (Defence) Act (1940), 16
empire *see* British Empire
Empire Service *see* Overseas Service
Empson, William, 26n4, 85
England, 8, 10
 Britain vs., 10, 53–4, 64n14
 Priestley and, 34, 39, 47, 49–50, 53–4, 190
English Journey (Priestley), 34, 46, 51, 63n13
Entertainments National Service Association (ENSA), 59
Ethiopia, 7, 15, 26n2, 84, 165
Evans, Walker, 114

facts
 in features, 65, 67–8, 71, 104, 115n12

in Johnston, 118–19, 120, 145–9, 150n3
knowledge vs., 135
multiplicity of, 147–8
propaganda uses of, 12, 20, 25, 68, 128, 134, 150n11, 151n14
see also information; propaganda: 'propaganda of truth'
Fanon, Frantz, 157–8, 159
Faust, 134, 138, 151n18
Features Department (BBC)
and North Region, 42, 68, 81n6
wartime growth, 65–6, 69–70
see also Alexander Nevsky; *Christopher Columbus*; features (radio genre); *Freedom Ferry*; Hanley, James; Johnston, Denis; MacNeice, Louis; *Stones Cry Out*
features (radio genre)
basis in fact, 65, 67–8, 71, 104, 115n12
development of features aesthetic, 24, 67–70, 80n1, 81n6
as propaganda, 21, 24, 65–6, 68, 71–2, 78–9 87–8, 97–8, 110–14, 114n7
as radiogenic genre, 65, 67, 68, 80
'shape' of, 67, 76–8, 84, 87, 113
see also Alexander Nevsky; *Christopher Columbus*; Features Department; *Freedom Ferry*; *Stones Cry Out*
Fielden, Lionel, 40–1
Fields, Gracie, 49–50
Figueroa, John, 154–5, 178–9
film, 4, 43
adaptation at BBC, 14, 98, 100, 103
context of intermediality, 4, 11, 12–14, 28n18, 36, 98–101, 103, 186, 191
and mass culture, 26n5, 34
and race, 166, 167, 180–2
see also Alexander Nevsky; GPO Film Unit; *West Indies Calling*
First World War
poetry, 51, 63n12
Priestley and, 51, 53, 63n13
propaganda, 15, 17, 18, 20, 27n16, 128, 142–3
Forces Programme *see* BBC; *see also* BBC: Light Programme
Fordham, John, 73, 77, 81n3
Forster, E. M., 19, 20, 29n27, 70, 157

France
Algerian broadcasting, 157–8
Allied invasion (1944), 123, 125, 126
as 'other' to Britain, 54
Vichy government, 16
Freedom Ferry (Hanley, MacNeice), 71–5, 81n10, 101, 106

gender, 5, 23
and *Calling the West Indies*, 155, 164–5, 166, 171
and cultural hierarchies, 38, 62n3
and national identity, 54, 55
George VI (king), 186, 187
Germany
in *Alexander Nevsky*, 97–103
Allied attacks on, 132–4
Atlantic, Battle of, 71–5
and First World War, 128
and Holocaust, 134–45
North African presence, 127, 129–30
overseas broadcasting, 7, 156
propaganda, 9, 21, 28n20, 30, 44, 62n2
UK perceptions of, 51, 63n12, 74–5, 129–31, 133–4, 137–42, 148
see also anti-fascism; Blitz; Holocaust
Ghana, 26n3, 165, 175
Gielgud, Val, 65, 69, 80n2
Gilliam, Laurence, 65–8, 71, 76–9, 88, 114n2, 114n4, 114n7
Gilroy, Paul, 25, 154, 178; *see also* black Atlantic
Goethe's Oak (Cook), 151n18
Goldie, Grace Wyndham, 93, 102–3
Good Companions, The (Priestley), 37, 40
Göring, Hermann, 139–40
GPO Film Unit, 46, 151n15
Greene, Graham, 45, 50
Grenfell-Williams, John, 162, 170–1, 179–80, 183n5
Griffith, Glyne, 155, 184n14
Grusin, Richard, 126–7, 151n13
Guthrie, Tyrone, 65, 80

Haley, William, 133–4
Hall, Stuart, 28n23, 178
Hanley, James, 4, 6, 24, 26n4
audile technique, 101
audioposition, 106
Boy, 70
censorship, 70, 79

Index   215

and Features Department, 65–7, 70–82, 83–5
Freedom Ferry, 71–5, 81n10, 101, 106
literary reputation, 70–1
My Name is Atkins, 77, 78–9
No Directions, 79, 80
Ocean, The, 74–5
Return to Danger, 76, 89
Sailor's Song, 80, 81n9
Shadows Before Sunrise, 76–7
struggles at the BBC, 75–80, 83–4, 87
Harding, E. A. F. (Archie), 42, 68
Harrisson, Tom, 48
Hart, Matthew, 177
'He Called Us Brethren!' (Marson), 167
He Had a Date (MacNeice), 80
Healey, Maurice, 44–5
hegemony, 17–18, 28n23, 177, 181–2
Hendy, David, 9, 27n10, 27n12, 81n4
'High, Low, Broad' (Priestley), 36
highbrows, 31, 34, 61, 62n3, 69, 191
  BBC as highbrow, 7, 43
  Priestley and, 33, 34–6, 37–8, 47
  see also Bourdieu; broadbrow; lowbrow; middlebrow; 'Eclipse of the Highbrow'
Hilmes, Michele, 5, 27nn10–11
Hitler, Adolf, 15
  anti-Semitism of, 140–1
  responsibility for war crimes, 131, 134
  UK writerly resistance to, 16, 85, 95
  see also Germany; Holocaust
Hollar, Constance, 174
Holocaust, 131, 134–45, 146–7, 151n18, 152nn21–5
Home Service *see* BBC
Homeless People, 68
Hughes, Richard, 101
hypermediacy, 126–7

immediacy, 120
  hypermediacy vs., 126–7
  technological, 122–7
  see also neutrality
imperialism *see* British Empire
India, 4, 10, 11, 26n3, 60, 156–7, 167, 172; *see also* Overseas Service: India Section
information, 21–2
  in Johnston, 119, 128, 149
  see also facts

intermediality, 4–5, 11, 12–15, 27n15, 27nn17–19, 31
  Alexander Nevsky as intermedial text, 14, 98–101
  coronation and, 186–7, 188
  metatextuality as response, 147–8
intimacy
  as effect of radio, 4–5, 9, 27n8, 27n12
  Olivier and, 108–9
  Priestley and, 31, 35, 36, 37
  racial in *West Indies Calling*, 180–1
Into the Wind (Reith), 33
Ireland, 120–2
  broadcasting to, 121, 150n8
  Johnston and Irish identity, 5, 10, 120–2, 146, 147
  neutrality of, 24, 27n13
  see also Northern Ireland
Italy, 133
  invasion of Ethiopia, 15, 165
  overseas broadcasting by, 7, 156
  propaganda, 150n11

Jamaica
  broadcasting reception, 160–1, 162
  literature, 174–7
  Marson's origins in, 5, 10, 153, 155, 165, 167
  see also Calling the West Indies; West Indies
Jameson, Storm, 45
Japan, 103, 105, 157, 172
Jarrett-Macauley, Delia, 165–6, 167, 183n9
Jews, 134, 140–5, 149, 152nn23–5; *see also* Holocaust
Johnston, Denis, 4, 6
  audience, attitude to, 12, 124–5
  autobiographical record of, 117–20, 150nn2–4
  Brazen Horn, The, 149, 149n1, 152n26
  censorship of, 19, 119, 125, 129–31, 138, 148
  Dionysia, 118–19, 124, 131, 150nn3–4, 152n27
  at Features Department, 121, 122
  Germany, attitude toward, 129–31, 133–4, 137–42
  Holocaust responses, 134–45, 146–7
  Irish identity, 5, 10, 120–2, 146, 147
  journalistic objectivity, faith in, 127–34

Moon in the Yellow River, The, 121
neutrality as goal, 24–5, 117–20, 122–52
Nine Rivers from Jordan, 25, 117–20, 128–51, 189
Old Lady Says No!, The, 121
and propaganda of truth, 6, 118–19, 120, 145–9, 150n3
recording technology, use of, 120, 122–7, 133–4, 151n12
television and, 121, 150n6, 188–9
'War Field Books', 117–18, 136, 139–40, 145, 148–9, 150nn2–3, 152n27
Johnson, James Weldon, 167
Joyce, William, 30, 44, 62n2

Kaleidoscope I (Sieveking), 67, 81n4
Kalliney, Peter, 155, 172–3, 183n2
Keane, Damien, 13–14, 26n2, 26n7, 28nn20–1, 122
Keys, The, 164, 165; *see also* League of Coloured Peoples
Kushner, Tony, 143, 144–5, 152n21, 152n23

Labour Party, 3, 60
LaCapra, Dominick, 144
Lacey, Kate, 9, 11, 90
Lambert, Calvin, 174
Lamming, George, 154–5
Lawrence-Curran, Zelda, 116n16
League of Coloured Peoples, 164, 165, 169
League of Nations, 165
LeMahieu, D. L., 27n17, 28n23, 33
Let the People Sing (Priestley), 1–2, 37–8, 51, 58
Let Us Now Praise Famous Men (Walker and Evans), 114
Levine, Caroline, 87
Lewis, Wyndham, 26n5
Light Programme *see* BBC; *see also* BBC: Forces Programme
'Lili Marleen', 129–30, 151n15
Listener, The (periodical), 11, 27n15, 93, 102, 110–11, 112, 186, 191nn1–2
Listener Research Department, 21, 97, 103
Alexander Nevsky, reports on, 103, 115n10
Christopher Columbus, reports on, 112–13

development of, 44
Priestley, reports on, 30, 47
USSR, reports on, 97–8
West Indies, reports on, 162
'Little Brown Girl' (Marson), 166–7
Littlewood, Joan, 68
London Calling (periodical), 11, 47, 89, 169, 186
'London Letter' (MacNeice), 45, 111
Longley, Edna, 86
Lorca, Federico García, 115n15
Lord Haw-Haw *see* Joyce, William
lowbrows, 31, 34–6, 38, 59, 62n3
Lumby, Christopher, 134, 138

Maas, Brigid, 76–7
MacKay, Claude, 176
MacKay, Marina, 3, 26n1
McLaine, Ian, 143, 152n23
MacNeice, Louis, 4, 6, 26n5, 45, 83–116, 172
Alexander Nevsky, 14–15, 19, 24, 85, 96–104, 114n1
audiences, attitude to, 12
Autumn Journal, 84
Autumn Sequel, 84
Christopher Columbus, 17, 24, 85, 87, 104–16
collaboration on radio, 17, 85–7
Cook's Tour of the London Subways, 96
Dark Tower, The, 101
at Features Department, 66–7, 83–5
He Had a Date, 80
Ireland, attitudes toward, 122
'London Letter', 45, 111
Modern Poetry, 86
'Plea for Sound, A', 185–6, 189
postwar, 185–7, 189
and propaganda, 21, 83, 98, 104–16
and radiogenic form, 84–7
Stones Cry Out, The, 24, 85, 87–96, 115nn2–7, 116nn8–9, 187
The Strings Are False, 89
Time Has Brought Me Hither, 186
McWhinnie, Donald, 66, 80
Madden, Cecil, 163–4
Marshall, Howard, 126, 127
Marson, Una, 4, 18, 153–84
At What a Price, 164
audiences, attitude to, 12, 162
censorship of, 19, 156, 170–2
'Cinema Eyes', 166

departure from BBC, 155
gender and feminism, 155, 164–5, 166, 171
'He Called Us Brethren!', 167
Jamaican identity, 5, 10, 153, 155, 165, 167
'Little Brown Girl', 166–7
poetry, 165–7
and race, 154, 163, 164, 166–7
voice, 5, 180
Marx, Karl, 57, 58
Mass Observation, 48, 61
Matheson, Hilda, 40–1
media ecology *see* intermediality
middlebrow
  BBC and, 30–6, 43
  broadbrow vs., 36–7
  demotic speech and, 40–3
  Priestley and, 33–9
  wartime appetite for, 31, 59
  Woolf on, 33–4, 36
'Middlebrow' (Woolf), 33–4
Miners' Wives, 68
Ministry of Information (MoI)
  Authors' Planning Committee, 46
  BBC relations with, 18–19
  and First World War, 128
  and Holocaust, 143, 152n23
  and Priestley, 21, 32, 45–7, 51, 57, 63n9
  and race, 164, 180–1
Modern Poetry (MacNeice), 86
modernism, 22, 85–6
  intermediality and, 11, 12–13, 14–15, 147–8
  mass culture and, 35, 37, 61
  propaganda and, 22–3
  radio and, 4, 28n19, 32–3
  transnational turn in, 26n7, 155
  war and, 17, 22–3, 31, 61
Moody, Harold, 169–70
Moody, Ronald, 170
Moon in the Yellow River, The (Johnston), 121
Moyne Commission, 159, 170–1, 183n4
Munich Crisis
  BBC response, 18–19
  MacNeice and, 84
Murphet, Julian, 13, 147–8
Murry, John Middleton, 26n5
music
  in *Alexander Nevsky*, 98–9
  on BBC, 6, 32–3, 44, 69

on *Calling the West Indies*, 154, 163, 169, 174
in *Christopher Columbus*, 104–8, 112, 116n16
in features and drama, 10–12, 14, 65, 86–8, 95
see also 'Lili Marleen'; Mussorgsky, Modest; Prokofiev, Sergei; Walton, William
Mussorgsky, Modest, 76–7
My Name is Atkins (Hanley), 77, 78–9

Naipaul, V. S., 155
nation language, 25, 63n10, 154–5, 156, 173–8
national identity
  accent and, 4–5, 23, 62n2, 63n7
  BBC and, 2–3, 5, 8–12
  British, 5, 8–12, 52–8, 190–1
National Programme *see* BBC
nations
  as imagined communities, 5
  radio and nation-formation, 5, 8–12, 190–1
  and transnationalism, 5
  see also radio: nation-formation via; national identity
neutrality
  Ireland and, 4, 10, 27n13, 28n20, 120–2, 147
  Johnston and, 10, 24–5, 117–20, 122–52
  journalistic objectivity as, 127–34
  technological immediacy as, 122–7
News Division (BBC), 20, 41, 63n7, 151n14
  Holocaust, response to, 138–9, 143–5, 152n25
  and mobile recording, 123–7, 133–4, 150n9,
  relation to military, 127–9
  War Reporting Unit, 120, 123, 126, 127
newspapers, *see* press; *Times* (London)
Nicholas, Siân, 30, 44, 57–8, 61, 62n1
Nicolls, Basil, 98
Nicolson, Harold, 61
Night and Fog (Resnais), 151n18
Nine Rivers from Jordan (Johnston), 25, 117–20, 128–49, 150nn3–4, 150nn11–12, 151nn18–20, 189
No Directions (Hanley), 79, 80
Northern Ireland
  and 'British' identity, 27n13

Johnston and, 117, 121, 150n5, 150n7
MacNeice and, 115n14
Regional Programme, 8, 42
wartime broadcasting, 9–10
North Region (BBC) *see* BBC

Ocean, The (Hanley), 74–5
Ofori Atta, Nana Sir, 165
Ogilvie, Frederick, 142
Old Lady Says No!, The (Johnston), 121
Olivier, Laurence, 104, 108–9, 112
Orwell, George, 26n4, 27n14, 29n27, 38, 41
  on British identity, 10, 16
  Calling the West Indies interview, 171–2, 184nn12–14
  India Section broadcasts, 10, 157, 171, 172, 180, 184n13
  on propaganda, 14, 18, 181
Ottley, Roi, 171, 184n11
Out of the People (Priestley), 55, 60
Overseas Service
  India Section, 10, 157, 171, 172, 180, 184n13
  propaganda, 156–7, 160
  US broadcasts, 10, 21, 46–7, 71–5, 87–96, 114n2
  West Indies broadcasts, 10, 156–64
Owen, Wilfred, 51, 63n12

Padmore, George, 159, 184n11
People's War, 2, 3, 16, 17, 26n1, 67, 68, 109–14
  Priestley and, 30, 43–7, 49, 52–8, 190
Peters, A. D., 46
Phoney War, 43–4, 161
photography, 13, 62n5, 126, 188
Pickles, Wilfred, 47
Picture Post (periodical), 111
'Plan for Britain, A', 111
'Plea for Sound, A' (MacNeice), 185–6, 189
politics, 19–20
  of cultural access, 38–9
  Priestley and, 19, 58–62
  and propaganda, 20–3
Pollentier, Caroline, 37, 62n5
'Poor We Country Folk' (Warren), 176–7
Poovey, Mary, 119, 128
Postscripts (Priestley), 1, 3, 23–4, 30, 39, 44–62, 110–11, 190

press, 2, 9, 11, 142–3, 162, 171, 174; *see also Times* (London)
Priestley, J. B. (John Boynton), 4, 6, 18, 23–4
  accent and voice, 5, 24, 30, 31–2, 40–3, 45, 47–9
  'Birmanpool', 38–9, 63n6
  Britain Speaks, 10, 21, 23–4, 45–6, 51, 54, 56, 57
  broadbrow philosophy of, 31, 35–9, 45, 49, 58–9, 62n3
  celebrity of, 30–1, 45, 48, 61
  censorship of, 19, 57–8, 61
  cultural politics of, 1–2, 4, 23–4, 31–2, 33–9, 56–62
  Daylight on Saturday, 38, 59
  English Journey, 34, 46, 51, 63n13
  Good Companions, The, 37, 40
  'High, Low, Broad', 36
  Let the People Sing, 1–2, 37–8, 51, 58
  Listener Research on, 30, 47
  and middlebrow, 30–2, 33–9
  MoI support of, 21, 32, 45–7, 51, 57, 63n9
  Northern origins of, 10, 42–3, 48
  Out of the People, 55, 60
  Postscripts, 1, 3, 23–4, 30, 39, 44–62, 110–11, 190
  postwar, 189–90
  propaganda by, 21, 32, 45–6, 48, 50–1
  'To a High-Brow', 33, 34–6, 38
  Topside, 190
Prokofiev, Sergei, 14, 98, 99
propaganda, 7–9, 13–14, 19–23, 26n6, 187
  audile technique and, 102
  'Black' propaganda, 29n25
  Calling the West Indies and, 163, 180–2, 183n4, 184n16
  constraints of, 3, 17, 71, 78–9, 156
  features as, 21, 24, 65–6, 68, 71–2, 78–9, 87–8, 97–8, 110–14, 114n7
  First World War vs. Second World War, 15, 17, 18, 20, 27n16, 128, 142–3
  'integration propaganda' (Ellul), 21–2
  Johnston and, 127–31
  MacNeice and, 21
  modernism and, 22–3
  MoI involvement in, 18–19, 21, 32, 45–7, 51, 57, 63n9, 128, 143, 152n23, 164, 180–1
  Overseas Service, 156–7, 160

and postwar planning, 85, 109–114
Priestley and, 21, 32, 46, 48, 50–1
'propaganda of truth', 6, 12, 20, 29n26, 118–19, 120, 145–9, 150n3, 150n11, 151n14
see also facts; Germany: propaganda; Joyce, William
publics, 11, 52–8, 110, 158, 163, 183n3
and counter-publics, 158
radio generation of, 2–3, 6–12, 157–8
Punch (periodical), 33

race
at BBC, 154, 163, 164
and *Calling the West Indies*, 168–180
and Marson's poetry, 166–7
and *West Indies Calling*, 180–2
see also black Atlantic
radio
development in UK, 6–8
domestic presence of, 1, 4
as middlebrow medium, 31, 32–6
and modern life, 34
nation-formation via, 5, 8–12, 190–1
publics, 6–12, 157–8
wartime role, 2–3, 8, 10, 22–3, 156–7, 190–1
see also BBC; Radio Luxembourg; Radio Normandy; Germany: broadcasting in
Radio Luxembourg, 8, 11
Radio Normandy, 8, 11
Radio Times (periodical), 11, 112, 186, 191n2
radiogenic form, 6, 24, 27n8
features as radiogenic, 65, 67–70, 80
MacNeice and, 84–7
recording, mobile, 68, 120, 122–7, 133–4, 151n12
Regional Programme see BBC
Reith, John, 6–7, 32–3, 40, 44
Into the Wind, 33
remediation, 11, 118, 186; see also intermediality
Remediation (Bolter and Grusin), 126, 127, 151n13
Rendall, R. A., 21, 89, 164, 179–80
Resnais, Alain, 151n18
Return to Danger (Baker-Smith and Hanley), 76, 89
'Romance Sonámbulo' (Lorca), 115n15
Rose, Sonya, 26n1, 181, 184n16

Sailor's Song (Hanley), 80, 81n9
St Paul's Cathedral, 93–6, 115n9
Salt, J. A. S., 98
Sassoon, Siegfried, 51, 63n12
Scannell, Paddy, 19, 27nn9–10, 27n12, 80n1, 81n6
Scotland, 8, 9–10, 42, 53
Seaton, Jean, 142, 143, 152n23
Second World War
Battle of the Atlantic, 71–5, 81n8
Battle of Britain, 50
D-Day, 123, 125, 126
declaration of, 1–2, 18–19, 43–4, 51–2
Dunkirk, 49–50
Emergency Powers (Defence) Act (1940), 16
Narvik, 161
North African campaign, 122–5, 128–30, 132–4, 141, 151n16
official war culture, 17, 30, 52, 55, 79, 119
Operation Barbarossa, 97
Pearl Harbor, 103
as People's War, 2, 3, 16, 17, 26n1, 30, 43–7, 49, 52–8, 67, 68, 109–14, 187, 190
Phoney War, 43–4, 161
as radio war, 2–3, 8, 10, 156–7, 190–1
as total war, 1, 5–6, 32, 153, 187
transformations during, 3, 16, 25–6, 58–62, 110–12, 181–2, 187–8
see also Allied bombing; Blitz; Holocaust
Selvon, Sam, 155
Shadow of the Swastika, 67
Shadows Before Sunrise (Hanley and Maas), 76–7
Shapley, Olive, 68, 81n6
Shaw, George Bernard, 45
Sherlock, Philip, 160–1
shortwave broadcasting, 115n8, 154, 159, 160, 168, 177
Sieveking, Lance, 65
Kaleidoscope I, 67, 81n4
Stuff of Radio, The, 81n5, 87
silence, 72, 90, 91, 114, 146
Spain, 89
in *Christopher Columbus*, 104–14
civil war, 15, 26n2, 84, 112, 115n15, 126, 171
Spender, Stephen, 26n4, 85, 172
Springer, Maida, 170

Sterne, Jonathan, 102
Stones Cry Out, The, 24, 85, 87–96, 115nn2–7, 116nn8–9, 187
Strings Are False, The (MacNeice), 89
Strong, L. A. G., 172, 180
Stuart, Francis, 28n20
Stuff of Radio, The (Sieveking), 81n5, 87
Swanzy, Henry, 155

Talks Department *see* BBC
television *see* BBC
Tennyson, Alfred Lord, 93, 95
Third Programme *see* BBC
'This is the Voice of Algeria' (Fanon), 157–8, 159
Thomas, Dylan, 66, 101
Time Has Brought Me Hither (MacNeice), 186
Times (London), 31, 61, 134, 142
'To a High-Brow' (Priestley), 33, 34–6, 38
Topside, 190
Trinidad, 162, 179, 180; *see also* Calling the West Indies; West Indies
Trotter, David, 28n18
truth *see* facts

Ullswater Committee, 41, 156
Under Milk Wood (Thomas), 66, 101
Union of Soviet Socialist Republics (USSR), 14, 96–8
    in *Alexander Nevsky*, 97–104
    in UK public opinion, 97–8
United Kingdom *see* Britain
United States of America (USA)
    in *Christopher Columbus*, 103, 105–6, 116n16
    entry into war, 103
    in *Let the People Sing*, 1–2
    see also Alexander Nevsky; Britain Speaks; Christopher Columbus; Freedom Ferry; Overseas Service; Stones Cry Out

Verma, Neil, 96
Voice (BBC), 171, 180, 184n14
voice and national identity, 4–5, 30; *see also* accent; intimacy

Wales, 8, 9–10, 42, 53, 77, 78, 81n7, 115n11
Walton, William, 104–8
'War Field Books' (Johnston), 117–18, 136, 139–40, 145, 148–9, 150nn2–3, 152n27
War Report (Hawkins), 126, 127, 144
Warner, Michael, 11, 55, 158, 163, 183n3
Warren, Robert, 176–7
welfare state, 3, 16, 25–6, 58–62, 187–8
Welsh, Sarah Lawson, 182n1, 183n9
West, Rebecca, 25, 62n2
West Indies, 182n1
    accents on radio, 163, 177–80, 182
    BBC broadcasts to, 25, 156–64
    literature, 154–5, 173–80
    regional identity, 25, 154–5, 156, 158–9, 168–9, 170, 173–4
    West Indian Royal Commission, 159, 170–1, 183n4
West Indies Calling, 180–2
Westminster Abbey, 89–93, 185–7
'Where Are the War Poets?' (Day Lewis), 15–16
Williams, Keith, 27n17, 42
Williams, Raymond, 28nn22–3
Wills, Clair, 122, 147, 150n8
Wilson, Ian, 139
Wolfe, Douglas Maurice, 71, 81n7
Wollaeger, Mark, 20, 22, 29n26, 128
Woodcock, George, 18
Woolf, Virginia, 36, 62n5
    'Middlebrow', 33–4
World War I *see* First World War
World War II *see* Second World War
Wren, Sir Christopher, 93, 95

Yugoslavia, 125, 132

EU representative:
Easy Access System Europe
Mustamäe tee 50, 10621 Tallinn, Estonia
Gpsr.requests@easproject.com

www.ingramcontent.com/pod-product-compliance
Lightning Source LLC
Chambersburg PA
CBHW051116230426
43667CB00014B/2603